Roy Hattersley was born ⋯⋯⋯ ⋯⋯⋯ ⋯⋯⋯
the Sheffield City Gramm⋯⋯⋯ ⋯⋯⋯ ⋯⋯⋯
sed for the Labour Party. ⋯⋯ ⋯⋯⋯ ⋯⋯⋯
Party, the Member of Parliament for Sparkbrook, Birmingham,
and was a Cabinet Minister from 1976 to 1979. Roy Hattersley
was a Visiting Fellow of the Institute of Politics at the University
of Harvard and is now a Visiting Fellow of Nuffield College,
Oxford. He is the author of four books of essays – *Goodbye to
Yorkshire*, *Politics Apart*, *Endpiece Revisited*, *Press Gang* – a
biography of Nelson and *Choose Freedom*, the future for
democratic socialism. His first novel, *The Maker's Mark*, will
be published by Macmillan in 1990 and Pan in 1991. He has
been a columnist for *The Spectator*, *Punch*, *The Listener* and
Guardian. He now writes weekly columns for the *Sunday
Correspondent*. He was Granada's 'Columnist of the Year' in
1981.

Roy Hattersley's mother, Mrs Enid Hattersley – who plays a
prominent part in *A Yorkshire Boyhood* – was Lord Mayor of
Sheffield in 1982.

Roy Hattersley

A YORKSHIRE BOYHOOD

with a new Foreword

PAN BOOKS
in association with Chatto & Windus

First published 1983 by Chatto & Windus Ltd,
and with a new Foreword in 1989
This edition published 1990 by Pan Books Ltd,
Cavaye Place, London sw10 9pg
in association with Chatto & Windus Ltd
9 8 7 6 5 4 3
© Roy Hattersley 1983, 1989
ISBN 0 330 31394 0

Printed and bound in Great Britain by
Cox & Wyman Ltd, Reading, Berkshire

*For
my father*

Contents

List of Illustrations

Foreword

———

If I were to write a sequel to *A Yorkshire Boyhood*, it would certainly be called *In Search Of My Father*. In the six years since the story of my childhood was published, few months have passed without a new discovery about Rex, the student at the English College in Rome; Father Hattersley, the parish priest at St Joseph's in Langwith Junction; or 'Staff' (short for Stafford Cripps, whom he was said to resemble), the constable in the Police War Reserve. I have been approached in railway trains by ancient monsignors and sent faded cuttings from local newspapers which have not been printed since the war. At my first public meeting in the 1987 General Election campaign, a member of the Mansfield audience told me that my father had taught him in Sunday school – mostly about football and cricket. The sister of a dead bishop wrote to me to say that her brother had defended my views on the abolition of public schools only in memory of the happy times which he had spent with my father. One old lady offered me a box of paper handkerchiefs in preparation for the tears which she was sure I would shed before our conversation was over.

Even before I wrote *A Yorkshire Boyhood*, I was fascinated by the idea of my father's years in the Church. Indeed I was in thrall to his secret past from the moment – a week after his death – when William Ellis, Bishop of Nottingham, wrote to express his condolences. At first I thought that the letter was a silly mistake. For it made no sense. 'I have said prayers for the repose of his soul . . . As you will know we were in Rome together . . . We were both young priests in this diocese . . .' But, before I reached the Maltese Cross which preceded the signature, I knew that it was all true. At that moment the search began.

The Catholic Church – as represented by a variety of bishops and monsignors – accepted what *A Yorkshire Boyhood* said about my father's apostasy with a broad-minded composure and a desperate determination to correct my errors. I now know that some of the 'facts' in Chapter One were an unintentionally romanticised – as well as compressed – account of my parents' unusual courtship. I have left that chapter as it was not out of sloth or fear of my mother's wrath – great though that might be. The account of the meeting and marriage is what I believed to be the truth when *A Yorkshire Boyhood* was written. Since the book is about what followed the flight to Sheffield – and most of the Sheffield story is my own recollection – I have left the original introductory romance intact.

I have now written the story of my father's years in the church – his preparation for the priesthood and his decision to abandon what he had believed to be his calling – in *The Maker's Mark*. That novel tells the story, in only slightly fictionalised form, of three generations of Hattersleys. It ends with an account of my parents' early relationship which, paradoxically, is more accurate than the version of their extraordinary courtship with which this book begins. But the spirit of *A Yorkshire Boyhood*'s first chapter reflects exactly the feelings which they had for each other. For over forty years, they filled each others' lives. Indeed, almost twenty years after his death, my father fills my mother's life still.

Their mutual devotion was the secure background to my boyhood, though the strength of their feeling did not always contribute to my confidence. The home in which I was brought up was as stable as the Pennines – despite the occasional tantrum which I now recognise as the product of my mother's intellectual frustration. But, occasionally, there was the feeling that I was – if not an intruder – at least an optional extra. I was special to my father because I was Enid's son. As a child, I never needed, or dared, to waste time on insecure questions about 'Who do you love most?' With both of them, I always knew the answer.

A couple of months before he died, my father provided me with a perfect example of his occasionally infuriating devotion. He had been mildly ill for several weeks and the results of a medical examination had prompted fears of cancer which were sufficiently strong to bring me back from holiday. By the time I got to Sheffield, a second series of tests had contradicted the diagnosis of the first. Unfortunately, the second prognosis proved incorrect. But during the period of false hope, we celebrated his reprieve by going to the opening football match of the season. On the way to Bramall Lane – euphoria had made us sufficiently undiscriminating to tolerate

Sheffield United – I asked my father what he had felt when he first thought that he was going to die.

His answer was immediate and explicit: 'I was glad that we'd bought that little Wolseley last week.' Close as we were, I had no idea of what he meant. So I asked him. He looked at me with open contempt for my lack of understanding. 'Your mother,' he said, 'wouldn't have had to bother about repairs for a year.' It was then that I realised that the old Catholic instinct had remained. Heaven was still the beatific vision. Only the source of blessed light had changed.

From the age of about ten, I felt a desperate desire to protect my father. Whether or not he needed protection is of no consequence. It was the feeling – the sort of love – which he aroused in me. I recalled one day when he rushed to see me in the mistaken belief that I was about to have my appendix removed. I was in fact suffering from nothing more serious than renal colic. But it hurt. My father – sitting on the side of the bed – was so obviously distressed by the sight of his agonised son that I sat up, put my arm round his shoulders and shouted downstairs for a cup of tea with which to comfort him. Yet that was the man who, thirty years earlier, had packed up his cassock and clerical collar and walked out of St Joseph's presbytery in Langwith Junction for the love of a woman who might never have married him. I wish that I had known of that moment of extraordinary heroism.

In these more tolerant days it is difficult to remember the penalties which society imposed on those who acted with a reckless disregard for conventional respectability. He risked – and he endured – years of unemployment. He risked – and he accepted – the disapproval of much of his family and of the church around which his whole life had been built.

At the heart of *A Yorkshire Boyhood* there is a heroine, not a hero. During the years which it describes, it was my mother who held the family's world suspended. It was my mother who effectively brought up my two young uncles when they – approaching rather than occupying holy orders – abandoned the church shortly after my father's apostasy. It was my mother who nursed – for twenty years – my grandmother, who was so badly crippled that she sat immobile in a small bed under the living-room window. And it was my mother who managed the family's meagre income with such success that we were able to buy the semi-detached suburban house in which I was brought up and in which she still lives. The habit of touring green-grocers in search of the least expensive vegetables still persists. Long before she was a great figure in the heroic traditions of Labour local government she was a remarkable woman in the heroic traditions of northern wives and mothers.

It has to be admitted that although *A Yorkshire Boyhood* is written in praise of my mother, my mother did not and does not like it. Her judgement on its artistic merits I have yet to hear. But I do know that she regards its contents as a sort of literary indecent exposure, and that she fears that some neighbours – and ex-neighbours – who are mentioned in the story have been offended by what I have written about their ancestors. None of them has denied the truth of my tales. But some of them have, apparently, been hurt by them. For that I am truly sorry – particularly in the case of the Moores, who lived next door to the Hattersleys when we inhabited 174 Wadsley Lane. I remember them with nothing but pleasure and gratitude. Their lodger, Mr Corcoran, helped me dig a pond at the top of my garden. Their daughter, Rosie, amused me on rainy days. Weighed against such boons and benefits, their son's late-night drum practice counted for nothing. I very much regret any distress which the book caused to them. The rest must take it in the spirit which I intended. With much of *A Yorkshire Boyhood*, as with most of what I write, the joke is on me. If a little of the ridicule spills over onto other people, I can only ask that they accept their lot with tolerance and understanding. At least I hope that they will believe that it was written with good intentions.

I thought about writing *A Yorkshire Boyhood* for almost twenty years before I began to construct sentences on paper rather than in my head. Throughout those two decades – in government and opposition – the idea of describing my early life and times disturbed my attempts to understand Cabinet papers (concerned with such fascinating topics as metrication and the reform of local government), and postponed the preparation of *Guardian* leader-page articles on equally absorbing topics. It would be wrong, as well as embarrassing, to say that my enthusiasm grew into an obsession. But by the time, in 1981, that I began to write, I was only just on the respectable side of the line which divides those two conditions.

The book which I wanted to write (indeed the book which I thought that I had written) was not an autobiography – a literary activity about which I have so many reservations that I am tempted to put the word literary in inverted commas. *A Yorkshire Boyhood* was meant to be the story of the generation which was born during the great depression, brought up in the war and propelled through adolescence by the gentle revolution which began in 1945. I was simply an example of life in those extraordinary times.

The great depression left only vicarious scars upon me, though I was reared on the stories of hunger marches, means tests and dole queues. The war affected me as it affected every other child who lived in an industrial city and avoided the trauma of evacuation, something which I feared far more than I feared Hitler's bombs. Certainly, I was sometimes afraid and when I heard jokes about bananas in 'Garrison Theatre' and 'Workers' Playtime', I felt deprived. But for most of what we called 'the duration' my only thoughts of war concerned playing at soldiers. It was not until peace was declared that I realised that I was a part of the great world outside the suburb of Sheffield in which I lived. And by then, the world was changing at such a speed that I was swept along in the wake of the irresistible waves of improvement. Indeed, looking back, I sometimes feel that the reforms of the 1940s were planned with me, exclusively, in mind.

I was born too late for Ostermilk. But I suspect that the early deficits on the health service budgets were largely my responsibility. I was asthmatic, and for several damp winters and pollen-heavy springs, the doctor and I were inseparable companions – though not friends on account of his habit of sticking hypodermic needles into my arm. More important – at least to my future, if not to the Treasury – when I no longer needed to take advantage of state medicine, I moved on to state education. I might have won a grammar school place had I been eleven in any year after 1935. For the Sheffield City Council anticipated the Butler Education Act by ten years. But I went to university because I was wise enough to grow up in an age when university places were both generally available and part of a natural progression which took boys like me from fifth form to lower sixth, lower sixth to upper sixth and upper sixth to some institution of higher education without requiring us to pause and think about anything more academic than the prospect of steady scholastic progress being interrupted by National Service.

We ought to have thought about our new status. For few of us came from families which, ten years before, would ever have imagined that their sons and daughters might go to university. The only graduates that we knew were the vicar and the few teachers at our schools who wore gowns in morning assembly. But by the first years of the 1950s, young men and women with minimum entrance requirements took it for granted that they were going to become bachelors of something. Expanding universities were looking for students. Grants were awarded by state and local authority. Going to university was positively fashionable. Bliss was it in that dawn to be eighteen, and to possess three A-levels and a charcoal grey suit was equally gratifying.

I seemed to be tailor-made for the temporary paradise. I was the only child of parents who, although to fortune and to fame unknown, were immensely ambitious for their only son. They were – as they needed to be – desperately careful with money. But there was always something to spend on those pursuits which they regarded as educative or enlightening. They did not encourage me to read the classic texts of middle-class childhood. So I did not meet Alice, Winnie the Pooh or even Toad until I was in my teens. But my father read *A Christmas Carol* to me in late December and, during the years of sickness, I struggled through *A Tale of Two Cities*, *The Scarlet Pimpernel* and *The Prisoner of Zenda*. My mother was usually complimentary when I did well and my father was invariably sympathetic when I did badly – though there were one or two bitter occasions when my mother blamed me for my failures. In short they were the ideal parents to help me drive my way through the years of opportunity. I chose – as well as the right time at which to enter the world – the right family into which to be born.

A Yorkshire Boyhood was intended to describe growing up at that extraordinary age and to suggest – very gently – that it was easier for some of us to succeed than for others. It was written in praise of the 1940s and their values. But it was also a threnody for principles and policies which, although admirable in their time, had to be changed. The book which I meant to write described the experiences of one ordinary member of an extraordinary society. However, when I read the reviews – including those which were exceptionally kind – I discovered that the book which I had written was the memoir of the son of a Catholic priest who had not found out about the abandoned calling until after his father's death.

Thinking about it again, *A Yorkshire Boyhood* may be about something unusual – the extent and nature of the affection that my parents had for each other. It was not without its penalties – for them and for those who intruded into their world. But when I was the beneficiary of the warm home that it created, I had no idea of how singular it was or that it had survived the most extraordinary trials and tribulations. To me they were a couple of ancients – well over forty – who held hands like teenagers at the youth club and took remarkable pains to spend time together.

Whilst the waves were beating around me, I was just as ignorant about the great tide of social revolution which was sweeping my life along. When I found out that I had bobbed about on waters which previous generations had not sailed, my enthusiasm to write about it was uncontainable. After twenty years I described my experience of those turbulent days. I now realise that I was the beneficiary of two remarkable phenomena – the 1945 social revolution and my parents. *A Yorkshire Boyhood* is about both.

R.H.
July 1989

I

Pulling up the Drawbridge

—

On a summer's day, a little over fifty years ago, the Catholic priest in the little Nottingham mining village of Shirebrook visited the local coal merchant to make early arrangements for the winter heating of his church and presbytery. He was twenty-seven, and robustly healthy. Yet he looked more contemplative than athletic. The impression of unworldly detachment was established by rimless spectacles and a lock of hair that fell over his forehead. It was enhanced by a slightly deprecating manner, common in Christians of deep conviction. Since his days at the English College in Rome he had been known as an anxious man who hated uncertainty, and was rarely confident about the outcome of events over which he had no personal control. So there was nothing surprising about his decision to order coal before the production of the Nottingham pits ran out. The visit to the coal merchant was an act of providence, in at least one of the meanings of the word.

The coal merchant was Ernest Brackenbury, a roisterous man who had, in his time, been the hope of the Communists in the coalfield and was to die, at the age of ninety-two, a pillar of the Labour Party's local government establishment. When the priest called, 'Brack' was between his two political periods, and his absence from home and office could not be attributed to either union or council business. His wife, Agnes (crippled and confined to bed with rheumatoid arthritis), hoped that he was searching the county for business. Enid, his daughter, assumed that he was gambling with his cronies; either playing pitch and toss at the pit-head or holding a hand of cards in one of the sheds on the nearby allotments.

Enid Brackenbury was in her early twenties. She struggled hard not to resent the obligation to stay at home as nurse and housekeeper to her crippled mother. Once, she had briefly been allowed to work in a draper's shop. But for most of her adult life, what energy was left over from cooking and cleaning was spent on reading every book that came to hand and playing tennis. At the local club she was a star

3

– partly because of her remarkable good looks, and partly because of her obsession with winning every point in every game in every match. An incessant talker, she had learned from hard experience the importance of financial reticence.

Although the two women disagreed about where the proprietor was to be found, they were united in their determination not to lose the customer. So they sat the young priest down, gave him a cup of tea and talked to him about dogs. Enid owned a wire-haired terrier called Mick, an animal whose violent disposition she blamed on her father's habit of encouraging attacks on neighbours' pets. Mother and daughter both delighted in finding homes for neglected or unwanted animals as other women rejoiced in providing husbands for unwanted spinsters. There was, they told their slightly overwhelmed visitor, a collie pup in need of a good Christian upbringing. By the end of the afternoon, the dog was saved and the order secured. But the main outcome of the meeting was the marriage of Enid Brackenbury and Father Frederick Hattersley. A by-product of the union was me.

Of course, they did not arrange the wedding there and then in front of the kitchen fire. But years later, when the need for ritual romance was long past, they both insisted that each of them had fallen in love on the day of that first meeting. However, before either of them dared speak of it, there were other casual meetings – the most important at the Shirebrook Tennis Club. Father Hattersley (known to everyone outside the church by his second name, Roy) had two younger brothers. William (called George everywhere but in the seminary at Valladolid) was about to take his final vows. Charles (Syd to everyone except the clerically-inclined staff at Ratcliffe College) was still a schoolboy. He spent the first days of his summer holidays in Shirebrook, and arrangements were made for him to play tennis there. In a scratch tournament, fate drew his name out of a hat to play with Enid Brackenbury.

I have seen photographs of my mother in her long pleated tennis dress, wearing a Suzanne Lenglen bandeau and guarded by Mick, sitting at her feet like a homicidal caricature of an advertisement for *His Master's Voice*. My father, standing admiring but anxious, outside the wire netting that surrounded the court, I can only imagine. I know that he wore pince-nez and I assume that he had a regulation black suit. But I have never seen a picture that provided proof of his ordained past. Indeed, it was not until he was dead and I was forty that I realised that my father was once in Holy Orders. Now the evidence of my childhood seems absolutely conclusive. Yet, at the time, I deduced nothing from the dog-eared postcard picture of Swiss Guards, the knowledge of Latin (unusual amongst local government clerks) or the hatred of Oliver Cromwell.

The discovery of a *Golden Treasury* inscribed to C. S. Hattersley as a prize for excellent work at Ratcliffe aroused no suspicions of early Catholicism. And the Sacred Hearts that decorated the book-plate did nothing to suggest that, for a working-class boy, the path to Ratcliffe was the road to Rome. Nor did the inscription in another old book, that is now engraved on my memory like a single hyphen-ated word — 'Panton College, Ragley, Lincs'. I thought that all such schools opened their gates to the able and ambitious sons of failed cutlers turned polishers at the Raleigh Cycle Works, Nottingham. The idea that my father and his brothers had ever been, or contem-plated becoming, priests never crossed my mind.

I knew that my parents had endured a brief but difficult courtship. I had heard stories of secret meetings in Mansfield cinemas, discreet teas in small Sherwood Forest cafés and long afternoons spent rowing on the Trent safe from the land-locked world. But I attributed their troubles to Agnes Brackenbury's sickness and her husband's demand that Enid should remain the spinster housekeeper. I knew my father had spent years in Rome. But the questions with which I followed his stories of the death of Matteotti and visits to the catacombs were always turned aside by talk of Thomas Cook's office in the Termini Station — a place where, in truth, he had only found a few weeks' employment between school and seminary.

In the days that followed my father's funeral, the messages that came from long-forgotten friends all referred to the years in the church. At first, I assumed that they were all the result of some com-mon confusion. When I had received too many for repeated error to be a plausible explanation, I realised that the mistake was mine. It was years before I raised the subject with my mother. Then, emboldened by the effects of a long lunch we had together, I showed her a note from the Catholic Bishop of Nottingham that I had carried round with me, hoping that the courage to discuss it would suddenly come.

My mother carefully read the reminiscences of Rome and the stories about days together as young priests in the same diocese. She slowly absorbed the final promise 'to say prayers for the repose of his good soul' and then stared, remorselessly, at the name signed next to the little Maltese cross below the benediction. 'That,' she said, 'is the man they sent to take your father back.' There was no suggestion of a half-forgotten fear that he might go — just fury at the suddenly remembered impertinence. I began to understand that it must have been a battlefield, back in Nottingham in the prim days of 1929, bombarded from one direction by Rome and respectability, and from the other by love, hope and inclination.

We talked for a little about the traumatic days. 'Not a word,' my mother said, smiling still at the memory of the achievement, 'ever appeared in a newspaper.' The determination to avoid notoriety turned into a preoccupation with hiding the past. For my father, I suspect, only part of the obsession was produced by the fear of gossip. He left the priesthood with no regrets. Indeed, he turned his back on Catholicism itself in a way that was too complete to allow the suspicion of reluctance. But to abandon the ingrained habits of even a reluctant vocation required him to put half of his life out of mind. As I grew up, he felt no obligation to tell me about something that he rarely admitted — even to himself — had ever happened.

If there were difficult days of early adjustment, they were eased by my mother filling the place which the church had hoped to occupy in my father's heart and mind. But that did not overcome the practical problems of the unusual union. Both partners came to the marriage with substantial obligations. Enid could not, or would not, leave her mother in the care of Ernest Brackenbury. My father discovered that his apostasy had set off a whole round of renunciation. George had come home from Spain, determined to be William no more. Syd refused to follow his brother to Rome and become Charles. Neither was happy to return to Nottingham where their widowed father had provided them with a stepmother for whom they could feel no filial enthusiasm.

So it was decided that the three Hattersley brothers, the new Hattersley wife and the recently acquired Hattersley mother-in-law would all stay together. But they could not stay together in Shirebrook and live notoriously in Nottingham. Instead, five human beings without a job or a prospect between them had to find a new home. And three of them, having just abandoned lives of total security for the uncertainty of the world, began their search with no savings and no intention of telling a prospective employer about their previous experience. They looked only in places where they were unknown and they began by exploring South Yorkshire. Reconnais-

sance parties went out on old bicycles searching for a house they
could afford to rent. When a suitable refuge was found, Mrs
Brackenbury was painfully transported from Shirebrook, hunched
and huddled across the back seat of a hired motor-car. Fifty years
after they moved into the city, Enid Hattersley became Lord Mayor
of Sheffield.

Sheffield, in the middle of the great depression, offered far worse
employment prospects than the nearby East Midlands towns of
Derby and Leicester. Yet they chose to move to South Yorkshire. The
real reason for that strange decision was, I suspect, the stories that all
of them had heard about it in their childhood. Both my grandfathers
were Sheffield exiles, unhappy expatriates who talked persuasively
about the virtues of their native city, underestimating neither its
beauty nor its bounties. No doubt after years of white rose propaganda the Ridings seemed the right new world in which to begin a
brave new life. The promised land also had the considerable advantage of being within easy reach of Worksop.

Worksop was the home of the only relatives on whom my parents,
and their new relations, could rely. At 89 Newcastle Avenue lived
Anne Skinner and Charlotte Hartill, my mother's aunts respectively
by birth and by adoption. For a time a third ancient shared their
home. Jenny, Charlotte's elder sister, was a retired nanny who spent
her brief respite between the nursery and the grave with the two triumphantly maiden ladies. I recall being ushered into Jenny's awesome
presence only twice. I remember her as a plump, navy blue Queen
Victoria who wore the lace hat and disapproving expression of the
Widow of Windsor in her recluse period. She was kept upstairs so as
not to impede the progress of the dressmaking and tailoring business
with which Aunts Annie and Lot met the sartorial demands of 'the
Dukeries'' middle classes. Their real life's work was contributing to
the greater glory of Annie's younger brother Ernest, known to us as
'Uncle Ern'. Their hobby was discovering and rescuing neglected and
ill-treated animals.

Uncle Ern was chief clerk at Hurst's, a firm of Retford builders and
timber merchants. He was accomplished in a wide range of Edwardian pursuits, particularly fretwork and the manipulation of Indian
clubs. On the historic occasion when the north Nottingham canal
froze over, he skated to work; a feat of daring that his doting sisters
never let the world forget. He possessed an upright bearing, a
bristling moustache, and a nearby house of his own at 7 Overend

Road. His brief marriage had ended with the death of his wife who, it was always hinted darkly, had died to cause him inconvenience. Uncle Ern and Aunts Annie and Lot were devout Christians of the sort that rarely goes to church on Sunday but makes up for the absence of formal piety by mortifying the flesh – particularly other people's. Jenny was on the scene far too briefly to establish a persona in the Hattersley men's minds. The other three were known, collectively (and slightly pejoratively) as 'Worksop'.

There can be little doubt that 'Worksop' was opposed to my parents' marriage; for 'Worksop' was opposed to marriage in general in much the same way as it disapproved of alcohol, theatrical productions, and reading novels on Sundays. But to my mother and father 'Worksop' practical help more than compensated for the moral opprobrium that was heaped upon them. It was to one of 'Worksop' houses that my parents went for their brief honeymoon, whilst 'Worksop' looked after Mrs Brackenbury. 'Worksop' made the wedding dress, and it was from the Newcastle Avenue workroom that the one bridesmaid came. She was known in family folklore as Miss Smith, although she became Mrs King shortly after my parents' marriage. In later years, although only separated by the breadth of Sheffield, Mrs King and Mrs Hattersley rarely met. But when 'Miss Smith' died my mother treated the news like the death of the last survivor from an outnumbered, yet eventually victorious, army. It helped me to understand what the weeks before the wedding were like and why 'Worksop', which hung over my childhood like a damp, grey cloud, was the object of her eternal gratitude.

None of the five recipients of 'Worksop' help and constant good advice had – despite their diverse backgrounds – previously endured grinding poverty. When the really penniless years were over, they repeated the facts and folklore of the period with a resigned humour which I doubt that they were able to sustain before the nostalgia set in. On Saturday afternoons, when Sheffield United were at home, the men hung around outside Bramall Lane waiting for the moment in the second half of the game when the gates were opened and the unemployed were let in free of charge. Rent was a constant anxiety. Once the humiliation of asking the landlord to call back again later in the week was only averted by the discovery of a cache of bottles and jam-jars, on each of which there was 'a penny back'. Visits from 'Worksop' contributed rabbits, 'home rendered' lard and 'home cured' bacon to the larder. Sometimes one of the elderly aunts brought, by bus and tram, delicacies which, although they were not designed to travel, were nevertheless taken by Uncle Ern to Retford each day – rice pudding, beef broth, and mutton stew.

Such gifts augmented unemployment benefit and odd jobs for nearly two years, the five of them living from day to day on the hope of soon 'finding something'. Then they found that they were about to become six, a discovery that (with the advantage of half-a-lifetime's hindsight) all of them insisted was received with general rejoicing and unrestrained delight. If that is true, the new arrival was anticipated with more emotion than practical judgment by the five adults who dominated his early life from within the closed circle of affectionate conspiracy in which they existed.

They had formed themselves into a psychologically self-contained community – protecting each other from the world and locked together by a secret which, although it was not shared by me, still held the whole family together. 'Worksop' (introspective for reasons of its own) was allowed to enter in from time to time. Once inside, it became temporarily part of a family that excluded all other friends and relations – my father's sisters in Nottingham, my mother's old admirers from the Shirebrook tennis club and anyone else who knew the story about 'Brack's daughter running off with the Catholic priest'.

In those early days, my father still looked the part, and although the theology and belief of the skin-deep conviction had been sloughed off, more practical characteristics of the lost vocation remained in his character and in the personalities of his brothers. They were passionate supporters of brisk, healthy exercise, and gentle intellectual improvement. During days' outings they all tried obsessively to draw the churches that they saw, and then hurried home to listen to the boxing match on the radio. They believed it was their duty to convert young heathens into cricketers who gripped the bat properly, and readers who preferred Conan Doyle to Zane Gray, and Father Brown to Sexton Blake. They accepted, without question, my mother's authority as head of the house. She, for her part, at the age of twenty-five, accepted responsibility for the welfare of three unemployed men and a terminally sick old lady. When she added an infant son to her obligations she continued to manage the family, the house and, above all, the money. 'Manage' became the word for both success and survival.

On the day that the closed community expected to welcome its novitiate, all the influences on my early life assembled in Sheffield – the city which more than anything else, except the family itself, affected my formative years. 'Worksop' was represented by Aunt Lot, who looked after the imminent grandmother, and Aunt Annie, who organised tea and hot water. Mrs Brackenbury wept to think that her grandchild would be born in the midst of smoke and grime and never see a cow or green fields. Syd and George were sent out for the day and walked across the open moorlands that lie within five miles of the Sheffield town hall. My father waited, white and anxious, then – when it was all over – expressed astonishment that his son was born complete, with nails both on his toes and fingers.

2
Babes and Sucklings

—

I remember nothing of the house where I was born. But my parents' reminiscences of Southview Road are now constantly confused in my mind with memories of my own. So I imagine that I really recall constantly burning my infant fingers on Syd's cigarettes. And I feel that I both witnessed and understood my mother's regular complaint about the way my father thrust his face into mine as if he were inviting me to snatch the gold-rimmed pince-nez from his nose and fling them to the ground, careless about the cost of repair. I am told that I was there when Aunt Lot, infuriated by my mother's rejection of some item of infant clothing, announced (as she wrapped the gift back in its parcel) that Jenny said she 'had seen exactly the same on the children of titled families'. To this day I feel guilty about Mick's sad end. He was 'put down' after being observed eyeing me in my pram as if I was a rat to be tossed in the air until my spine broke. My mother still owns the obese Buddha which George taught me to identify as 'dad' – though it has not been regularly on display since the time during the war when I scratched a Cross of Lorraine on the bulging chest.

And I still retain a vivid, if retrospectively painted, picture of unhappy early evenings spent sitting in an enamel bath which had been filled in the kitchen and dragged, full of water, to a place before the living-room fire. Slopping about in the warm suds would have amused me for a few minutes had I not known that the bakelite rowing boat and clockwork paddle-steamer were a prelude to water being poured over my head. I hated my hair being washed and screamed – every night – from the first touch of the soap to the last rub of towel. Attempts were made to insulate me from the feeling that I was being simultaneously blinded and drowned. Sometimes one of the uncles was called in to hold a towel over my eyes, as if I was in front of a firing-squad and could not face the sight of the signal to shoot. But the soapy water still seeped through. For years I was reminded of the nightly trauma when a shirt or pullover stuck over my head as I was in the act of undressing, and I was once again possessed by panic at the prospect of asphyxiation.

Perhaps it is only the stories of my hysteria, rather than the hysteria itself, that I recall. I may not even really remember the feeling of general concern I felt for Syd's welfare. Certainly, my mother was always so positively protective towards him that the projection of her iron will influenced us all. But I really think that in one of the misty recesses of my memory there is a genuine recollection of Bramley apples being prepared for a pie and Syd sitting by the kitchen table eating the green peel as it curled off knife. Syd, I thought, deserved something better – real apples not peel. I can no longer vouch that the incident took place. But it typifies the feeling I had for my youngest uncle from the moment that my feelings began. Like the rest of the family, I wanted to look after him.

However authentic the earliest memories may be, recorded time really began for me when we moved across Sheffield for the most welcome of all reasons. At last, work was in prospect. My father and his brother George had been offered temporary employment by the Public Assistance Committee at an outpost of the Central Sheffield Labour Exchange, set up to do what little was done in those days for the growing legions of unemployed. On the day that the glad news came, although Enid felt an obligation to stay at home with her mother, the rest of the Hattersleys celebrated with a visit to the local cinema to see Richard Tauber as Schubert in *Lilac Time*. The composer wore spectacles like my father and strode at the head of a column of children through the Vienna Woods playing the 'Marche Militaire' on the violin that was tucked inconveniently under his chin. For the next forty years, whenever the 'Marche Militaire' was on the radio, my father described the scene and the circumstances in which he had first heard the 'PAC march'.

But the rejoicing was short-lived. Ironically, when the general prospect of work improved, the temporary staff in the old Corn Exchange were made redundant. After a few weeks of renewed depression, both brothers were offered similar jobs in Barnsley, a town fifteen miles beyond Sheffield's northern boundary and, therefore, over twenty miles away from the southern suburbs. For some months they cycled to Barnsley and back each day – my father on a bike with a buckled front wheel which, as it had been knocked oval, threw its rider into the air like a circus performer. But there was no money for a new wheel; so the daily journey was made moving up and down as well as forward, covering about as much distance in the vertical plane as in the horizontal. Then the Barnsley prospect began to look permanent and the daily journey of over forty miles seemed an unnecessary waste of time, energy and inner tubes.

So we rented 174 Wadsley Lane, a large, dilapidated, late Victorian villa in a continuous – though irregular – terrace that ran up one of the steeply sloping roads which give Sheffield suburbs their distinctive character. We left Wadsley Lane when I was six, but by the time that we moved to the superior security of owner-occupation I had developed a clear perception of the social hierarchy within our little group of families. On one side of us lived the Moores, a large family which included an elder son with ambition to become a dance band drummer. He practised assiduously late at night in his bedroom. They lived higher up the hill, but lower down some imaginary league table. Nobody doubted that our arrival had improved the tone of the neighbourhood. The previous tenants of 174 had, we were told, gone to *The Horse and Jockey* every night, leaving their children to amuse themselves with hammers and nails. When we moved in, the skirting boards and the door jambs were riddled with holes as if they had been ravaged by giant woodworm.

'Next door below', but socially above, were the Shipleys, the head of whose household was distantly associated with one of the professions. The Shipleys had a daughter, Mary. I think of her now as pretty, with a short skirt and bobbed hair. Arch jokes were made about her attraction for and to Syd because they visited Hillsborough public baths together on mixed bathing afternoons. I was too young fully to understand the implications of the banter Syd endured as he followed his various unemployment hobbies – drawing village scenes on old bits of paper, and learning Esperanto. I suppose that, like the Wadsley Lane social register, it all seemed unnoticed through my innocent pores.

I recall only one social event in which Moores, Shipleys and Hattersleys all co-operated. On one distant pre-war November 5th, the three families stood outside our back door and watched the sparks fly from a bonfire that Syd and George had built. As it was dark, I assumed at the time that we were taking part in an all-night debauchery. Now I suspect that the festivities began a little after five o'clock and ended at about seven, for just after the celebration had got into full swing the 'bin men' arrived to remove our household refuse. In those days dust-bins were emptied with as much contempt for health and hygiene as the wit of the Town Hall could translate into working practice. The 'bins' were first tipped into open skips, made out of rusty tin in the shape of a shallow baby's bath. The skips were then carried to the 'bin van' on the shoulders of 'bin men' who wore specially designed leather epaulettes to protect their necks and collar-bones from the pressure of half-a-hundredweight of empty salmon tins and rotting potato peelings. Eventually, the skips were upended into the open van. But before the rubbish was scattered across the public highway, half of the bins' original contents were dropped or strewn about and stamped into the yards, paths and gardens from whence it was collected. I assume that it was the ritual spreading of the refuse which undermined my mother's patience with me.

Whatever the true cause of her exasperation, it came to a head after we had all burned our fingers on the baked potatoes and despaired of the home-made toffee ever setting hard enough to break into brittle, teeth-destroying fragments. I was frightened by – or pretended to be frightened by – the exploding rockets from other people's gardens which cascaded their golden showers through the early evening sky. Whenever one began to make the fiery arc across the sky, I hid behind my mother's skirts, sometimes clutching her with one hand whilst I held an ignited 'sparkler' or a piece of still-molten toffee in the other. She was entirely unsympathetic. Fear of the great toadstools that parasited on the trees in Wadsley Lane, fear that my 'jumping' tooth would give another sudden pang, fear that I could have bad dreams or not wake up in the morning – none of them ever struck a sympathetic chord in my mother. Pain itself moved her to real compassion. She was sufficiently concerned about suffering itself to suffer in sympathy with the sufferer. But the anticipation of misfortune did not move her. In the traumatic days, back in Shirebrook, she had overcome her own fear and she expected her son to do the same – particularly in front of the Moores, to whom we should set an example.

The Moores owned an Alsatian dog which we, inevitably, believed to be ill-treated. They also possessed a lodger by the name of Mr Corkran who worked in the building trade. One Friday he brought home from work various items of 'surplus material' with which he created, within the space of a weekend, a beautiful pond complete with willow-pattern bridge and desert island vegetated with miniature plants from Woolworths. I screamed for a pond of my own and was rewarded with what might have been (had I behaved better) a sign that infancy was now over and boyhood had begun. My old zinc bath (chipped from a daily journey from kitchen to place of honour in front of the living-room fire) was sunk into a distant corner of the garden and stocked with the best goldfish the rag-and-bone man could provide in return for various articles of unwanted clothing. Syd went to great trouble to hide the bath's handles with two little cairns of stones.

When Aunt Lot came on her next visit, she said that it was cruel to keep fish in captivity. Fortunately they died before Aunt Annie had a chance to reinforce the condemnation. As far as animals were concerned, 'Worksop' believed that death was without sting and graves were denied victory. 'Putting them out of their misery' was a regular occupation that despatched unwanted litters of kittens, half-hibernated hedgehogs and dormant wasps. I had no doubt who was responsible for the anonymous tip-off that brought the RSPCA Inspector hurrying around to examine the condition of the Moores' Alsatian. But if the eventually exonerated family had any suspicions about who the misinformers were, they did not allow the affront to prejudice the jovial neighbourly relationship. Indeed, as if to reciprocate our flattering imitation of their fishpond, one of the younger Moore boys decided to follow my example and begin a rudimentary stamp collection. Mr Corkran, temporarily laid off work because of bad weather, was unwise enough to bring his National Insurance card home and leave it behind the clock on the kitchen mantelpiece. When the young philatelist found it, he methodically steamed off the carefully preserved evidence of regular payment and brought them round to me – rolled up, wrinkled and wholly unacceptable to the Ministry of Health. He smiled to think that he had begun a worthwhile hobby.

It was in Wadsley Lane that I took up a spare time occupation that was as unrewarding as it is impossible to give up – support for Sheffield Wednesday Football Club. I was brought up within a family of football partisans who huddled round the radio each Saturday evening anxiously awaiting the results. If a good fairy had offered them two wishes, they would have included a first dividend of twenty thousand pounds on Littlewoods pools. If they had only been granted one magic boon, the unanimous request would have been a 'Nottingham double' – both County and Forest winning on the same afternoon. After the results broadcast was over (speaking while it was on being a capital offence) I was initiated into the sub-culture of football fanaticism. Syd spent hours teaching me to say 'Hamilton Academicals' and George convinced me that Father Christmas was represented in the Football League by a team called Queen's Park Reindeers. When I was five, I knew far more about the history of the two Nottingham Clubs than I did about the record of the recent Cup Winners whose ground was less than a mile from my own front door. But Wednesday had an attraction with which neither Notts County nor Nottingham Forest could compete – nearby noise.

When I was three, my father wheeled me in my pushchair to the bottom of Wadsley Lane and there, outside Oates' grocery shop, opposite the tram stop, the public lavatory and the park gates, I witnessed the return of the victorious Sheffield Wednesday team that had won the F.A. Cup. My mother assures me that as the bus went past and Ron Starling held the silver trophy in the air I raised my arm in a chubby Roman salute. Although I often talk about the glory of that morning, I have no recollection of even being there. But I do remember the winter Saturdays when Wednesday were at home, and the men in caps and raincoats who hurried down the hill outside our house. Three hours later, they were on the long climb back, either stepping out smartly in the elation of victory or stumbling home in the despair that comes from defeat. In between their journeys to and from the match, they made noises which, long before I started school, I could identify instantly at half-a-mile's distance as lucky escape, near miss and Wednesday goal. The cries of hope and grief, curling up from under the stands like heat out of an oven were the most exciting sounds I ever heard.

I lived surrounded by Wednesday. Mr Stokes who lodged down the road played for the reserves before he joined the police force. Mr Driver who lived across the street in one of the council houses that looked down on Wadsley Lane from the top of a steep grass bank was transferred to Bury. Mr Catlin, in his time the best left-back in England, would sit on the wall at the end of his front garden, and I used to see him dangling his famous feet on the pavement almost every time that I was taken to the Wisewood Coop. But it was the cheers and groans rolling up from the bottom of the valley that made me a Wednesdayite for ever.

Of course, during the years in Wadsley Lane, I was never allowed to see them play. Great effort was expended on sheltered amusement.

Indeed, with Syd still unemployed at home all day and my grand-mother anxious to do anything that relieved the tedium of her immobility, I was almost entirely the centre of too much anxious attention. I was read to. I was drawn for. I was instructed in the use of the smallest and cheapest Meccano set. I was taken to see Shirley Temple, and was frightened by the newsreel reports of the Spanish Civil War which preceded 'the big picture'. I was even taken to a circus because I agitated to see the elephants. The afternoon was a dismal failure because the outrage that my mother felt at the sight of performing animals was transmitted to me. I cried and, much to her relief, was brought home before the tigers stood on their tubs.

There was a long succession of gifts – a kitten that ran up the curtain and eventually met a fate that I do not recall, a puppy that developed some sort of head infection and (on 'Worksop's' advice) was 'put out of its misery', and an old radio. When we bought the new Marconi that was designed to look like an Inca temple, the old instrument (designed to look like a model coffin and worked by knobs on the top) was given to me for evisceration during a wet Sunday afternoon. Dry Sundays, if they were not spent in the garden, where whiled away on Wadsley Common.

Wadsley Common began, about a mile away from the Lane that bore its name, as a strip of sandy heather and broom covered hills. It was bordered on one side by the Hillsborough Golf Club and on the other by high fields of khaki-coloured grass which are now largely covered by rows of houses. After an uneven mile, 'the common' widened out into playing fields on the southern approaches and farmland to the north. Beyond the playing fields was a steep wooded escarpment broken by little cliffs and heaps of fallen boulders. On the other side of the farmlands rows of derelict brickworks still littered the countryside. As I grew up, more and more of Wadsley Common opened out to me. I learned to play football and cricket on its sloping pitches, and I spent Friday evenings, first with the Cubs, then with the Scouts, playing elaborate war games across its scarred surface. It was a place for quiet walks (ideally hand in hand) after evening service and it was to Wadsley Common that we went on the last day of Syd's embarkation leave. But during the days in Wadsley Lane I just wanted to potter about on the sandy slopes of its first acre.

Perhaps it was the boredom of taking me to Wadsley Common every day that put the idea of a sandpit into someone's head. Syd was nominated to bring a little of 'the common' to me. So, having done the mining at a spot suitably beyond the view of both road and golf club, he carried the sacks of stolen common property home on his back, leaving a tell-tale golden trail behind him. When the blisters on his shoulders had healed, he dug a shallow hole in the garden and covered its floor and sides with a light layer of what was left after the spillage. In the night it rained, and my sandpit was washed away for ever.

It was from Wadsley Lane that I first went to see the eternal sands of Bridlington. When, in 1937, we were able to afford our first seaside holiday, 'Worksop' was called in to take temporary care of my grandmother and to feed the hungry and now fully employed uncles – for Syd had found work in a cloth warehouse, and had been sent off on his first day of employment wearing a suit that had been freshly patched and pressed by the professional tailor's hand of Aunty Annie. A box Brownie was obtained by the assiduous collection of coupons from other people's copies of *John Bull*, and the three of us set off east in the direction of sea and sunshine.

I have an uneasy feeling that I behaved badly for most of the week. I certainly scattered crumbs onto the boarding-house floor with an abandon that provoked so massive a rebuke from the landlady that my mother felt obliged to defend her mores and my manners. A few steps up the narrow staircase that leads to the top of Flamborough lighthouse I refused to proceed a day further, forcing my father to carry me up to the lamp room on his back, rather than hold back the waiting queue of holiday-makers until I was persuaded or coerced into taxing my energy again. I found religion, and sang manically with the Church Army Mission on the beach. I demanded donkey rides and trips on miniature trains which we could not afford and in the evenings I refused to go to sleep. My nocturnal enthusiasm was submerging a model deep-sea diver in the wash-jug, blowing and sucking on the end of the rubber tube that came out of his head with an obsession that must have given him the plastic bends. But my greatest joy was sitting in the stern of the *Yorkshireman* or the *Princess Marina* watching the white foam rush away from under the propeller as the wind-up gramophone on deck played 'Cheek to Cheek' and 'September in the Rain'.

My mother sent pencil-written postcards home each day. They revealed deep concern about how my grandmother was 'managing' without her and expressed complete satisfaction at the behaviour of 'Roydie' – a name which, like 'Little Roy', I grew to hate with the years. 'Big Roy' added a brief formal greeting in a small neat hand. Its affectionate, but slightly detached, tone typified his attitude towards his mother-in-law. Although he was constantly and intimately concerned with her physical welfare – bodily lifting her whilst my mother acted as nurse – I never heard him call her Agnes or mother. His call for an evacuation of the living-room, 'Mrs Brackenbury wants a lift', rang out several times in each of my childhood days.

Bridlington was a happy holiday. Indeed, most of the days in Wadsley Lane provided a secure and certain beginning to my life. But physically events at Wadsley Lane marked me for life. I have the scar of it on my right instep and I breathe heavily in its memory whenever the pollen count rises. The scar was acquired as a by-product of one of the great family rituals – Sunday dinner, a meal eaten in the middle of the day and centred around a small joint of meat augmented by massive amounts of carbohydrate. The Hattersleys ate vast quantities of bread, much of it baked by my mother after the dough had risen in its cloth-covered pansion. Yorkshire pudding was not served as an independent delicacy that made up a course of its own, but was consumed with beef or mutton. Potatoes – roast (called baked), baked (called roast), mashed, boiled, chipped and fried – were an addiction which was least resistable when slices were frizzled in the joint's own juices immediately before we sat down for the weekly ritual.

One warm day, as I was playing in the garden, my mother, (making her final preparations for Sunday dinner) knelt in front of the kitchen oven as if it were a pagan altar and drew out the roasting meat for the addition of the essential potatoes. Finding the baking tin hotter than she expected, she rested it, for a moment, on the floor. That was the moment which I chose to bound through the back door and place my foot in the hot fat with the precision of a fast bowler who has practised for years to get his final stride exactly right. My grandmother later claimed that my white sock was 'shrivelled to a cinder'. I can only vouch for the feeling of the foot inside, in response to which I urged my father to cut it off with the carving knife.

Syd and George rushed out to a passing ice-cream cart and bought me a sixpenny vanilla sandwich to ease the pain. I was prevented from eating it by my grandmother, who knew that all Italians were unhealthy and was not prepared to risk my scalded foot being complicated by typhoid fever. I was carried off not to an expensive doctor but to a chemist who prescribed Antiflagistine, a proprietary brand of oily mud with which, in one form or another, I was to grow very familiar. My old pushchair was brought back into use for a week or so but I was soon leaping about again, proudly displaying a mark on my leg like a pair of white snakes wrestling with each other. When I started school, I used to show them to my classmates, proudly explaining that they marked the spot where 'm' mum scalded me with hot fat'.

That act of regular disloyalty took place at Hillsborough High School, a private establishment owned and run by Miss Bertha Roberts, Licentiate of the College of Preceptors. I made my first appearance there in the late spring of 1938, complete with bottle-green blazer and cap and the feeling of being different that was cultivated at fee-paying establishments. I was later to pay heavily for the priggishness. For Hillsborough High School, Miss Roberts and the green blazer were all a considerable mistake. That such a mistake was allowed to continue for five years – and was paid for in good money by a family with little cash to spare – was very largely the result of incidents that took place in 174 Wadsley Lane on or about Christmas Day 1937.

3
Bearing Gifts

—

By the standards of Christmas Eves in general, there was nothing
unusual that anyone can recall about Christmas Eve 1937. Gillie
Potter broadcast to England from Hogsnorton. The carol singers
dashed through a single verse of *Silent Night* before they asked for
money. In the Hattersley household, where there was a strict prohibition on decorating the living room before the 24th, paper streamers
were strung from wall to wall and glass baubles were hung on a tree
that had been planted in a soil-filled, crêpe paper-covered biscuit
box. The planting was as important a ritual as the tying-on of the
silver bells and golden apples. Each year, my mother infuriated Mr
English, the greengrocer, by sorting through all the trees which were
heaped against his front window 'looking for one which has not been
doctored'. Her object was the discovery of a tree which was healthy
enough to be transplanted into the back garden on Twelfth Night,
and would therefore relieve us, forever, of the cost of buying
Christmas trees. As the years passed, Mr English must have come to
realise that the stratagem never succeeded. By my birthday on 28th
December, the pine needles had always begun to pile up on the floor
under the branches which, by New Year's Day, were usually too
withered to bear the weight of the tawdry decorations. At some point
my mother would admit that she had failed. But there and then she
would announce her determination 'to get one without boiled roots'
next year.

But on Christmas Eve, we were always full of hope for the tree and
for ourselves. In the kitchen, 'home-made' mince pies were jostling
jam tarts for space in the oven. The term 'home-made' was a matter
of great pride and believed to be absolute, not relative. It encompassed both the pastry and the sticky conglomeration of dried and
crystallised fruit within it. I believed devoutly in the superiority of
'home-made' cakes and pastry. And, I was equally convinced that we
practised the home-made arts to a higher degree than any of our
neighbours. As, each November, I watched my mother turning the

handle of the cast-iron mincing machine, I really did believe that 'Worksop' grew the sticky ingredients on raisin trees and candied peel bushes.

In later years, when disloyal additions to the family actually expressed a preference for 'bought' mincemeat, mince pies were produced complete with coded messages – two 'jimps' cut in the top for 'bought' and three for 'home-made'. But in 1937 the collapse of culinary standards had not even begun. It seemed that the only problems were the usual problems. I was reluctant to stay still and quiet whilst my father read me the abridged version of *A Christmas Carol* and there was the annual argument over the 'Worksop' cathedral – a glorious structure made of papier-mâché (I suspect by Uncle Ern's own hand) with transparent sweet-papers providing a brilliant imitation of stained glass. The architect of this genuinely beautiful object had clearly intended that the whole building should be illuminated by a series of small candles – each one of which would shine through part of the 'stained glass'. Standing in the front window on Christmas Eve it would have been the envy of the neighbourhood – had it not been for a single design fault. If one of the candles had been lit within it, the whole edifice would have caught fire. Every Christmas Eve, I wanted to take the risk. Every Christmas Eve I was forbidden to go anywhere near the drawer where we kept the matches.

No doubt, there was much rejoicing when I eventually went to bed, and some relief when I was not awake and rushing round the house at five o'clock the following morning. When I was still asleep at eight, astonishment quickly turned into concern. At nine, I was complaining of headaches and a sore throat, pains in the back and feeling cold. Then I complained of feeling hot. When I began to make a noise like a winded cart-horse, it was decided that a doctor was needed; but nobody was quite sure which doctor it should be. My grandmother, although completely crippled, endured a stable condition that required only rare and routine medical attention. In those days, long before the National Health Service was invented, an ancient Dr Anderson from Worksop made occasional visits – arranged and financed, I now suspect, by Mrs Bráckenbury's eccentric siblings. Since there was no local doctor on whom we had a claim that came from familiarity, my father walked to Wisewood where the 'panel doctor', (provided for him because of his employment with the P.A.C.) had his home and surgery. The panel doctor was at home.

But he was not available on Christmas Day for casual patients. My father ran down the hill past the house where Christmas Day had not even begun to what I had always thought was a castle but was, in fact, the turreted residence of Dr Hall. He was out, but his assistant, Dr McBaine, had not yet left for the festivities at the Royal Infirmary. When my father described my symptoms, they ran back up Wadsley Lane together.

I was propped up in a living room armchair, performing the full repertoire of respiratory noises that I later came to call 'wheezing'. The tracheotomy that Dr McBaine had feared he might be required to perform for the first time in his life, was mercifully unnecessary. He looked at me and mouthed silently to my mother 'B-E-D'. I said 'bed' without arguing against the suggestion, and could not even raise the energy to complain when a ball of cotton wool on the end of a stick was pushed down my throat. Syd and George cycled off to the Royal Hospital with the carefully wrapped 'swab' in one of the tool bags that hung down from their saddles. In the late afternoon, my father was told what the tests revealed. I had diphtheria. Dr Hall himself came to see me in the early evening, pronounced that I should not be moved and announced to no one in particular that I was getting much worse. He promised to return in about an hour with serum and Dr McBaine. When they arrived, my mother told me that Dr McBaine was missing a party to attend upon me and made me wheeze 'thank you'.

Dr Hall was a small squat ex-naval surgeon with a square jaw and heavy watch chain. He took from his leather bag an instrument which I now know to have been a hypodermic syringe. Waving it in the air, he announced that he was going to stick its needle in my stomach. Still holding the hypodermic aloft as if it were a torch and he was the Statue of Liberty, he put his other hand in his waistcoat pocket and drew forth a couple of sweets of the expensive sort that had pictures of fruit on the wrappers. 'If you don't cry', he said, 'you can have these'. Dr McBaine held my shoulders. My father, his usual anxiety turned into terror, held down my feet with the aid of a towel Dr Hall had wrapped round my ankles. The needle was sunk into my stomach. I cried. Dr Hall, being a just man, put the sweets back in his waistcoat pocket.

I wheezed my way into Boxing Day and was injected again twenty-four hours after the first puncture. Late that night the rasping noise that reverberated from my larynx suddenly stopped. For a moment my father, part of the vigil by my bedside, thought that I had died. It was my mother who dared to make a closer inspection. I was breathing normally and sleeping peacefully. On the morning of the 27th I began to complain about missing Christmas, and preparations were made for a gentle celebration with me lying, weak and infectious, on my back.

The following day, I received gifts that had been intended for both birthdays – the 25th and the 28th. There were boxes of two dimensional soldiers – shiny coloured pictures of Green Jackets and Grenadier Guards stuck on plywood and cut out at rigid attention. There was a tin gramophone from Syd and George complete with a miniature record. During the next few weeks, the whole family grew to hate 'Auf Wiedersehen', the 'Stein Song' and the beer hall quartet which sang them. The prize amongst all the presents was a battered old, hand-driven, cinematograph.

In later years I met well-off youths who possessed electrically powered film projectors that were bought brand new. But my second-hand cinematograph possessed a quality with which none of the more modern models could compete. It spun around its spools and caught in its cog-wheels pieces cut from the ends of real motion pictures shown in real cinemas. It came to me with two round tins. One held six feet of Lon Chaney as a speechless Charlie Chan. The other held three yards of a silent Maurice Chevalier. Our first attempt to become the Wadsley Lane Cinema was disaster. A sheet, to act as the silver screen, was pinned to the bedroom wall. A bulb was removed from the landing light and twisted into place behind the lens. But as soon as it was switched on, every fuse in the house capitulated. We spent my birthday evening in candle-relieved gloom.

The following day, workmen came to complete the repairs which were far beyond our technical skills. When they had restored the power supply they demanded to see the offending apparatus in action. So, complete with mince pies and cups of tea, they tiptoed into my bedroom and together with Syd and George, my mother and my father began to breathe in the germ-laden air. Somehow Sheffield escaped the epidemic that the 'electricity men' might have started on its lethal way. The city even survived the way we responded to officialdom's instructions about finally preventing all risk of the infection spreading. When I was pronounced recovered, a dark blue van (embarrassingly like the vehicles used for fumigating rat-ridden or bug-infested slums) was parked outside 174 Wadsley Lane.

Working on the virtuous assumption that we had kept all potentially contaminated material in a restricted area, the driver announced his intention of taking all the portable material from my bedroom to the incinerator. The room would then be fumigated.

I possessed three objects which, since they were objects of embarrassed affection, I kept secret: Joey, a rubber cherub who looked as if he had fallen off a baroque altar; Duke, a handsome (though diminutive) Airedale bought by 'Worksop' to increase my canine consciousness; and a teddy bear that bore the imaginative name of Teddy. Following my visit to the circus I had demanded a small soft elephant to take to bed at night. But the message had been garbled on its way to 'Worksop', who sent me an ebony paperweight with real ivory tusks and toenails. Teddy was my true and constant friend. If he had been taken away for burning, diphtheria would certainly have been followed by a nervous breakdown. My original idea was to offer them the elephant as a sort of alternative hostage. But my mother, realising that his sacrifice would be in vain, saved Teddy with an act of athletic and ingenious irresponsibility. Whilst the 'sanitary men' staggered downstairs with one load of contaminated material, she opened the loft trap-door in the bedroom ceiling and hid Teddy in the roof like an allied airman in occupied Europe.

So both Teddy and I survived – Teddy probably less scathed than me. For months I retained an hysterical fear of doctors. One of Aunt Lot's distant Canadian relatives was forced to cut his Sheffield visit short because I associated his dark suit and leather bag with the medical profession and screamed uncontrollably whenever he approached. The sound of passing grocery or milk vans (the only form of internal combustion engine regularly to pass our door) had much the same effect. I insisted on making long detours so that we avoided passing Dr Hall's turreted surgery. But the aversion to doctors was not the worst outcome of the infection. Diphtheria confirmed the decision that I should be enrolled in Hillsborough High School where, it was assumed, my delicate chest would be treated with the kind of respect that was prohibited in state schools.

All the evidence suggests that I was destined for Hillsborough High School even before the fateful infection. Diphtheria struck three days before my fifth birthday and there can be little doubt that conscientious parents had decided on my primary school fate long before then. It is said that both grandma and 'Worksop' (for my mother always an irresistible combination) favoured Miss Roberts's establishment, though what actual benefit they expected it to bestow is far from clear. Its prospectus proudly boasted that it taught both French and Art – and would arrange piano and elocution classes for a small additional charge. But none of those enticing prospects could have really justified the fees. I suspect that the attraction was the visible difference (the bottle-green blazer and the extra week's holiday in September) and the act of sacrifice itself. If the front room was left unfurnished so that money could be found to pay the fees, the family huddled in the back room all knew that they were doing their best for Roydie. And when the mistake was recognised, the supposed delicacy of my constitution made the desirable transfer to Marcliffe Road Infants and Juniors too controversial to contemplate.

I vividly remember my first day at Hillsborough High School. The whole school – children ranging in age from four to sixteen – were accommodated within three classrooms within the rambling old house that accommodated Miss Bertha Roberts and her sister. Children between the ages of four and eight inhabited what must have once been the servants' hall – a large square room slightly below ground floor level, with barred windows which looked out onto the less attractive parts of the garden where coal and coke were stored – and enjoyed direct access to the lean-to shed where the housekeeper lived. From the housekeeper's quarters we received milk and arrowroot biscuits each morning – an optional extra for which Miss Roberts made a small charge. The smallest children worked at a long table under the window. Those about to 'move up' to senior classes occupied desks along a wall broken by what had once been a 'tradesmen's entrance'.

We were all under the supervision of Mrs Bramhall, a qualified teacher who had been forced to leave the state education system when she married. For socialist Sheffield of the 1930s obliged working wives to make way for single women and male breadwinners, and drove Mrs Bramhall and her like to take refuge in private establishments. Many of her pupils were equally in search of a sort of shelter which their parents feared the state would not provide. Betty was a bright and chubby cripple with steel callipers on both legs. Bessy, had she enrolled with the Local Education Authority, would have been sent to what unthinking locals call 'the daft school'. They were not typical of my fellow-pupils. More characteristic were the Broadbents (son and daughter of an Anglican vicar) and the children whose fur-collared mothers brought them back from lunch before they began afternoons of unremitting tea and gossip. But I remember Betty and Bessy because, looking back on Hillsborough High School, I cannot recall a single occasion when either of them was harassed or harried. Now, it seems to make up for some of its other educational inadequacies. At the time, nothing made up for the lack of physical activity. For all that Miss Roberts's pupils were allowed was a gentle swaying to the rhythm of Anne Driver and 'Music and Movement' on BBC's school broadcasts.

My first year at Hillsborough High School was the beginning of what seemed an age of constant asthma attacks. They grew in both severity and frequency until they reached a crescendo of coughing in 1941. But in the eighteen months before the war, the occasional spasms that assaulted my lungs and larynx terrified my parents more than they frightened me. The attacks lasted for about three days before I, apparently, recovered completely, and remained in my memory for nothing like the period necessary to prejudice me against physical activity. For half of the year I was an infant sports enthusiast with a Woolworth's cricket bat and three male adults willing to bowl to me. During the other six months, I was a football fan with a real football – a relic of George's youth that he had carried to Spain and back. I listened incessantly to sports broadcasts on the radio. All I lacked was the chance to push and shove other little boys in the pretence that I was playing organised games.

The absence of rewarding physical activity at school was, in part, mitigated by the ingenuity of the amusements provided at home. I was the only child in the life of two generations of adults; all of whom, in their different ways, felt an obligation to keep me amused and improve my education. Syd and George took turns in attempts at teaching me how to draw market crosses, horse troughs and other relics of rural England. My father, conscious of my affection for bears, cut the cartoons about Rupert from a workmate's *Daily Express*, painted them with water colours and stuck them in an old 'Worksop' pattern book. Uncle Ern made, with his own hand, a set of miniature Indian clubs which caused much distress to the whole family and almost made me a schizophrenic. Normally, I was forbidden to touch them, for I could not whirl them around my head without dealing myself stunning blows. But when the agile benefactor came to visit me I was required to perform in front of him to show how assiduously I had practised with his lethal gift. And, just before we left Wadsley Lane, there was the yacht.

The biggest model yacht which I had ever seen was made by Triang and bought from Redgate's in Fitzallen Square for a reduced price because of the damaged paint work on its hull. Its complicated masts and rigging could be trimmed and on its deck was a device that could, in theory, be used to make it tack in the wind or sail in circles. Operating the steering mechanism was entirely beyond us. So we usually sailed *Margaret* like an ordinary yacht on Hillsborough Park Pond, protected from becoming beached on one of the ornamental islands by a ball of waxed string that was fastened to her elegant stern and enabled me to haul her back from any danger. But on one great day I was taken across Sheffield by tramcar to Millhouses, where the yacht pool was innocent of dangerous islands. *Margaret*, leaning into the wind, sped for the distant shore and I raced around the lake to make sure that her prow was not damaged on the opposite bank. Of course, cutting corners, I fell in. Apart from my Hillsborough High School cap, I was totally submerged. The journey home, wrapped in my father's jacket, was one of my earliest lessons about the complicated and complementary characters of my parents. My father was so hopelessly anxious about my welfare that I felt a duty to comfort him in some way. My mother was simply determined to keep me as warm and dry as decency permitted – massaging my legs as much as was compatible with the avoidance of indecent exposure. I was affectionately concerned about him and absolutely certain that she would get me home before I was sick again.

4
Up in the World

—

Prolonged attendance at Hillsborough High School was the penalty I paid for diphtheria. The bonus, which all the family enjoyed, was Airedale Road. Inevitably the call of owner occupation grew louder and louder with the increase of financial certainty. The two older brothers moved from Barnsley to more secure employment. My father remained with the Public Assistance Committee but was made 'permanent' and transferred to the Hillsborough office where he worked in a converted chapel and played billiards on the youth club's table when business was slack. George became an 'established' clerical officer in the Ministry of Labour, working in the Hillsborough office, where he played table tennis in the rest room when there was no immediate demand for his services. Sooner or later we would have bought a house of our own whether or not I had been struck down in December 1937. But the infection – blamed for no very good reason on the Wadsley Lane drains – added urgency to a decision that had already been taken in my mother's mind and gave her an unanswerable argument with which to counter my father's caution and persuade 'Worksop' that they should lend us the money for the deposit at once.

The search for the house of our own was, of course, led by Uncle Ern, who strode with us across building sites, reinforcing his reputation on matters related to joinery by staring at oak and ash trees and estimating how many coffin boards they contained. Houses, contemplated by us in the expert's absence, were struck off the list if they were covered in stucco, since he could not be certain about the quality of brickwork that lay beneath. One house, on which we were just about to make the deposit, was vetoed after Uncle Ern made a surprise late night visit to the site. He was outraged to discover that the tarmacadam path, instead of being laid with the aid of brazier and roller, was being heated on a shovel over a woodfire and stamped into the ground by a labourer in hobnail boots. Then George found Airedale Road.

George, apparently like his father before him, was a great believer in bargains. He searched the evening paper for news about job-lots of sawn-up timber and bulk purchases of curtain material. He urged my mother to postpone purchase of the weekend joint until late on Saturday evening when, according to him, butchers were desperate to unload haunches of unwanted meat. In my active stamp collecting days, he often bought me packets of '500 for sixpence', 450 of which were the same and all of which I already possessed. So, naturally enough, when he discovered a stucco-free, brand new semi-detached house with garden front and back, we greeted his initial enthusiasm with experienced scepticism. His insistence that we could move (at a price we could afford) to the quiet road a mile or so nearer Wadsley Common and open country seemed wholly incredible.

George showed no resentment at the implied criticism made of his judgment by his brothers and sister-in-law. Indeed, he never seemed to resent anything. He faced life from behind a secret smile that always implied that he knew something that was denied to the rest of us. I was over forty when he died. But I still felt wholly incapable of understanding what he was really thinking and, in consequence, could not shake off a feeling of juvenile inferiority. Like my father, he possessed the Hattersley head. It was a characteristic as pronounced as the Habsburg jaw, and caused me much distress at grammar school. In art classes we were taught to draw skulls, like eggs balanced at forty-five degrees on their necks. I was the only boy in the form whose head was really that shape and bulged over the back of his collar. With typically unnerving self-confidence, George emphasised the infirmity by maintaining his short priest's hair-cut throughout his life. As a boy, I used to stare at that oval head without having the slightest idea about what was going on inside.

His judgment about Airedale Road was entirely vindicated by Uncle Ern's unqualified approval. But before it was thought right to spend the sage's time on a detailed inspection, we were taken on a detailed tour by Mr Swift the builder. I remember him sitting in our Wadsley Lane living room, waiting for my mother to descend hatted and coated for the expedition and watching me play on the floor with my model motor-cars. He was fascinated to notice that because of the steeply sloping floorboards the toys sped across the carpet like toboggans on the Cresta Run. When my mother came in, he announced that in his houses the floors were absolutely flat. She had no idea what he meant, but was clearly deeply impressed.

Mr Swift drew our attention to the solid mahogany lavatory seat which (no doubt with recent diphtheria in mind) he insisted was particularly germ-resistant. Uncle Ern (when it was eventually decided that his intervention was justified), made one of the workmen pull up a number of floorboards and descended into the darkness between the joists. On his eventual reappearance, he announced that 'you could eat your dinner down there' and, George's judgment being vindicated by the discovery of this important advantage, we decided to buy. I accompanied my parents to Slater and Elliot's (who for many years afterwards I thought of as 'our solicitors') and watched them go through the complicated formalities of buying a house. For much of the time my delighted attention was concentrated on velvet objects hanging on each side of the fireplace, which my father had told me (in the subdued whispers that he thought appropriate to a solicitor's office) were cricket caps. The afternoon was, however, spoilt by the discovery that our lease lasted for only nine hundred and ninety-nine years. The acquisition of a house of our own seemed such a monumental achievement, that the idea of it being snatched away from us in little more time than had passed since the Norman Conquest was unbearable.

In truth it was neither the superb ventilation of the foundations nor the absence of stucco, the mahogany lavatory seat nor the perfectly horizontal floorboards that made us buy 101 Airedale Road. The decision to purchase, like all the Hattersley decisions, was taken by my mother. Her mind was made up by the churchyard (which argued for Airedale Road in general) and the elderberry tree which gave Number 101 an advantage over the rest of Mr Swift's speculative development. The churchyard, overgrown with weeds so high that it was almost impossible to see the Victorian broken columns and celtic crosses, began immediately beyond the wall at the bottom of the garden. So instead of our washing and back windows being in the clear view of the back windows and washing lines of another semi-detached row running parallel to ours, we were spied upon by nothing more inquisitive than weeping angels. Wadsley churchyard offered us the privacy of not being 'overlooked'. When I first read that the grave was 'a fine and private place', I thought that the poet was alluding to the advantages of having a cemetery at the bottom of the garden – particularly one with a dense covering of tall weeds know to the botanically ignorant as 'bamboo'. Uncle Ern could make a whistle or blow-pipe out of the plant's hollow stem with a few shrewd cuts of the penknife. But I was allowed to blow into neither the instrument nor the weapon, as my grandmother was convinced that the plant from which they were made exuded a lethal poison.

The way into the cemetery for me (and subsequently for my parents, who used the narrow paths between the overgrown groves as a short cut to the bus stop) was the elder tree which, although we did not know it, had become positively geriatric by the time of our arrival. In Battle of Britain year, its green berries failed to ripen into an appropriate shade of purple. In the summer that we celebrated Victory in Europe the white blossom did not even turn into green fruit. When Winston Churchill became Prime Minister again, the tree withered and died. But in 1938 it stood, apparently sturdy, reminding my mother of her past in the Nottingham coalfield (which she increasingly recalled as entirely arcadian), symbolising our promotion to the ranks of property and providing me with a living ladder which I could use for my ascent to the churchyard. It was also 'something for Mrs Brackenbury to look at'.

My grandmother's narrow bed (specially made in Uncle Ern's joinery company to his own design) had a permanent place under the living room window. In it she half sat and half lay for every night and day of our first six years at Airedale Road – her legs drawn up at a permanent ninety degrees, making the sheets and blankets into a little tent, her arms immobile by her sides and her head held slightly forward but neither moving to left nor right. Sometimes she used a long thin toasting fork to convey small morsels of food from plate to mouth with a painful wriggle of her one half-mobile wrist. But most of her meals were fed to her by my mother. For the rest of the day she read and listened to the wireless – or stared out of the window at the garden and the elderberry tree. It never seemed the least strange to me that she should be living her motionless life right there amongst us. Once she told us of a dream in which local children had laughed at her and called her a cripple. We were horrified not so much by their cruelty as by their choice of language. She was not a cripple, she was my grandmother.

Airedale Road, being built to the classic design of the interwar suburban semi-detached, had two groundfloor rooms of almost identical size. The one at the front had a bay window which gave it a feeling of spacious pleasure. The one at the back had, when we first moved in, a coal oven, identical in principle to a black-leaded grate of Shirebrook, though made out of a speckled vitreous enamel that gave it a 1930s gloss. Either room would have made my grandmother a suitable retreat. But we never thought of her being kept apart from the family in lonely, hygienic isolation. She was part of us and she lived in our living room. So for the first few months the 'front room' was never used at all. When we could afford the furniture, it became just the 'dining room' and then, as the odd chairs at the back of the house were thrown away, the big oak table took their place and a brand new three-piece suite qualified it for the title of 'sitting room'. Some of our younger neighbours developed 'lounges'. But my grand-mother persisted with her more basic descriptions. The kitchen she called the scullery. The room in which she lived was the kitchen. The place we sometimes sat in on Sundays (but which was never used for activities which involved paint, water or sand) was simply 'the room'. Like Hannibal, it possessed a grandeur that needed no more than a single word description.

Actually getting my grandmother into the Airedale Road back room was a major logistical achievement. But although it was the greatest difficulty that we faced during our transmigration, it was by no means the only one. The Wadsley Lane plants and shrubs posed a major problem. For it said, quite specifically, on the back of our rent book, that no sooner had a tenant planted a bush or tree than it became the property of the landlord. But we could see no justice in that. So I was posted on guard at the front window to give early warning of the rent collector's final visit whilst my father dug furiously but furtively in the garden. We took the rose bush and the laburnum, the lilac and half the privet hedge. Although stolen, they grow still in Airedale Road; no doubt the legal property of whoever now occupies the Hattersleys' last rented house, but blooming nonetheless for that.

The problem of transporting my grandmother was solved by borrowing a wicker bath-chair from the Wadsley Church Vicarage; an object kept by the rector – George Cherry Weaver MA (Oxon) – for the occasional transportation of the itinerant poor. The three Hattersley men lifted Mrs Brackenbury aboard with great care and immense difficulty. Because of the curve in which her spine was fixed she had to be strapped in like a parcel in a basket. The back of the wheelchair was festooned with stolen greenery, that gave its rear view the air of an extravagantly camouflaged tank. Together we pushed the bundle of Wadsley Lane flora and fauna past *The Horse and Jockey*, the Hillsborough High School, the fish and chip shop

33

that my mother so heartily despised and Wadsley Church with which
we had an ambivalent relationship that I could not at the time have
hoped to understand.

We arrived before the building work was quite finished. A painter
(who for some reason my mother thought impertinent) spent a week
finishing off the woodwork in the rear windows and teaching me
parodies on popular songs of the day like 'Music, Mousetrap,
Cheese'. The steep drive, which was such a feature of the new houses
as it implied that the owners would one day own a motor car, was not
completely 'settled'. A heavy roller stood by the double gates waiting
to give the final coat of tar and gravel a suitably heavy pounding.
When Mr Swift went bankrupt (confirming George's claim to detect
underpriced offers as diviners sense the presence of water) we im-
pounded the roller as part payment for the inadequately surfaced drive.

We believed that the roller would provide valuable assistance in
the creation of the two gardens which we decided to construct in
conformity with the classic suburban design. That required grass
(known as 'lawn' to our neighbours) to be laid at both front and
back. Between the bay window and the road the grass, being
essentially decorative, would be surrounded by a hedge of 'miniature' golden privet that delineated the boundaries of our property but
in no way obscured the view of the central flowerbed and its standard
rose. The back garden, being an essentially utilitarian place for the
erection of deck-chairs in summer and the drying of clothes on
Monday mornings all the year round, had as much as possible of its
privacy preserved by green privet which we believed would grow six
feet tall. Between hedge and grass herbaceous borders bloomed with
the help of Suttons' and Bees' seed catalogues. The annual cycle was
invariable. In the spring they were raked into little furrows of
carefully prepared soil – their temporary resting place marked by the
picture on the packet which was speared into the earth by half a
wooden clothes peg and blew in the May wind like a decorated sail
on a toy galleon. Strangely enough the flowers usually lived up to the
promise of their illustration. Only the back border, dark and dank
under the churchyard wall, proved barren. The shame of constant
failure was camouflaged by calling it 'Roydie's garden' and pretending that the wilting sweet peas and stunted marigolds were a
concession to my botanical education.

Growing successful grass is – as every amateur gardener will testify
– one of the most difficult of all horticultural tasks. Turf being

beyond our pocket, we bought from Woolworth vast brown-paper packets of seed which we proposed to broadcast in the manner described in New Testament parables. But before the sowers went forth, they had to minimise the amount of stony ground on which it might fall. That required the whole back garden to be dug over and then replaced smoothly horizontal. The roller proved a disaster. Instead of flattening the earth until it looked like the foundations of a billiard table waiting to be covered in baize, it created deep undulations with the single virtue of uniformity. The regular repetition of troughs and peaks gave the unhappy impression that the whole of the back garden had been buried under a vast sheet of corrugated cardboard. Sitting in the back room in exasperated despair, my father suddenly noticed Syd and George demonstrating why necessity is sometimes ashamed to acknowledge its material connection with invention. They had fastened to their feet pieces of plywood torn from the tea-chests in which our chattels had been transported from Wadsley Lane, and were attempting to stamp the earth flat. It must have looked like a fertility rite, performed by some primitive tribe to ensure the fecundity of recently captured ground. And in a way it was.

That patch of grass became the scene of the last rite in our ritual wash day. On 'good drying days', the clothes line was stretched across it from the hook in the house wall to a branch in the elderberry tree. My mother then ran beneath it, duster held high, cleaning the rope in anticipation of dangling clean clothes from its spotless fibres. The 'duster' was really the remnant of an old sheet or worn-out shirt. We cannibalised the same source for the 'handkerchiefs' which we used during the streaming colds which afflicted my father and me each winter. Then we described them with more simplicity. They were 'rags'. When wash day coincided with a cold I never dared go near the kitchen. Outside it was bright and dry. But around my mother's tub, the world was awash. She beat the dirty clothes on an old zinc wash-board and agitated the soapy water with a 'dolly-peg' – a little five-legged stool at the end of a wooden handle which, if rotated amongst the washing ensured that no fold or crease escaped the carbolic douche. Inevitably, she performed all these operations with such manic vigour that the kitchen floor ran with water. The whole operation was carried on in something approaching secrecy. For the shape of the tub, dolly-peg, wash-board and mother could only dimly be discerned through the steam that filled the kitchen as

35

the washing was prepared for the lawn which we had created with such single-minded determination.

We never made the back lawn really flat. Though we did create an uneven plateau by chopping away the earth at the top of the garden and piling it behind a containing wall that we built from 'antique' stone at the bottom. As the wall was about to be finished I was allowed to use a dollop of surplus cement to stick a pale green pot rabbit on one of its uneven coping stones. The rabbit was a prize from Wadsley Fair, and my grandmother insisted that she would enjoy watching it through the window. It was generally agreed that the rabbit let down the tone of the new wall and the incipient garden beyond. Indeed it was only spoken of with affection after I, for some inexplicable reason, smashed it to pieces with a shovel. Its paw marks are visible still.

The garden once 'laid out', there were other signs of arrival and symbols of property which had to be paid proper respect. We bought a toolshed through the post – replying to an advertisement in the *Daily Herald* – and erected its prefabricated sections where the path, into which the drive had narrowed as it passed to the side of the house, met the first cultivated earth of the recently landscaped garden. The path itself ran parallel to a thin strip of earth, divided from our 'detached' neighbour's thin patch of earth by concrete posts through which the boundary wires were slung. On the far side of their identical patch of earth was their identical narrow path. The 'back' doors of both properties (actually at the side of the house, but maintaining their tribal description) stared at each other across mirror images of tarmacadam, earth, boundary posts, earth and tarmacadam. We decided to fence in what came, partly because it was enclosed, to be called the yard. In order to avoid offence to the neighbours, from whom we were clearly trying to isolate ourselves, we built our stockade out of 'rustic' poles – lengths of straight timber from which the bark had not been removed. The fence, complete with home-made gate, cut across the top of the drive just below the back door and turned at right angles to run along the line of the boundary posts. It created only the illusion of privacy, for we lacked the courage to nail the posts close together, and left two-feet gaps through which our activities could be easily seen. But once the rustic gate was shut we felt shielded from the eyes of a road almost entirely composed of similar families making similar attempts to occupy a new world of property and possession.

5

Flora and Fauna

—

Through the gaps in the rustic fence and beyond the patches of earth and strips of tarmacadam lived the Browns – George, Nellie and their teenage son, Cyril. George Brown as an insurance supervisor whom I wrongly believed to be Scottish. I made the mistake about his origins, partly because our paths first crossed whilst I was passing through my Highland phase – a brief obsession induced by the possession of a 'Worksop'-made kilt. Because of the cardboard claymore and the tales of Bonnie Prince Charlie that my father supplied to augment the Royal Stuart tartan I felt a desperate need to know at least one Scotsman. Mr Brown seemed to qualify because he had sandy hair and even sandier 'plus-four' trousers. These, I later learned, were intended to proclaim his passion for golf.

George Brown passed all his weekends and most of his evenings at the Hillsborough Golf Club. The few moments actually spent at home were occupied almost exclusively by practising the swing of his drive. I can still hear the swish of club cutting through the air – a noise remarkably similar to the hiss of a scythe reaping high grass. I can recall my mother actually confusing the two sounds and hoping that, at last, the dense, weed spreading undergrowth that made up most of the Brown land was being mowed down. But golf left no time for George Brown to till the soil or plough the wilderness. To keep up appearances he had most of the front garden covered in concrete, vaguely camouflaged with haphazard indentations in the vain hope that it would look like carefully laid crazy paving. Mr Brown's habits were as regular as the grass on the eighteenth green. Each evening at ten, his labours on the tees and fairways over, he would march up to his own front door (an amenity used by his neighbours only on ceremonial occasions) and ring his own bell. I took it as a sign that he was truly the master of Number 99.

On the other side of 101, and locked to us like a Siamese twin, were the Fredericks. Mr Frederick was a young metallurgist in a steel works. His father – by occupation a lady's hairdresser and, therefore, the object of general contempt – bought Mrs Frederick Junior a dog as a birthday gift. We had no doubt that it would be ill-treated and neglected – fears later said to be confirmed by the decision to call the unfortunate Scottish type of terrier Whisky. We believed that the purchase of animals as presents was a sure sign of the irresponsibility of the eventual owner, second only as an indication of callous disregard to the choice of the luckless pet's name. Long after I had come to understand the absurdity of blaming the recipient for the behaviour of the donor, I still believed that cherished and respected dogs were called Mick, Chum and Bruce, or something similarly sober. A fancy name meant that this year's cuddly pup would become next year's neglected stray.

However, the possession of a suitably sensible name was no guarantee of good treatment. On the other side of Airedale Road, in one of the older owner-occupied houses, a cairn terrier called Bessy was believed, by us, to be in an advanced state of battered malnutrition. Bessy demonstrated her deep deprivation by eating all the meat we gave her and wagging her tail whenever we stroked her shaggy coat. Dogs, we believed emphatically, could recognise their friends. We set ourselves up as Bessy's refuge and she became a virtually permanent protected resident. I have never been sure if her owners' failure to prosecute us for alienation of canine affection was an indication of their sensible tolerance or lack of interest.

The Frederick's other neighbour ('next door but one' to us in the road) were the Davises; mother, father and Hilary, a girl of exactly my age. Mr Davis was a retired Petty Officer, who had become a postman and used his Royal Navy gratuity to buy his house outright. True to the maritime tradition, he performed domestic tasks that his male neighbours would have found embarrassing. Each Sunday, he washed all the family's laundry and – if the weather was warm – he did it in public, occupying the space by the back door which, unlike us, the Davises left visible to the road. One sunny morning, with sleeves rolled up and hairy forearms covered with foam, he was approached by a tract-selling Jehovah's Witness. The evangelist, undeterred by the Davis brisk 'No thank you', set up a portable gramophone on the garden wall and began to broadcast a message to Wadsley and to the world. Mr Davis offered the missionary the choice of removing the instrument or having it kicked to Barnsley, in a voice that could be heard through the walls of the intervening houses. My father took me into our front room and made me promise 'never to use any of those words'.

Our reservation about the Davises concerned more than the occasional use of quarter-deck language. It was said that they had been seen together going into public houses – most flagrantly *Marples* in FitzAllen Square. Mrs Davis once called round with some underwear which she had purchased in the 'rag-market' and asked Syd, an embarrassed bachelor, to use his experience as a clerk in a cloth warehouse to judge whether or not she had bought a bargain. Talk of Davis depravity ('he could hardly get his key in the door last night') was rife amongst their more middle-class neighbours, but hotly refuted by other ex-servicemen in the road. Eddie Gill – who lived opposite and had been gassed in the First World War – 'understood' why a recently retired regular sailor who had served at Jutland might take refuge in an occasional bottle of stout. Mr Gill, who had become a Town Hall clerk after years of unemployment, was (he always added) too worried about next week's rent to similarly indulge himself. In any event, he had to be constantly alert and ready to respond to the sudden medical demands of his wife, 'who was not of the strongest'.

I used to fancy that the further I looked up and down Airedale Road from our central position of orthodox respectability, the more colourful the characters of our neighbours became. Three houses to the north was Eddie Wheatley, the go-getting owner of a small spring manufacturing company. Four houses to the south lived Eric Taylor, then secretary, but eventually General Manager, of the Sheffield Wednesday Football Club. If my cup ran over at the thought of living in the same sort of house as a Sheffield Wednesday functionary, it produced a positive flood of pride at the recollection that I shared a road with a man who had played cricket for Yorkshire Colts. Walter Colley was Airedale Road's only manual worker – the single resident who came home 'in his muck' with his 'sweat rag' still around his neck. At the top end of the road, he was held up as an awful example of the fate that befell the intemperate. For, as well as showing youthful promise as a fast bowler, he had once possessed a voice which – local legend claimed – had won him an audition with the Sadlers Wells Opera Company. Both gifts had, however, been sacrificed to the demon drink. But as I grew up, I came to regard Walter Colley as a personification of the Yorkshire virtues. He spoke with the broad vowel sounds of the Ridings. He still talked about his youthful delights – cricket and choral music. And he worked at

Daniel Doncasters, 'makers of high quality stampings, pressings and forgings, established 1779', as second or third man on a steam hammer. I developed an increased admiration for his army of sons – all of them what my father called 'typical Sheffield tykes'. They had moustaches, which were not fashionable outside Sheffield at that time, and double-breasted suits with high padded shoulders and accentuated waists which have never been fashionable anywhere except Sheffield.

On Sundays when George Brown was playing golf, ex-Petty Officer Davis was washing his dirty linen in public and the more respectable residents of Airedale Road were doing whatever reasonable task was essential to the welfare of their homes and gardens, the Colleys were on Wadsley Common playing 'knur and spell', otherwise known as 'nipsey'. Knur and spell was a primitive pastime popular amongst competitive Yorkshire miners. Players took it in turns to lob a missile into the air and strike it with a weighted rod for the greatest distance that eye, muscle and reflex would allow. In its pure form the trajectile was tapered at one end and elevated for the *coup de grace* by a smart tap from the weapon that eventually sent it hurtling two hundred yards through the air. In the sophisticated (perhaps even corrupt) form of the game, the flying object was initially elevated by a spring-loaded device which gave the striker valuable extra seconds to prepare his massive swing. Sometimes, during our Sunday morning walks 'across the common', we saw the Colleys in competitive action; jackets off, ties loosened and braces exposed. We suspected that they gambled on the rival distance. I was, and remain, in perpetual shock, at my inability to remember whether the 'knur' was an object to be struck, or a weapon with which to strike the 'spell'.

Ernest Wheatley was, in his way, an equally typical son of Sheffield. His special talent – apart from, or perhaps related to, the gift of getting on – was the ability to 'lay his hands' on objects that his neighbours needed but could not afford to buy at normal market price. George, having discovered a novel entitled *I Can Get It For You Wholesale* on the shelves of the Hillsborough Public Library spent several Saturday mornings searching second-hand bookshops for a copy which he swore he would sell to Wheatley at an inflated price. Whilst he pursued his unremunerative search, Ernest Wheatley himself was delivering rolls of wire netting, sheets of glass, lengths of garden hose and bags of cement; for all of which the grateful homebuilders paid instant cash. The fruits of these various labours ripened into a slightly battered S.S. Jaguar, with a solid brick garage to keep it in, innumerable items of uncut moquette furniture, one of the few private telephones in the road and a huge mahogany radiogram. One evening, Mr Wheatley actually engaged the services of ex-Petty Officer Davis to help him manhandle the radiogram down the street and into our living room where – out of the goodness of his heart – he gave my grandmother a recital of Nelson Eddy and Jeannette MacDonald. After he left, George was reproved for affecting surprise that there had been neither charge for admission nor the sale of chocolates and cigarettes.

I suspect that both Mrs Brackenbury and her daughter felt that if cigarettes had been on offer, Syd, George and 'big Roy' would have queued up to buy them at any price. Smoking was the only Airedale Road indulgence tolerated by the young matriarch and her mother. But it was always kept under supervision and in tight control. Each Friday, Hemmings, the Co-op or whoever was currently supplying our groceries delivered the weekly supply of unperishable food – the tinned salmon which my father enjoyed more than any other delicacy, and the pineapple chunks which were a feature of Sunday afternoon tea. Somewhere buried under the Carnation Milk and the Skipper Sardines, there were several cartons of Woodbines, which were handed out in a weekend ritual like rations in a beleaguered fortress. There was usually a mighty argument about whether or not I could open all the packets immediately and extract the cigarette cards, of which I became a collector at a precociously early age. However, I never possessed a complete set. For I could not sustain sufficient interest in Policemen of the World and Birds of Britain to pursue the missing Mountie or search for the rare willow warbler. Swapping, a practice essential to cigarette card success, was forbidden because my grandmother feared that I might lick an adhesive surface that had already been moistened by the spittle of an infectious acquaintance. In any case, I knew that stamp collecting was a superior pursuit with first claim on my time and enthusiasm.

Stamp collecting was believed to be educational and was, therefore, encouraged to the furthest extent of the family's financial ability. Each Saturday, when my father's five-and-a-half-day week had ended in the receipt of his pay packet, he would buy me a cheap stamp which I had found attractive in the Stanley Gibbons catalogue that I pored over in the Hillsborough Public Library. Buying the stamp was the only violation of his pay packet that my father allowed himself. For as he handed me the small cellophane envelope that contained the little picture of the Temple of the Tooth at candy or the tiny reproduction of Whistler's Mother he also handed over his weekly earnings to the head of our household. For years, George and Syd did the same, receiving in return a few shillings for their essential expenses and occasional indulgences. Apart from the cigarettes (aggregated in the total household budget) their only extravagances were weekly visits to the local cinema, winter Saturday afternoons at Hillsborough or Bramall Lane, and regular browsing through the Market Hall second-hand bookstall.

The Market Hall bookstall was also one of our sources of stamps. From an early age, I was taught to avoid the adjective 'foreign', for as with King George V (who, I was reminded, possessed an entirely colonial collection) I realised that the postal arrangements of the Empire were, like its people, British, not alien. My philatelic tastes were slightly more catholic than the King's, but I heartily despised the lurid religious series printed by South American republics. And I believed that no self-respecting envelopes would adhere for long to the crudely commercial products of Andorra, Monaco, Lichenstein and the Vatican City. I liked to fill pages of my album with precise rows of small stamps, distinguished from each other not by their design but by their colour and value. Most of all, I prized 'Penny Reds' – engravings of the young Victoria identical in every particular apart from the letters in their perforated corners. 'Penny Reds' were virtually worthless, but they looked as if they ought to be locked away at night. I was a stamp snob.

Stamps from the Market Hall bookstall were given an unequivocal Airedale Road welcome. But the second-hand books themselves were treated with frightened suspicion. 'Worksop' suggested that any volume that had been read before it passed into our vulnerable hands should be sterilised by baking in the oven to ensure the death of the germs that surely lurked between the pages. The ingenuous precaution was vetoed by my grandmother, who feared that even the temperature generated by 'Barnsley brights' would be insufficient to kill the more hardy microbes. She had a clear mental picture of the resilient bacilli residing in the cracks and crevices of the fire-bricks ready to infect unsuspecting Yorkshire pudding and to contaminate innocent baked potatoes.

Fortunately for my future, enthusiasm to develop a healthy mind triumphed over concern about the maintenance of a healthy body, and elderly editions of standard works began to litter the living room. The prize pieces in the collection were three volumes of Harmsworth's Encyclopedia, bound in what looked like leather and embossed with what might have been gold. I pored over those heavy tomes for half a decade of wet Saturdays, but only improved my education in subjects with initials from the top end of the alphabet. However, there was little human knowledge that could be encompassed within the headings A–BAN, BAN–CAV and CAV–DRI that did not pass swiftly through my mind during those years. The title pages of the sections afforded me particular delight. Each one was, in itself, a general knowledge game which allowed me to demonstrate my ability to recognise the drawings of St Augustine, King Alfred and Matthew Arnold, Queen Boadicea, Napoleon Bonaparte and the Venerable Bede, Julius Caesar, Caxton and Edith Cavell, Dante, Disraeli and Donatello's David. My deep, but narrow, erudition was shared with Harold Woolhouse from Number 84. I suspect that, had we possessed the entire set, he might well have become a professor of zoology, rather than of botany.

Harold Woolhouse was a tall, rawboned boy with a tall, rawboned father (who taught in the school for the mentally handicapped) and a tall, rawboned grandfather who lived next door. Each rawboned generation had a passion for plants and animals. Harold's father shared his spare time between greenhouse, allotment, rabbits, hens and racing pigeons. He also possessed a disreputable-looking dog that was possibly a cross between a whippet and a lurcher but would not have been acknowledged as a relation by respectable members of either breed. The pigeons disturbed the entire road. The pleasure of sharing their postal address with a genuine 'professional man' was more than counteracted by the indignity of living in a road with bobbins on the telegraph wires to protect the homing racers from crashing into the invisible hazard as they swooped for home. The bobbins hung between the posts like a social stigma.

We, of course, were more worried about the welfare of sixteen pigeons and took particular exception to Mr Woolhouse's habit of throwing stones at those birds which, at the end of a race, loitered on nearby roofs rather than descending to their loft so that the identity bracelet they wore could be passed through the special clock which recorded their arrival time. But it was the butterflies and caterpillars that gave us sleepless nights. Harold, under his father's supervision, collected butterflies with methodical zeal. Running about the churchyard or Wadsley Common with net and fey expression was not his style. He collected leaves from plants which, on the balance of scientific probability, were likely to be the resting place of species that his collection lacked. He then waited for the eggs to turn into caterpillars and the caterpillars to metamorphose into butterflies and moths. When the jam-jar-bred chrysalis finally burst and the Red Admiral or Cabbage White spread its wings, the creature was gassed with ammonia and staked out on a cork board until *rigor mortis* set in. To preserve my friendship with Harold Woolhouse, we had to keep his habits from my grandmother. She thought of him as the little boy who could identify different sorts of *auriculae* and took me hunting for them on overgrown graves. They were the only plants that grew successfully on my strip of garden under the cemetery wall.

6
Reared by Hand

—

During our first two years at Airedale Road, I began to develop the bronchial asthma that kept me indoors in foggy autumn evenings and wet winter afternoons throughout the early Forties. Dr Hall of the hypodermic syringe and the returnable fruit pastilles retired and sold his practice to a short man with a neat moustache, Dr McArthur, in whom none of us had any confidence. For instead of being Scottish, like a proper doctor, he talked with a thick Dublin accent and openly admitted that he was a graduate of Trinity College. It may have been the years in Rome and Valladolid that convinced George and my father that the Irish medical schools were the refuge of students who were unable to fulfil the exacting requirements of Great Britain's teaching hospitals. Whatever the cause of their contempt, it was both considerable and contagious. So, after a visit to the mahogany consulting room of Dr Anderson in Worksop (financed by the aunts so that 'their minds could be put at rest') we transferred all our custom to Dr Andrew Stephen, whose name proclaimed his paper qualifications. Dr Stephen – and his numerous assistants – ministered to me for the rest of my boyhood. Most of the ministrations came from the assistants, for the principal in the practice felt most medically fulfilled when treating the pulled muscles and torn ligaments of the Sheffield Wednesday Football Club. Thirty years later, as the knighted Chairman of the Football Association he, like me, was the luncheon guest of the British Waterways Board. 'Have you' an official enquired, 'met the Secretary of State for Prices and Consumer Protection?' The reply was only a slight exaggeration: 'Met him,' Sir Andrew replied, 'I delivered him.'

All the doctors diagnosed the same condition: I suffered from bronchial asthma. No one had any idea about its cause. Therefore, all-out war was declared on the symptoms. I was tested for a whole range of allergies – hay, rhubarb, cats, pollen, bananas, feathers, strawberries – and found, to some extent, vulnerable to all of them. But although I slept on a flock pillow and made wide detours around lilac trees, the 'asthma attacks' persisted. I do not know if they struck twenty or two hundred times. For each episode of coughing and wheezing now seems identical – save for the single occasion when I was given a double dose of the palliative with which my respiration was encouraged to return to a normal pattern of behaviour, and very nearly gave up wheezing and coughing for ever. All the other spasms took exactly the same course. They began with a congested awakening in what I imagined to be the middle of the night, but was usually about nine o'clock in the evening. As my breathing became more and more constricted, I shouted for my mother and banged on the floor in panic that she could not hear or would not come. When it was confirmed that my inability to draw steady breath was more than a nightmare's memory, I was carried downstairs clinging to my mother like an agitated monkey and held in a combination of maternal embrace and fireman's lift.

For the next couple of hours I remained in the same position, half asleep yet half upright as I was passed from parental hand to parental hand and wheezed and spluttered over different shoulders. The tablets – like so many things in our lives, spoken of with generic simplicity as 'the tablets', as if mine was the only prescription in the world – were always administered with reluctance. But if after sixty minutes or so I still sounded like a winded carthorse, they were washed down my throat in tiny crushed fragments. When that failed to bring my breathing back to normal, my father walked to the kiosk at the end of the road and telephoned for Dr Stephen who arrived, briskly injected me in the arm, watched my visible recovery and returned home to dream of Cup Finals and League Championships.

Since (at least in their presence) we treated the medical profession with proper respect, the actual injection was performed in the front room where – during the desperate winters – a special 'day-bed' was kept open in anticipation of the regular emergencies. But the comfort and the tablets were administered in the living room, with my mother and father walking up and down with their breathless burden across the few feet of unoccupied carpet. Syd and George sat each side of the table at the back of the room, reading with the self-conscious air of men who suspect that they should be taking part in the nearby drama but who are uncertain about which role to play. My grandmother evoked her concern without the slightest restraint, demanding regular bulletins on my progress and prophesying my immediate death. Next morning, no matter how severe the sudden attack or how deep the sleep it had half interrupted, I woke remembering every detail and feeling far healthier than anyone would believe.

My treatment was immensely complicated by the confusion of the two illnesses – or the double illness – from which I suffered. Asthma seemed to be an unpredictable act of God, a malady that attacked in a way which no precautions could prevent and disappeared as quickly as it arrived. It was called 'bronchial' because it induced breathlessness. But bronchitis itself was a distinctly different disease. Bronchitis came with a high temperature and a cough that echoed up from phlegm filled lungs. It was 'brought on' by wet feet, damp sheets and draughty corridors. And it could be 'guarded against'. I spent weeks of my life guarding against bronchitis with every proprietary medicine known to medical science.

I can still recall the sticky white taste of Scott's Emulsion and the bitter brown flavour of Owbridge's Lung Tonic. If the British pharmacopoeia contained a repulsion chart both would occupy an equally high place. But at least they were administered by the overflowing teaspoonful. Codliver oil and malt, which possessed the viscosity of tar on a warm day, came in a soupspoon. I tried to chew it straight from the EPNS. I tried to drink it after the minimum dose had been mixed with just enough milk to make it look, and taste, like engine oil. Either way, it always made me sick. So did the 'friars balsam' that I inhaled from the spout of an old kettle, after burying my head in a towel to prevent dissipation of the fumes. On the other hand, the smell of Vick swirling up from my chest was always welcome. For it signified that I was in no immediate danger of being encased, front and back, in hot Antiflagistine. Perhaps the congestion in my lungs was relieved by the application of slow cooling, quick drying medicinal cement. But from the moment the scalding compresses were strapped upon me, to the time (twelve hours later) when the clammy congested poultices were peeled off, I cursed the bearded fisherman with the great cod on his back for advertising an emulsion that did not cure bronchitis without the help of fire and brimstone.

In the earliest days of my illness, very few activities were completely prohibited by my 'weak chest'. I ran about the road in the pretence of playing football. I built secret lairs in Wadsley Churchyard. I fished for frog spawn on Wadsley Common. But I did not do any of those things with certain regularity. I was not allowed out in the rain. In the summer I did not climb the churchyard wall until my friend

Fred Guest, the elderly verger, had scythed down the long grass. If an asthma attack was imagined to be imminent or a bout of bronchitis had just passed I was kept at best in sight and at worst indoors. When I was house bound, Harold Woolhouse called in from time to time and discussed our stamp collections or described the birth of a new litter of rabbits. But little boys of six or seven take their obligation to sick friends notoriously lightly. So on the days when I was thought to be 'not very well', I generally made my own amusements or had them made for me by the family.

Some time during the late Thirties I acquired my first lead soldiers – not 'sets' in Britain's boxes of eight, but individual servicemen chosen by me for the bellicose positions in which they had been cast. On the last Christmas Day of pre-war peace I received a clockwork train. It was later the cause of great amusement to my more opulent friends for it had only four wheels and no bogey. But it was loved by me not least because of its bright green LNER livery. It pulled four coal trucks and a guard's van around a tight circle of slightly warped line, passing on its way a signal box and a replica of the high water cisterns which were used to fill the boilers of steam driven loco-motives. My little toy – like the massive red cisterns on which it was modelled – worked on the simple gravity principle and con-sisted of no more than a tank and a tube. Unfortunately clock-work trains have no need of water. The result was regular patches of damp on the carpet and constant friction between my mother and me.

I suppose that the hand that guided me was all the heavier because of the need to protect my grandmother from the ravages of a rampant little boy, kept indoors despite his instincts to throw stones at cats and chalk wickets on other people's walls. My mother's simul-taneous protection of her mother and me was aggressive and inge-nious in turn. When I first went to Sunday School she went too, and sat in the back of the class as the coloured pictures of 'Jesus with His Disciples' and the good attendance stars were given out. My enthu-siasm for Wadsley Common was diverted, whenever possible, from desperate determination to test wind and stamina by racing up and down the hills to gentle interest in the elderly donkey that was spending its retirement in a shed at the foot of the first slope. The idea, though not the reality, of out-of-doors athleticism was encour-aged by the purchase of a large green tent that was erected with much difficulty in the back garden. We only hammered the pegs into the herbaceous borders in the summer. And even then, despite the acquisition of a ground sheet, I was never allowed to lie on the grass if it had been dampened by rain, dew or condensation.

Reading was urged upon me by all of the five obsessively reading adults with whom I lived. Great attempts were made to guide me in the right direction. But I found Arthur Mee's *Children's Newspaper* incomprehensible and after much agitation had it replaced with *The Magnet* and took my vicarious place in the Greyfriars 'Remove' alongside Billy Bunter, Bob Cherry and Harry Wharton. Strange though my enthusiasm for Frank Richards was, he was by no means the most improbable of my favourite authors. My greatest indoor delight was readings, by my father, from the works of Jeffrey Farnol, whose romantic fiction was the sort of sentimental trash that 'Worksop' believed undermined the moral fibre of the nation. Somehow all of his historical novels – identically bound in scarlet cloth – had forced their way amongst the copies of Carlyle's *French Revolution* and Thomas Babington, Lord Macaulay's *Lays of Ancient Rome and Greece*. They were my constant delight.

Occasionally I was persuaded to move slightly up the literary market to the works of the Baroness Orczy. Indeed, I can recall a passionate argument between my mother and father concerning the desirability of expurgating a passage in which Sir Percy Blakeny kissed the ground on which the disdainful object of his rejected affections had walked. But although the Scarlet Pimpernel also occupied a world which I vaguely described as 'a hundred years ago', he could not compete with the improbable heroes of *The Broad Highway*, *The Amateur Gentleman* and *Beltaine the Smith*. I enjoyed the pathos most. Pursued by insistent creditors, the last acre of family land mortgaged and a ruthless usurer refusing to wait a moment more for full satisfaction an officer 'who had served England well' gambled his few remaining possessions on a point-to-point race in which he competed as a forlorn outsider. Leading at the last fence, he fell and broke his neck. As his friends bore him off 'on a hurdle', he announced with his final breath that the 'debts to Jasper Gaunt are paid for good and all'. I had no idea what any of it meant. But between my sixth and eighth years I knew of no line in English literature that could equal its emotive force – save possibly for 'his mother who was patient being dead', a fragment of poetry that I particularly enjoyed because it glorified a badly-treated child. Certainly, *Lamb's Tales from Shakespeare*, *Swallows and Amazons*, and shortened versions of *A Tale of Two Cities* and *Nicholas Nickleby* could not compete with stuff like that.

Despite the protective prohibitions, I usually enjoyed my time spent at home. The one occasion when I can remember waking up both sickly and sad ended in near disaster for my mother not me. Parodying the instructions of the BBC keep-fit class, she spilled a kettle of boiling water on her feet. Having smeared the scalded extremities with the all-purpose Antiflagistine, she carried on with her normal day as she always carried on after one of her frequent self-inflicted minor injuries. My mother specialised in falling up short flights of stairs and stumbling down shallow pairs of steps. She received innumerable electric shocks from light fittings, set fire to chip pans and, one May morning, hung herself by the wedding ring to the hook in the back wall over which she was attempting to loop the washing line. Until she wriggled herself free from the hook (removing the wedding ring was unthinkable) she stood on tip-toe against the house, with her arms raised in a salute of the sort which was about to become ominously familiar. On the way to 'Worksop' her hand was trapped in the railway carriage door. Familiar as I was with her indomitable spirit, I could barely believe that she did not use the split fingers as an excuse for an immediate return home.

For I hated visiting 'Worksop', and I could not imagine that anyone escaped the feeling of deep despair that always overcame me as the train puffed through Swallownest, Woodhouse, Aston and Anston. At 'Worksop' my mother – normally the dominant rock on which every wave broke – was not in command. Others gave instructions and, to my disturbed astonishment, she accepted them. And as well as disturbing the proper order of things, 'Worksop' was intolerably boring. My early excursions were to Newcastle Avenue, where the aunts still maintained the remnants of their dressmaking business. The 'work room' filled with seamstresses had gone. But a 'fitting room' still occupied the front of the house. When a customer called, I was sent to the kitchen to sit on a huge horsehair sofa (that prickled the back of my bare knees) and bidden to remain absolutely silent. A dog called Chum (equal in proportions to the sofa and also exiled to the rear) licked my face as if to take advantage of my inability to complain. Knowing Lot and Annie to be very old, I longed for them to die.

Sundays were the most difficult of all 'Worksop' days. The rule of courtesy that I was obliged to observe seemed to me wholly unreasonable, even then. At Airedale Road I was required to respect the aunts' wishes because they were my guests. At Newcastle Avenue, I was required to conform to their views because I was their visitor. Their views about Sunday were absolute and incapable of adjustment. Games of chance, no matter how innocent, were forbidden. The construction of models, being manual labour, was prohibited. Only serious reading material was tolerated. The usual prohibitions on slang and singing were, of course, maintained. The stream which flowed through the property – justifying the name 'Brook House' – had to be given a normal wide berth in case I should fall in and drown or, worse, contemplate catching the small fish and keeping them in captivity. Only once did I see either of the aunts at the centre of a cheerful scene.

That was in the early summer of 1939 when our neighbours, the Fredericks, decided that Whisky was a liability on their social life that they could tolerate no longer. Their worst suspicions confirmed, the gloriously vindicated old ladies offered the dog a good home in place of the recently deceased Chum. However, they found his name an unacceptable embarrassment.

Anxious to avoid the animal suffering the psychological damage that might have been caused by a total change of title, they decided to call him Frisky – a name which, for all its frivolity, at least had no alcoholic association. Unfortunately, the dog proved to possess a highly developed ear for consonants and refused absolutely to answer to the new name – indeed it has to be admitted that he answered to his own name only rarely. The happiest 'Worksop' scene which I ever recall was my father, Syd and George in hysterical pursuit of the missing adoptee. As the brothers were conducting a desultory search of the churchyard, they had suddenly beheld two hatted and gloved elderly ladies with dresses brushing the pavement, standing in Airedale Road crying 'Whisky! Whisky! Whisky!' into the cold night air.

7
Into Battle

—

I talk now about the late 1930s as if they were the years when I came to know the jagged hills and the bracken-covered moors that border Sheffield to the south and west. In truth, before the war I visited Derbyshire only once. For we lived in the north of the city, nearer to the Barnsley coalfield than either the Peak District or the great houses that the Elizabethan aristocracy built north of the Trent as places of regular recreation and occasional refuge. And the journey from Wadsley to the grandeur of the moorland above Baslow and Bakewell, or the magnificence of Chatsworth House and Haddon Hall was, for the immobile working classes, immensely difficult.

It began with a half-mile descent to the Middlewood tram terminus, where the '101' was said to 'turn round'. In reality it did no such thing. The transfer of the burnished brass steering arm from one identical end to the other converted bow into stern, and allowed the most serene of vehicles to make its certain way in the opposite direction. Tramcars were the most subtle as well as the most adaptable form of public transport. They contrived to look majestic without being menacing. As they clanked and swayed out of the Middlewood terminus they sounded their melodious bells to warn not to frighten, to protect rather than to startle. Sparks flashed from beneath their mighty wheels whenever a pebble was crushed against the gleaming tram-lines. Little blue lightning flashes danced at the point where they drew electricity from the overhead wires. I always thought of the tramcar as the proper chariot for the ascent into heaven of the bearers on the City coat-of-arms – Vulcan and Thor.

The tram that took us into Derbyshire made its calm progress along the Don Valley, past the old barracks where Bassetts made their Liquorice Allsorts and Burdalls mixed its gravy salt, the Royal Infirmary and the police headquarters at West Bar. Half a mile away from the city centre, it swung up Snig Hill – a gradient so formidable that it took its name from the verb 'to snig', the practice of hiring extra horses to help a carriage up a slope that the normal team would

find beyond its pulling power. Even the trams slowed down on Snig
Hill and paused when they reached the summit. The peak was the
city terminus where shoppers 'alighted', and expeditions to Derbyshire took strategic decisions about which of the little limestone
villages would become their base camps. Travellers from Wadsley
who wanted to explore Hathersage and Bamford simply dropped
their tickets on the tram floor and bought new ones for the second
half of what was, essentially, the same journey. For the '101' was a
cross-city service that 'terminated' in Ecclesall, the gateway to the
more accessible parts of the golden frame which was said to surround
Sheffield's dirty picture.

The Ecclesall route – through the stucco and glass of the 1920s and
the heavy grey Edwardian mansions that stood on the very edge of
the open country – was the path chosen for my second visit. In
September 1939 we abandoned the tram at the top of Snig Hill and
carried our raincoats and sandwiches to Pond Street – once the site of
the wells that provided water to Sheffield Castle, then the sodden
ground that bore the darkest dankest slums in northern England and,
after the Council cleared the hovels away, the municipal bus station.
At Pond Street we began the last lap of our journey to Castleton.

For part of our complicated odyssey we were surrounded by
devotees of Sheffield's favourite sport, coarse fishing. Even now, I
can only admit with shame that the most popular pastime in my
native city is catching fish. Sheffielders do not stand waist deep in
swiftly running rivers, trying to imitate flies in the hope of deceiving
salmon and trout. They sit, quiet and contemplative by the still
waters of Nottingham and Lincolnshire canals and scatter their
bread (known to the *cognoscenti* as 'ground bait') upon the water.
Then they wait for the greedy carp, roach and bream to swallow
down the hooks along with stale lumps of tea-cake and remnants of
last Sunday's scones.

In later years, fighting my way through the piled up wicker-baskets
that filled the tram's back platform, I looked with contempt upon the
owners. They should have been practising trapping with the inside of
the foot or perfecting the forward defensive shot. I felt much the same
about the posses of touring cyclists who peddled their manic way
along Sheffield's streets and the packs of road walkers who waddled
along, dressed like Olympic runners but competing in a race which
forbade them to run. All these essentially south Yorkshire pursuits
were witnessed by my father in a spirit of incredulous awe. He

referred to the people who practised them as 'professionals' because of their obvious dedication. Whenever he saw 'professional' fishermen bowed down with rod, basket, umbrella and keeping net he would point them out to whoever was nearby and exclaim 'the fishermen of England'. Between my fifth and my fortieth birthdays, he must have said it to me a thousand times.

On my first trip to Derbyshire, the 'fishermen of England' left us at the city terminus to make their way to the railway station and the flat land to the east. Some 'professional' hikers – identified by my father from their thick woollen socks, hob-nailed boots and ruck-sacks – certainly travelled all the way to Castleton. That little village lay at the foot of Winnat's Pass, an ancient escape route from Lancashire and a valley cut through hills so complicated in their construction that they provided vertical cliffs for athletes who liked to spend their spare time dangling at the end of ropes, and gentle inclines for the older and less adventurous holiday-makers who simply wanted to find a high place from which they could look out across the uneven magnificence of the Pennine foothills.

Under those hills a complicated pattern of subterranean streams washed their way through a labyrinth of caves, cut by a previous generation of underground rivers into the rock along the line where the soft porous limestone met the hard impervious millstone grit. In some places torrents rushed through narrow tunnels, filling them from floor to ceiling like flood-water in a sewer. But beneath Castleton the water flowed, shallow and gentle, in caves that were as high as the apse in York Minster. And because of their complex configuration, they were given names from ecclesiastical architecture. The 'Castleton Caves' had become the centre of tourist industry of sorts. Day-trippers were paddled through them in flat-bottomed boats to marvel at the great mineral-stained stalactites that spiralled down from the cavern roofs. And they peered past the spluttering candles in the natural niches in the hope of spotting pieces of sparkling 'blue-john' embedded in a wet wall.

I hated the caves. My father was sure that I would fall down the flight of wet steps by which the gloomy landing-stage was approached and his anxiety was transmitted to me. The farther we burrowed under the Pennines, the more I felt the full weight of Derbyshire pressing down on me. According to my mother, I was suffering from something called claustrophobia, which would miraculously pass when we regained the surface. The diagnosis proved only partly correct. The gloomy influence of the caves pursued me into the sunlight as I approached the real object of our pilgrimage – the Norman remains, after which the village was named.

At the age of six, I believed myself to be an authority on Norman England. The church which watched over the mortal remains of 'Worksop's' ancestors was a perfect example of eleventh-century round-arched piety. Whenever I visited Steetley with grave gardeners or flower replenishers, I was required to identify both the architectural characteristics at that chapel and the marks made on its walls by Cromwell's cannon-balls. Woolworth's produced picture books of English history full of line drawings based on the Bayeaux Tapestry. 'Children's Hour' seemed to broadcast a five o'clock feature on keeps and baillies at least once a week in 'Castles of England' or 'Hilltops of Britain'. But, most important of all, I wore Norman vests and pants. My underwear bore the brand name 'de Montfort', and the Leicester factory that wove it fastened a little picture of the square-jawed, flat-helmeted hero to every garment. I believed that the portraits that rubbed against various parts of my person qualified me as an expert on the Conquest. But they did not act as a talisman that ensured a joyous visit to my first Norman remains. Half-way up the grassy slope, on which what was left of the castle stood, I developed almost uncontrollable diarrhoea. I was a fastidious as well as a learned child and we had to descend the mound at once in search of an acceptable lavatory. Nothing was left except the bus ride home.

All that I really recall of the return journey is the superficial misery of infant inconvenience. But because of the week in which it took place, I later associated it with every incident that should have happened at such a historic time. I began to believe that Mr Chamberlain's fateful broadcast was relayed to us as we sat 'inside' or on one of the sets of seats that faced across the tram's gangway. And I started to fancy that I really could recall beacons being lit on the hamlets through which we drove as the Territorials, still buttoning their tunics and setting their service caps straight, ran to muster in the village squares. The fantasies remained with me for forty years.

During the night, I discovered – or thought that I discovered – the reality of Airedale Road at war. The sirens sounded shortly after midnight. The following day we were told, or we read, that the Luftwaffe had been turned back along a salient that ran from Cleethorpes to Whitby. In fact, the Germans did not come at all. The alarm was either fake or sounded as a test of our preparations. The

Hattersleys were ready. My father went off to man the 'rest centre', a refuge for 'bombed out' families which was run by the staff of the Public Assistance Committee during their off-duty hours. Syd and George prowled the road with other residents, ready to dowse any incendiary bombs that landed on the recently acquired real estate. It was their first experience of 'fire watching', an activity which, from then on, occupied an increasing amount of our neighbours' time and energy.

Most of the 'fire watchers' were young managers in steel or engineering companies and, therefore, enjoyed the security of 're-served occupations'. Despite, or perhaps because of, their per-manently non-belligerent status, they developed an extraordinary enthusiasm for their patriotic duties. The nightly 'fire watching' rota was prepared and circulated, revised and re-circulated, amended and circulated yet again. Equipment was bought with the aid of a special Town Hall grant. The new owner-occupiers haggled over custody of the various items with the enthusiasm of families who realised that when the war was over the stirrup-pump could be used for watering roses and a ladder would help with the removal of leaves from blocked guttering. My father, unsuited to the infighting necessary to acquire apparatus of permanent value, became custodian of an instrument invented by Mr Wheatley.

The 'Wheatley shovel' was a giant pole with what appeared to be a small coal-scuttle fastened to one end. It was designed (using the word loosely) to enable a fire watcher to pick up an incendiary bomb and toss it out of harm's way without risk to his person. Mr Wheatley (a practical man who despised theories) was unfamiliar with the work of Isaac Newton and did not realise that if the handle was held at a safe distance, eight feet from the flames, the scoop and the flaming contents became too heavy to control. On the other hand, if the operator held the device near enough to the shovel to make manipulation possible, his hands were burned off. There was also a conceptual flaw in the decision to construct the handle of highly combustible timber. But Mr Wheatley brushed all criticism aside with the assurance that he proposed to charge his neighbours only cost price for the use of his invention – despite his fear that the Germans would break the patent.

Mr Wheatley was, naturally enough, a 'captain' of one of the fire watching teams. The other group was led by Eddie Gill, the gassed veteran of the Somme whose military reminiscences increased as he assumed the new authority. Although, for the first year, the *blitzkrieg* never came, constant vigilance was maintained. Only one 'fire watcher' was ever absent unaccounted for. That was our immediate neighbour, George Brown, who eventually responded to suggestions that his attendance record should improve by sending Mrs Brown to fill his place on the rota. This substitution caused great embarrassment to my father who, since the names Brown and Hattersley usually appeared together on the duty list, was often required to patrol the pitch-black road side-by-side with his neighbour's wife. After suffering in silence for some time, he consulted higher authority. Mr Gill called the 'team' together. Their reaction was instant and violent — for Mr Brown's plus-fours and golf club manner were much resented, and he had slighted or insulted most of the road's residents during the two years he had condescended to inhabit Airedale Road. They decided upon immediate confrontation.

When the lynch mob arrived at Number 99, my father, who had declined to take part, was overcome with guilt. I crouched just below the front room windowsill, anxious to witness the first ritual killing to take place in a Sheffield suburb. When the vigilantes arrived their victim was in the back garden practising his golf swing. He sauntered towards his tormentors, resplendent in check pullover, swishing a niblick in one hand. Nonplussed, little Eddie Gill made his complaint in language more restrained than I had expected from a retired corporal. Mr Brown paused in preparation for his measured reply. Waving the golf club in the direction of his garage (a prefabricated construction, bought in sections from a firm that advertised in the *Daily Telegraph*) he inquired if his tormentors had any idea what it contained. I knew that it housed an old Morris Opal, for I had seen the car through the cobweb-covered windows when I fought my way past our hedge in pursuit of a missing ball. Not possessing that advantage, the vengeful patriots were caught wrong-footed by the apparent irrelevance of the question. Mr Brown pounced. 'I should not be telling you any of this,' he said, 'but you force my hand. That building is full of equipment which I must man whenever enemy action seems imminent.' The lynch mob apologised and slunk home. From then onwards, my father fire-watched alone.

The window through which I had peered in the hope of seeing real blood was hung with 'black-out' curtains and the panes were criss-crossed with strips of brown paper which were supposed to prevent fragments of blast-shattered glass from flying through the air. During the 'phoney war', preparing for the holocaust that we knew was bound to hit the great industrial cities became a cottage industry. In gardens all over Sheffield great holes were dug for the imminent receipt of Anderson shelters. On our side of Airedale Road, only two families declined delivery. Mr Wheatley had a special bunker built by workmen from his factory who constructed a steel and concrete redoubt from materials bought at a bargain price from a bankrupt builder. We decided that since my grandmother could not be moved, we must all stay together in what we hoped would remain the livingroom. Mr Wheatley suggested that corrugated iron sheets – hung every night over the window in which she sat – would provide much needed protection, and offered to provide a pair. They were delivered one Friday evening and immediately given the generic name 'tins'. On the following Sunday afternoon a bill (which we could not afford to pay) was pushed through the front door.

Fortunately we did not have to rely on our home-made protection for long. Officials of the City Engineer's Department designed a bespoke shelter within which all the Hattersleys could take refuge. The original free enterprise 'tins' which had been hung on nails crudely hammered into the outside wall, were replaced by municipal steel shutters that swung silently into place on well oiled hinges. Four iron columns (known to us as 'the posts') were sunk through holes in the living-room floorboards and embedded in the foundations. The 'posts' supported two steel girders that ran along the ceiling. We were assured that the scientifically determined relationship between the girders and the joists that held up the bedroom floor would prevent the whole weight of a collapsing house falling in on us. No doubt the arrangement provided great psychological comfort. But during the two days of its installation it did more damage to our house and caused more injuries in our family than the Third Reich managed in six years.

Unfortunately, one of the workmen misread the diagram which described the way in which girders were to be embedded at the point where the much-prized 'moulding' smoothed off the angle between ceiling and wall. Instead of cutting a neat cavity, four inches square, he began to chop at the inside of our almost-new house with a pickaxe in the belief that a four-foot chasm was needed. My mother, having first physically restrained him from doing further damage, drew his attention to the correct specification on his working drawing as calmly as she could. The wall having been prepared, the girders were sent for. As they were being manhandled across the room, I noticed that half-a-dozen of my lead soldiers were in the direct firing line of the workmen's boots. Rushing to the rescue I fell into one of the holes which had been cut into the floorboards for eventual receipt of 'the posts'. Had I fallen all the way through, I could, no doubt, have confirmed Uncle Ern's judgment about the quality of the foundations. Unfortunately, just one leg made the descent, whilst the rest of me remained above the surface. Only Mrs Davies, visiting to watch the girders swing into place, was prepared to ask specific questions about the nature of my injuries. My mother, furious at the scene I had caused, marched me off to the kitchen for private examination. The soldiers remained in jeopardy.

Those lead (or 'tin' soldiers as we called them with our strange enthusiasm for verbally debasing our possessions) were no more than the advance guard of my eventual army. They had been bought, singly, not in regiments, at Thomas's, the local electrical shop. Most of them were still moulded in the pre-war patterns – Highlanders in the uniform of the Indian Mutiny, foot guards in scarlet tunics, and bandsmen blowing the tunes of ceremonial peace. In keeping with the mood of the time (and the map of the Western Front that we had cut from the *Daily Express*, stuck to a piece of plywood and propped up on the sideboard) my father began to bring me a toy soldier each Saturday instead of a postage stamp. One Friday night, George (promoted to 'Government Auditor' and posted to Watford) came home for the weekend with a suitcase that contained two small field guns wrapped inside his dirty laundry. That was in the early spring of 1940. The mechanisation of my army always seemed to me to mark the point at which Airedale Road really went to war.

8

Finest Hour

Throughout the war I was ill for part of every winter. If 1940 was medically exceptional, it was because the asthma attacks were so frequent and prolonged that we were not quite sure when one ended and another began. I missed a full six months of school and the day bed which, in previous years, had been 'pulled out' for the occasional emergency, was kept in permanent use. It was dragged from the front room into the back so that I could be sick in the patent shelter that the benevolent Corporation had built above my grandmother. An important by-product of the concentration of both patients under a single ceiling was the restoration of the front room to its proper, though recently acquired, glory. Just before war broke out we at last acquired the three-piece suite which was essential to our self-esteem. I went with my mother to buy a 'bureau' from the Sheffield and Ecclesall Co-op, its possession signifying that we had valuable papers to keep safe. After what seemed to be an eternity of turnings over, we chose a carpet to occupy the space within the linoleum surround which my father had laid. I was told that the carpet was 'Axminster' and realised from the tone of my mother's voice that I was being given this piece of information in order that I should be proud, impressed and careful not to spill anything. Remembering the anguish with which she discovered that Harold Woolhouse had been allowed to see inside the unfinished front room, I understand her relief at moving messy me and my sticky medicine out of the pristine surroundings into the living-room.

By the time that the air raids became a regular hazard, preparing for bed each night had become a complicated ritual. If I resisted the detailed and heavy-handed washing that my mother administered before she filled the stone hot water bottle, I was sternly told to remember 'that something might happen in the night'. The thought of the Air Raid Warden's contempt when he dug me from the rubble and discovered that I had dirty hands and feet always made me submit to the flannel. My father invariably winced with disapproval whenever my likely death was used as an argument for improved hygiene. But the desperate expedient never frightened me. It merely made me conscious of my duty to prepare for the worst. Part of my preparations involved equipping my teddy bear for sudden evacuation. Teddy must have been the best dressed bear in wartime Sheffield. He had a home-made siren-suit (of the sort that Winston Churchill popularised), several pairs of pyjamas and a couple of garments which, from a distance, looked like the army's battle dress. On closer inspection, they all turned out to be made on the same (Worksop) pattern. But when his stiff arms had been pushed into the pyjamas, I always insisted that the rest of his wardrobe was bundled up and tied round him like an evacuee's pathetic parcel. With Teddy ready for a good getaway, I slept peacefully until asthma, or the Luftwaffe, attacked.

I rarely slept through a raid, not least because of the comings and goings of fire watchers. One night Mr Wheatley brought me a jagged bomb splinter which, since it was still too hot to hold, he juggled between one hand and the other. Mr Gill outdid him by bringing me anti-aircraft shrapnel which he had picked up in our garden. I kept it, although my mother said that it rightly belonged to his son Eric. But Wadsley remained generally unscathed as the bombers sought, and usually found, the industrial east end. At first the attacks amounted to little more than hit-and-run raids. But when, early in the second December of the war, the BBC played the Coventry Carol and we heard what had happened to the city from which it came, we knew that nights of hard pounding were not far away.

I suppose that the older Hattersleys were often frightened. But they never communicated that fear to me. We busied ourselves with trivial acts of patriotism, clubbing together to buy Petty Officer Davies cigarettes to take with him when he rejoined the fleet and shaking the hands of bewildered Free French sailors who were left wandering shipless in Britain's most land-locked city. One of our neighbours was rumoured to have run out onto the road during a particularly heavy anti-aircraft barrage and cried at the searchlight beams – like a dog baying at the moon – 'Why don't they give in whilst there are a few of us left?' But the episode was treated like a bad joke which was no more suitable for conversation than the bar room stories about what happened when Blackburn Meadows sewage farm received a direct hit. Whilst idling away the bored hours of a visit to Worksop, I was actually standing at my aunts' front gate when a convoy of muddy soldiers passed on their way to temporary refuge in the grounds of Welbeck Abbey. They were, Uncle Ern told us on his return from Retford, some of the heroes who had been evacuated through the French port and holiday resort at Dunkirk. The idea that they were part of a beaten army never struck me.

The history books tell us that our spirits were kept at fighting pitch by the oratory of Winston Churchill. I cannot remember one of his broadcasts. By 1940, my mother's antipathy to the arch-villain of 1926 had begun to moderate. So there is no doubt that, like the rest of Britain, we sat around our wireless set and were inspired to renewed defiance and increased confidence. But the only message that I remember came from the King: 'I said to the man who stood at the gate of the year,' he told us one New Year's Eve, 'Give me a light that I may enter . . .' The watchman's reply was beyond my understanding and contrary to my parents' religious taste. But they bought a printed copy of George VI's message set out like a medieval manuscript, with the first letter of each paragraph illuminated as if it had been written by a monk. They framed it with *passe-partout* and hung it over the living room mantelpiece. We were all beginning to take the war seriously.

The blitz began on the late evening of Thursday, 12 December 1940. Coventry having provided a warning, we expected every alert to be the prelude to immediate obliteration. But at first it seemed like any other air raid. The siren sounded, and a long silence followed. Then, just as we began to reassure ourselves that the Germans had, once again, passed over Sheffield *en route* for somewhere else, the pattern changed. As the bombs began to fall, the drama of our night was heightened by the behaviour of Joey, a stray budgerigar which we had caught in the churchyard and befriended. Joey lived in a tassled cage which we had bought secondhand from Mr Wheatley. Although he stubbornly refused to speak in human tones, he was an enthusiastic campanologist. When his sand was changed or his millet replenished, he rang his bell in a way which my grandmother recognised as a 'song of gratitude'. On the night of 12 December 1940 she was proved wrong. Joey was an hysteric with particularly acute hearing.

The Luftwaffe came in waves. After a period of silence, we heard their engines, then the anti-aircraft guns, then the explosion of their bombs on the city centre. Joey always anticipated the menacing cycle with a joyous peal on his tin bell. At first we believed it to be no more than a coincidence. Then the pattern persisted with such regularity that we realised Joey picked up the sound of the enemy's approach before it was audible to human eardrums. We all stared at him, silently awaiting the warning of the next attack. Just before midnight awe turned into hatred and there was talk of Joey being strangled. Syd was forbidden to go within a yard of his cage. As if to relieve the tension my uncle consulted his watch and announced that we had all entered the morning of Friday the Thirteenth.

The raid ended, like most raids, in time for the German crews to get home for breakfast. After the All-Clear sounded its simple constant note, I was allowed to go into the front room and see the red glow that hung over what had previously been Sheffield's shopping centre. The steelworks and the factories had largely escaped, but the Castle Street headquarters of the Brightside and Carbrook Co-operative Society had been destroyed. So had Foster's — the store from which we bought my clothes when 'Worksop' contributed to the cost — and *Marples*, the city centre public house into which Mr and Mrs Davies had been known to go. Thirty men and women were killed in *Marples*'s vault that night. Mr Davies was securely back at sea and his wife was huddled with their daughter in the Wheatley's super-shelter, forty yards up Airedale Road. But from then on I always looked upon her as an example of the deathly wages paid by sin. At the age of nine, I really believed that a divine hand punished the ungodly but spared those who repented.

I suppose that I picked up all my infant piety from my grand-mother and from 'Worksop'. The viler side of my character was always attributed (in hushed whispers which I invariably overheard) to the misfortunes of having descended from Ernest Brackenbury. I never met my grandfather. My grandmother (in the manner of an earlier autocrat when faced with the inconvenience of the Pyrenees) announced to the world and to herself that he no longer existed. But when, for instance, I opened the little toy sandbags that 'Worksop' had made to go with my lead soldiers and (with the wilful intention of distressing the sick old lady) emptied their contents on the carpet, the wickedness was recognised as the direct consequence of Bracken-bury blood flowing in my veins. My father (for once more active than contemplative) reacted by striking me a sharp back-handed blow across the left ear; an assault known in South Yorkshire as the 'clip'. It was the only time in my life that my father ever hit me and what followed was as much the result of my surprise as the weight of his blow. How far I would have travelled had my progress not been diverted by one of the 'posts' it is impossible to say. The noise made by my head hitting the cold steel confirmed the contention that the posts were (as I had always argued) hollow rather than solid, as my grandmother had been known to boast. As I came round, I heard my grandmother denouncing her son-in-law's violent disposition. The brutal father himself was on his knees, trying to revive his dazed child and weeping at the thought of the brain damage he had done. As soon as I could speak, I assured him, coldly, that I was perfectly well, accepted that his behaviour was an unfortunate but understandable lapse and gave him unqualified absolution. I sensed that my mother was tempted to hit me again. But in the light of my magnanimity, I could not understand why.

In December 1940, the Germans showed no such self-restraint and hit Sheffield a second time on the following Sunday. In between the two *blitzkriegs*, half of the city made the difficult journey to the site of the first night's devastation, and stared bewildered at the twisted tramlines, the shells of bombed-out buildings (that were being pulled down before they fell on passers-by) and the piles of rubble which, a week before, had been offices and department stores. On the Saturday, George travelled North from Watford to make sure that his brothers and their relations had survived. He arrived at the Midland Station after the black-out had begun and started out on the long dark walk to Hillsborough. Two hours later, exasperated by the detours and road blocks, he ducked under the sign that warned of unexploded bombs ahead and put his fate in the hands of whichever deity watches over close-knit families. Uncle Ern proceeded with greater caution but more eventual inconvenience. He made the anxious journey from Worksop early on the Sunday morning (by which time he believed that the respite was permanent) and left Airedale Road before dusk on the same day, determined to be secure in front of his own fire before dark. His train pulled out of Sheffield Victoria, just as the siren sounded to herald the second blitz. It made straight for the Woodhouse sidings. He spent the night flat on the carriage floor, alongside a person he later described as a 'total stranger' whilst the incendiary bombs set the nearby marshalling yards on fire.

Undoubtedly, Uncle Ern arrived weighed down by the Gladstone bag which he took to work every day and the wicker basket that 'Worksop' employed for the transportation of the fresh food they believed the Hattersleys to lack. 'Worksop' regularly augmented our rations with genuine farm produce and the output of market gardens and smallholdings. The hard-bottomed Gladstone bag was used as a vehicle for the transportation of the 'good', 'nourishing' and 'home-made' delicacies that were thought essential to our diet. The only obligation placed on the recipients by the donors themselves was visible enjoyment. But my mother in her capacity of recipient-in-chief required us to be constantly and audibly both grateful for the generosity and full of wonder at the quality of the alms we received. Syd was once branded an ingrate for complaining about the taste and texture of what his sister-in-law insisted was cooked ham. It turned out to be raw bacon which had acquired a deceptive patina because of brief proximity to a warm pork pie. My father found half-a-dozen pins in a packet of genuine beef sausage meat (sausages themselves were prohibited because of the synthetic nature of wartime skins). From then on he examined every food parcel for other lethal relics of the tailor's and dressmaker's arts. But he always did it surrep-titiously.

'Worksop' eggs, even when they had travelled from some distant Nottinghamshire poultry farm, were always judged to be bigger and fresher than ordinary eggs, and to possess a higher incidence of double yolks than eggs from other places. Often they tasted of fish. When I drew attention to this interesting phenomenon Syd began to explain that if the rigours of war obliged the poultry-farmer to feed his hens exclusively on fish meal, they – and their produce – would take on the characteristics of their diet. He told me of 'Ilkley Moor Ba't At', in which Mary Jane's suitor was reminded of what would happen if he died of pneumonia and was buried above Wharfedale. The 'worms would eat him up'. The ducks would 'eat the worms'. Sooner or later, his friends would 'eat the ducks', and then, they explain, 'we will 'ave eaten thee'. The interesting discussion on rebirth and renewal was interrupted by my mother. Since Worksop eggs could not possibly taste of fish, the whole conversation was pointless and, what was worse, disloyal.

How much material, as distinct from moral, help 'Worksop' provided is difficult to assess. Certainly they gave me their sweet coupons. So did Syd, George and my father, whilst my grand-mother's passion for mint-rock was gratified by her daughter's sacrifice. But often the 'Worksop' contribution to our nutrition was, like 'Worksop', wholly bizarre. We received a blood-stained postal package that turned out to contain a pair of partridges. The pigeons that they sent as the ingredients for a pie were never plucked and I was sworn to secrecy about the dustbin becoming their final resting place. We were given jam so old that a layer of sugar had formed at the top of the jar like cream on a jug of milk. 'Worksop' were always full of good intentions. But the goodness which they intended was defined according to their own idiosyncratic values. As a result, the recipient was often left more bewildered than blessed.

Being the children of a head gardener on a great estate, 'Worksop' encouraged us to supplement our rations by digging for victory. The aunts' house at Newcastle Avenue and Uncle Ern's increasingly neglected house in Overend Road were both surrounded by jungles of dockweed and twitch-grass. But that in no way prevented the residents from offering endless advice about the advantages of growing turnips, broad beans and other nutritional vegetables. So we rented an allotment. Syd had left his precarious employment in the cloth warehouse to join the Auxiliary Fire Service and, after a hard night up and down the ladders, showed no enthusiasm for the rake or hoe. My mother had even less time available for horticultural matters, but she had a great urge to live off the land which we were required to gratify. When the pollen had blown away and the weather was warm and dry I was sent to help my father make a Walder's Avenue wilderness bloom. We hacked away at undergrowth that had not felt a scythe for ten years. The earth was just beginning to show when a man of uncouth appearance and bellicose disposition appeared at the edge of our almost cultivated plot and claimed it as his own. He threatened my father with violence if we so much as watered our peas or brussel sprouts again. When I told my mother about the terrifying incident, she reacted with remarkable composure. If necessary, she said, my father would have defended us with his spade. Then – before I knew about how my father had behaved in Mansfield back in the 1920s – I could not imagine him fighting for his land and family like the hero of a cowboy comic. I was immensely relieved when his conscription into the Police War Reserve brought our horticultural endeavours to an end.

For the rest of the family recruitment into PWR provided relief of a different sort. In early 1941 the call-up was extended to my father's comparatively elderly age group. We knew that without him to 'lift' her, my grandmother was doomed to an institution for the chronically incapable. That judgment, although reinforced by Dr Stephen and his numerous assistants, was either rejected or discounted by the Ministry of Labour. At first my father was ordered to Hull to become a railway shunter. We appealed. Whilst the appeal was pending, he applied to join the police and every walk that we took in Wadsley and every tram ride that we made to town became another search for the bespectacled constable who would confirm that shortsightedness was not a disqualification. We never found one. Perhaps PWR 5076 was the first myopic recruit to be accepted into wartime police service. Having passed muster, he was allocated, by pure chance, to the Hillsborough Division of Sheffield. Grandma's 'lifts' were safe for the duration.

By the end of the year, the Hattersleys were the only family on Airedale Road with three men in uniform. George left the civil service for the Royal Army Ordnance Corps and Syd (still anxious to secure his future) resigned from the Fire Service for a permanent prospect in West Riding local government. He knew that within weeks he would be required to put it all behind him and wear the King's Coat. But it was the road to post-war security, and he proposed to take it despite the temporary obstacles that lay in his path. At the end of the year my military prospects also made a dramatic improvement with the arrival of much needed reinforcements. The remnants of my original lead army were mostly wounded, with heads only attached to their bodies by matchsticks.

The new recruits came at Christmas in neat boxes of eight – one officer and seven other ranks. Some of them were relics of the piping days of peace. But the red-tunied Gloucesters and York and Lancasters were augmented by battle-hardened veterans in forage caps and webbing, gas-masked machine-gunners lying rigid behind their Brownings and steel-helmeted bomb throwers poised to lob their grenades at the still advancing enemy. They were all housed in a plywood and stucco castle that I knew had not been built according to the exacting requirements of Norman architecture. But they were supported by a bren carrier, an anti-tank gun that fired wooden shells and a clockwork tank with rubber tracks that kept falling from its wheels. I felt immensely confident about the future.

There was only one moment when I feared defeat. It was in the afternoon of our greatest naval disaster, the sinking of the *Prince of Wales* and the *Repulse*. The tragedy was reported to me by Harold Woolhouse's mother as I sat by her son's bedside during his recovery from some trivial youthful illness. We were playing 'Springtime in the Rockies' on his gramophone and talking about stamps or rabbits or butterflies, when Mrs Woolhouse announced the appalling news she had heard on the wireless. That evening, as the desperate story was being repeated on a later bulletin, I asked 'Are we going to win, dad?' He assured me that we were, though I cannot vouch for the conviction with which he answered.

9
Money Can Buy

—

For most of the war, I was more frightened by the French than by the Germans. French was taught at Hillsborough High School as part of the standard curriculum – one of the minor items on the *table d'hôte* menu which obscured the general low quality of the cuisine and the inadequacy of the *à la carte* alternative. It was taught to everyone in the school except the kindergarten – which, to her credit, Headmistress Bertha Roberts (Member of the Royal College of Preceptors) did not rename the nursery after the blitz. So I opened my attack on the language of Balzac, Lamartine and Molière at the age of nine – a year later than more fortunate pupils who had not been held back by asthma-enforced absence. The assault was led by Mme Wurtier, a refugee from previous hostilities against the Germans, whose minimal command of the English language (by which she had been surrounded since the occupation of Belgium in 1914) did nothing to inspire confidence in either her linguistic abilities or the essential simplicity of learning to speak a different tongue.

Like other members of the Hillsborough High School staff, Mme Wurtier was part-time to the point of absenteeism. Her place in the curriculum was justified by a confrontation with the entire 'upper school' in 'Miss Roberts's classroom' each Friday afternoon. She brought with her a pile of cards, which depicted every day life in France. Beneath each picture was printed a juxtaposition of letters which, to me at least, was beyond comprehension. Indeed they were so unnaturally arranged that I could not properly focus my eyes upon them. Mme Wurtier dealt out her visual aids like a dealer in a poker school, sometimes palming one from the bottom of the pack in an attempt to set a sixteen-year-old girl a more difficult test of pronunciation than that which she imposed on a seven-year-old boy. I was the dunce of the class and always got *wagon lit* – which, for two years, I believed to derive its name from an integral lighting system which distinguished it from other Paris tramcars. With our cards on the desks before us, we took turns to make gargling noises based on the title of our picture. Each of us then held up for general recognition the picture which we had been allocated, and imitated, with our fellow linguists, the gargling noises made by our teacher as she obsessively checked her watch to see how much more of our company she was obliged to endure.

The seventy minutes of the double lesson was the most bewildering time of the week. The three minutes which preceded them were one hundred and eighty seconds of pure terror. Mme Wurtier was always late. Miss Roberts always left the previous lesson at the moment that the time for its appointed end was reached. Invariably, we were 'put on our honour' not to speak a word during the transition. Invariably, everyone (except me) shouted and screamed until the classic, black-swathed figure of a Belgian widow swept through the door. My silence was the product neither of instinctive obedience nor natural taciturnity. I was so frightened that my vocal chords atrophied. For I knew the terrible retribution which would follow the discovery of our awful crime. The punishment involved what is still, for me, the most terrible torture of all – uncertainty.

Mme Wurtier did not punish us herself. Our behaviour was reported to Miss Roberts when she returned at four o'clock – in theory for the final dismissal of the week. Her reaction never varied. First of all we were harangued for our failure to keep a promise that we had never made. Driven on by desperation, I often had an insane desire to rise in my desk and argue that since we were not willing parties to the broken compact, the punishment should be reduced. But, I always shrank from the ultimate lunacy of expecting Miss Roberts to be reasonable. Instead, I sank back amongst the other miscreants and waited the next inevitable stage in the ritual drama. Each week we were invited to confess our disobedience. When no guilty hands were raised, the path of honour was abandoned and an invitation was offered to those who had remained obediently silent to indicate their virtuous record and turn Headmistress' evidence on the real culprits. All eyes were turned on me. But I never grassed. By then I was immobilised by the prospect of the horror ahead. We would be 'kept in' – but not 'kept in' for a prescribed fifteen minutes or specific half hour. We would be detained at Miss Roberts's pleasure.

And we were kept there in the upstairs room, without the comforting presence of Miss Roberts herself. Perhaps more composed children welcomed the absence of their tormentor. But to me the sight of her sitting, erect and disapproving behind her desk would have been immensely reassuring. It would have prevented the renewed talking that inevitably broke out the moment she left, the angry expressions of anguished outrage when she returned and found us in a blatant conversation and the prolonged detention that was the invariable outcome of the other offences being taken into consideration. More important, as long as Miss Roberts was there, looking at her errant pupils, I was confident that we had not been forgotten. Without her, I grew increasingly certain that she would never return to release us, and that our lifeless bodies would be discovered by a search-party of parents long after the weekend was over.

Sometimes I tried to escape – pretending, when I was caught on the stairs that I was on my urgent way to the lavatory. When Mme Wurtier increased her workload to two part-afternoons a week my nerve totally broke. On the day her extra duties began, I set off for school as usual but, once around the corner of Airedale Road, I doubled back into Wadsley Churchyard. It was a dark damp morning and I shuffled along the paths that divided church and vicarage, water-butt and faded-flower dump, kicking the wet leaves into which I sank up to my ankles. It was a huge churchyard and it offered a nine-year-old with an active imagination unlimited opportunities for fantasy. The following year the cemetery was to become a battlefield in which I led an irregular army. But throughout my days of 'truancy' (as my mother always woundingly called it after my apprehension) I dreamed more peaceful dreams. During the two days which I spent amongst the laurels and cypresses, I determined to write a standard work on the English tombstone. I found a memorial to a local cricketer into which bat, ball and stumps had been carved and a headstone engraved in the pattern of blacksmith's tools that marked the last resting place of a farrier who had served with Kitchener at Omdurman. A single tomb eclept a whole family that had perished together in the great flood when the dams above Sheffield burst and the water swept through the northern valleys of the city like a tidal wave. Interred within it was 'an infant of about one year'. I was fascinated by the melancholy mystery of the churchyard, but I accepted the book in which its mortal remains were immortalised would have to omit all references to military memorials and interment of paupers. The little patch of war graves to the south of the church with its stone tablets (identical apart from the regimental badges that they wore like medals) was far too near the road for prolonged investigation by anyone who needed to keep his whereabouts a secret. And the rough acre of unloved and uncut twitch grass that covered the last unmarked resting place of the Victorian inmates of the Wadsley Asylum was too open a piece of country to be crossed by a man on the run.

I remained a fugitive from Miss Roberts's justice for almost two days. Then half way through the second afternoon my mother appeared and gently led me home. I was astonished to discover that she was more worried about the anguish which she assumed had provoked the complicated deception than she was about the truancy itself. But I was even more amazed that I had been discovered. Throughout the whole episode I had spoken to only three human beings. Two of them were Air Raid Wardens, who had made a command post in the old church school. When our paths crossed on the first morning, they addressed me by an unfamiliar name and asked me 'if I was locked out again'. I nodded and hurried on, trying to work out the cause of their error and the logic of their question. They could not have caused my capture. Mr Guest, the one person party to my guilty secret, would not have betrayed me. Mr Guest was my friend.

Fred Guest was the church verger. He was a round, red-faced man in his late seventies who was ready to retire and pass on the almost hereditary office to his son Bob, who could thus escape from work in a nearby brick-yard. Fred spent most of his working day 're-opening' graves; for Wadsley Churchyard was 'full-up', and its only funerals were the burials of wives and husbands, sons and daughters lowered to rest above relatives who, in the words of the In Memoriam columns of the *Sheffield Telegraph* and *The Star* had 'gone before' or were 'waiting on the other side'.

I often spent half a day watching Mr Guest dig his careful way down through the first five feet of soil and then pause whilst he took sounding to discover how near he had approached the coffin that was slowly disintegrating below his feet. He possessed a long iron pole, especially for the delicate task of probing the floors of almost re-opened graves. Standing in the cavity he had dug, his bald head barely visible above ground level, he banged at the clay that he suspected provided a bare cover for the oak and brass, bones and muscles. If the probe brought forth the dull thud of iron hitting earth he dug, carefully on. If it gave out a hollow echo, digging ended and scraping began. Sometimes the coffin collapsed under Mr Guest's weight and he pulled his boots out of the debris cursing and vowing that 'young Bob' (who was in his early fifties) could not take over too soon.

I think that Mr Guest must have enjoyed both audience and company. For he certainly encouraged me to sit on the mounds of earth that he gradually piled up on each side of the grave. If days passed without our meeting, he usually appeared at the wall that separated our garden from the churchyard and offered us small seasonable gifts gathered in his cemetery – dandelion leaves in summer for Peter my giant rabbit, holly at Christmas to put behind the pictures in the living-room and horse-chestnuts in the autumn to turn into the biggest and hardest 'conkers' in Wadsley. It was 'conker' time when I played truant, and our house was littered with the shiny brown nuts which I expected to shrivel into indestructible missiles hard enough to shatter any rival with an owner rash enough to make a challenge. I would have loved Mr Guest for the 'conkers' if for nothing else. And, despite his clear disapproval of my refusal to go to school, it never struck me that he was the one who knocked on the back door of Airedale Road and told my mother about her wandering son.

Long after I was forgiven, I was told of Mr Guest, literally cap in hand, knocking on the door during the second morning of my absence and saying that he hoped that he was 'doing right'. But in the days immediately after the offence was discovered, I was simply cross-examined about the terrors and traumas that had driven me to such a desperate escapade. The only tangible fear that I was able to express – the horror that I would go to school on the Friday afternoon and never return – was dismissed as a fanciful alternative to describing what was really wrong. My general objection to Hillsborough High School would, I knew, be equally incomprehensible. I hated it because of all the qualities that made it so attractive to 'Worksop' and my grandmother. It was different. It required its pupils to wear a distinctive uniform. It taught elocution and the piano for a small additional fee. It even charged for the general education that my contemporaries received free. It set me apart. In particular, it provided the special cossetting that my delicate health was thought to require. There were no rough games or dangerous physical jerks. I did not have to visit the baths and swim. If asthma struck one night, the following day's absence was accepted without the need for complicated demonstrations that I had not been kept at home to mind the baby or clean the windows. I was required to live immersed in perpetual debilitating protection.

The deprivation which distressed me the most was the denial of energetic activity. Hillsborough High School was essentially designed for girls. So for the senior pupils there was the occasional visit of a lady from the Women's League of Health and Beauty. And there was (naturally enough at an extra fee) tennis on a Tuesday afternoon. I was enrolled for the tennis and accompanied Mrs Ratcliffe and a gaggle of teenage girls to a local sports club for a knock-about on a weed-covered court left neglected by sportsmen who preferred 'seven no trumps' to 'forty-fifteen'. Mrs Ratcliffe, the heavily-made-up matron who taught the 'intermediate class', clearly believed that a nine-year-old boy had no right to intrude on an otherwise girlish outing. In vain did I beg to demonstrate the weight of my service and the power of my volley. Mrs Ratcliffe would not believe that I knew the difference between a tennis racket and a frying pan. In fact, early in the spring of my tenth year, I had travelled with my mother and father to a little rural park, called Glen How. And there, after I had watched them re-live the half-volleys and passing shots of their youth, I had been allowed a few swings of my own. Knowing that I could acquit myself at least as well as Mrs Ratcliffe's giggling adolescents, I was driven to undisguised fury at being relegated to the role of ball-boy and intentionally intercepted what passed for rallies by lobbing back balls as the incompetents essayed their ungainly strokes. I consoled myself with the thought that, really, I did not want to play tennis at all. I wanted to play cricket.

I actually suggested to Miss Roberts that cricket ought to be added to the curriculum and offered to lend my few elementary items of equipment to whoever was allowed to join me on the Wadsley Common one afternoon. Miss Roberts was never averse to the acceptance of suggestions that extended the range of school activities. Indeed during a phase in my life when the construction of balsa-wood model aeroplanes had been my uncontrollable obsession she had agreed to 'handicraft sessions' in her dining room. Only one session actually took place. At the end of an afternoon spent carving, sticking and covering the fragile 'frames' with tissue paper, the two or three handicraftsmen threw their debris into the gas fire. As I tried to explain, none of us had ever seen such a sophisticated piece of apparatus before. Kneeling in front of her hearth and poking with a knitting needle at what had once been the holes through which the gas bubbled and burnt, Miss Roberts removed 'handicraft' from the syllabus.

Covering my figures with balsa-wood cement (which I could later peel off and show to my grandmother in the pretence that it was skin scraped from my person by one of the razor blades that were essential tools in the construction of model aircraft) was all very well for rainy afternoons. When the summer sun shone, I wanted to be playing cricket. My addiction to the game was, I suppose, the product of both heredity and environment. I can remember my father saying – and only pretending it was a joke when my mother looked at him despairingly – that all aspirations to greatness ought to be abandoned because, like Percy Fender (in that ex-England Captain's famous explanation of his own inadequacy) 'I did not have a bat in my hand until I was six.'

I cannot remember when I first took guard and was told to space my hands evenly on the bat handle and point my shoulder towards the bowler; but I do recall an early expedition to play on Wadsley Common sometime before my tenth birthday, because it took place on a Sunday when games were not usually permitted and because George (who was home on brief leave and therefore justified the breaking of the Sabbath rule) was coach and guardian. It was usually Syd or my father who spent the time and had the patience to bowl the endless overs that I was prepared to pat back down the pitch with what I called a 'forward defensive stroke'. But on that remarkable Sunday, moved by an absent soldier's sentiment, George took their place. Gordon, the younger of the Woolhouse brothers, came with us. Gordon and I were asked a question that pinpointed the year in my memory and led on to the first metaphor that I can remember. Having determined that Gordon was eight and I was nine, George observed that neither of us 'was in double figures'. Realising that we were being treated like runs, against a batman's name, I rolled about in uncontrollable laughter. When I had recovered George bowled, Gordon Woolhouse kept wicket in old foundry gloves that provided protection for neither palm nor finger and I, as always, batted. As I pushed my defensive shot forward, George (the least expert cricketer of the three brothers) expressed his admiration. Praise from the detached, aloof Uncle George was different from praise from Syd or my father. I decided, there and then, to take cricket very seriously next summer.

But before next summer came, my world changed again. Syd

received his inevitable 'call-up' papers and left for service with the RAF, first at Wilmslow then at Padgate. After six months in England, he appeared unexpectedly one Friday night and confounded our pleasure at the surprising reunion with the news that he was on embarkation leave. The Sunday before he left he climbed a tree on Wadsley Common, and my mother allowed herself the unpatriotic thought that if a branch broke and he fractured a leg, the war might, at least, be over for him. Over the years Syd – longer unemployed than the rest, younger than the rest, less self-contained than the rest – had become, to my mother, like a brother of her own. I suspect that she felt real regret when he returned to earth unscathed.

Syd had no idea where fate and the Royal Air Force were sending him. So he, and my father, constructed a complicated little code by which he could tell us his destination once he was at sea and the secret was revealed to him. The scheme, by which they planned to deceive both the enemy and the censor, matched possible postings with affectionate messages. We feared that we would receive a letter that ended 'thinking of you all', for that meant that the troopship was on its way to the Far East. We hoped for 'all the best', which would signify that Leading Aircraftsman Hattersley was on his way to man the stores in Gibraltar; a station, which for all its dangers, seemed comfortingly close to home. When the belated letter arrived it ended 'keep smiling'. Syd was destined for Egypt and my father indicated that the message had been received and understood by referring in his reply to 'the land of smiles'. From then on, it was the war in the desert on which we pinned our hopes of allied victory. When I played with my fort it was always Tobruk. My lead soldiers fought for the possession of Sidi Barrani and Mersa Matruh.

One day I took a piece of flat sandstone that had been unearthed in the churchyard and – copying the work of the stonemasons whom I had often watched as they added a name to a tombstone – I carved 'WAVELL' on it. When I had propped it up in the little strip of sunless garden in the shadow of the churchyard wall which was said to be mine, I called my mother to marvel at my handiwork. She was furious. For us, there was only one hero in North Africa. So I took the old screw-driver that I had used as a chisel and inscribed 'SYD' on the other side. My mother helped to embed it in her rockery. I had learned another lesson about the rigid rules of our closely-knit community.

10

Having Been a Soldier

—

By 1942, I too was in uniform. On Friday evenings I wore the blue jumper of the Wadsley Church Wolf Cub Pack and at odd moments during the week I struggled into the full regimentals of a para-military unit of my own creation, The Boys' Own Army. I was not a distinguished Wolf Cub. Prevented from winning my 'first star' by a paranoid fear of performing the forward roll (an essential accomplishment in those who were awarded that distinction) I remained resolutely in the 'other ranks' whilst more recent recruits put on the yellow armbands of 'Sixers' – leaders of boys whom, it was confidently predicted, would grow into leaders of men. But in The Boys' Own Army I was Field Marshal and Commander-in-Chief.

My three qualifications for assuming command were unimpeachable. I owned most of the weapons and equipment in our armoury – a real steel helmet (from which the letters 'ARP' had almost faded), a toy double-barrelled shot gun with a spring-loaded trigger that incongruously simulated machine gun fire, a goatskin covered water bottle from Millet's army surplus store, two cowboy-type six-shooters and a rubber bayonet. Equally important, my garden gave easy access to the churchyard, the scene of our disorganised manoeuvres. And the private army was my idea. Had I patented the invention, I would not have guarded it with more proprietory care.

Most of the recruits were younger boys who, in the manner of their leader, were kitted out in old jackets and blazers to which they had persuaded their mothers to add a martial dimension. It was an age of old army badges, discarded chevrons and second-hand regimental insignia. We all bought, begged or stole a dozen small items of inappropriate military regalia which were then sewn on pockets and sleeves. The more flamboyant volunteers added items of exotica in the manner of the much decorated (and even more despised) Field Marshal Goering. The pink silk tassel, from the bottom of Joey's budgie cage, was fastened to my left shoulder in the manner of an ADC's aiguillettes.

77

Uniformed – but obviously improperly dressed – we made furtive patrols through the churchyard, taking cover behind the larger gravestones before we fired a round or two at some imaginary enemy. The real attraction of the cemetery was the slime-green jam-jars that held the rotting remains of long-withered flowers. Lobbed, like Mills bombs, they exploded against the granite monuments and the marble headstones with a most satisfying sound. Once we had discovered the Chivers' and Hartley's grenades, we became guerillas, darting in and out of the cemetery's shadows. For we then faced two enemy forces – the people who thought that we ought not to be in the churchyard at all, and the people who thought that if we were to be tolerated on consecrated ground we should not desecrate the tombstones by using them for target practice.

I invariably played at being a soldier. The Navy held no charms for me, and despite the Battle of Britain's glamour I remained resolutely khaki, not Air Force blue. The balsa-wood and tissue-paper fighter plane that my father helped me to build was a Hawker Hurricane, not the more fashionable Spitfire and, despite the similarity of the two types, I never pretended that I owned a replica of the aircraft which saved civilisation. From time to time I was bought Dinky models of ancient engines of war – a Gloucester Gladiator, a Sopwith Camel and a Sunderland Flying-boat. But I thought of them as no more than tactical support for my infantry.

Next door below, Cyril Brown constructed complicated flying machines that bore little resemblance to real aeroplanes but flew long distances powered by rubber-bands which he stretched inside their fragile frames from tail to propeller. One day he saw me in my garden loading the usual balls of rolled-up silver paper into the muzzle of my spring-loaded Woolworth anti-aircraft gun. Was I, he smiled, proposing to shoot down his air force? I was too overawed to reply. But in my heart, I longed to open fire.

Before the war was half over, Cyril was called to sterner aerial duties. His dream was to become a fighter pilot. But although he passed the ingenious tests by which potential aircrews were selected, he was sent to America to train for the essentially secondary role of navigator. Mrs Brown gave us regular bulletins on his progress and always seemed inordinately proud that he had been chosen to manipulate the complicated compasses and intricate sextants with which we guided our bombers to Saarbruken, Cologne and the Ruhr. Yet on the day when the Ministry of Information issued a film which

78

extolled the indispensable heroism of men who wore a single wing above their tunic pockets, Mrs Brown welcomed the public recognition of Cyril's contribution to the war effort with such uninhibited relief that even the nine-year-old next door recognised it was a sign of her previous insecurity. A little earlier, Tommy Trinder had starred in a similar production that featured an Auxiliary Fireman too brave and public-spirited to abandon the fires of the Home Front for the fleshpots of active service. We had thought of it as a paeon of praise composed specifically for Syd.

But most of my early war memories are only obliquely concerned with the struggle against Nazi Germany. Whilst my father worked for the local Assistance Committee he regularly brought home food parcels from the free world. They were part of an 'allocation' made to the NAB staff who organised the distribution of American bounty. But when I opened our share of the transatlantic largesse, I thought of its contents in much the same way as I thought of any other edible gift. They were not romantic reinforcements from 'the arsenal of freedom' but long-denied opportunities for gluttony which were taken as soon as my mother's back was turned.

After my father was conscripted into the police force we were in a constant state of anxiety about his welfare, and mounted a front window watch at about the time he was expected home each day. What I recall most vividly is not relief at safe return but the afternoon when my mother suggested that I run down the road to meet him — and tip his constabulary cap over his eyes. Typically, I tipped too hard and the cap fell to the ground. And uncharacteristically my father was offended by my minor assault. The feeling of injured embarrassment which followed my mother's denial of complicity remains in my mind far more clearly than whatever emotion I felt when Dunkirk fell or when the Germans were driven back at El Alamein.

And much of my life during those desperate days had nothing at all to do with the war — unless the continual entanglement of home-made model parachutes on telephone wires and the gradual acquisition of a taste for bitter 'ration chocolate' are regarded as bellicose activities. It was in the early Forties that I began to 'play out' on the road — at first against the express wishes of my mother (who thought that pavement football was an activity fit only for urchins) and then, with her tacit agreement, subject only to my hooliganism being kept secret from 'Worksop'. The first games of competitive football and cricket that I played were contested on tarmacadam and granite chips. In winter gates were our goals. In summer the gate-posts became wickets. During both seasons we ballooned our balding tennis balls into unsympathetic front gardens and then made strategic calculations about whether it was best to ask polite permission for their return or make lightning rescue raids between flowerbeds and bushes.

The Browns — with the worst-kept garden in the road — were the most aggressive protesters of territorial integrity and often refused, point-blank, to return what was clearly not their property. Other neighbours tried to extend their sovereignty to the piece of public highway that bounded their front gardens. The injunction to 'go and play outside your own house' made no allowance for the difficulty of pitching wickets and siting goals on the steeply sloping parts of our roads. It also demonstrated a proprietorial view of common property which I deplored. It was as much our road as theirs, and we possessed a perfect right to awaken sleeping shift-workers, disturb babies' afternoon rests and make muddy ball-marks on other people's walls and gates.

Of course, communal property had its finest flowering in the Hillsborough branch of the Sheffield City Libraries (Children's Section). During the years of inter-war poverty the three brothers had made an occasional visit to 'no charge for admission' concerts at the City Hall. They had heard tirades from Harry Pollit and Sir Oswald Mosley; slinking out before the collections as they were too poor and too antagonistic to contribute, and too afraid of the muscular steward openly to refuse a donation. They had attended a gramophone recital given by Christopher Stone and crept out before the radio personality's assistants passed amongst the audience with cut-price records for sale. But such exotic opportunities came only once or twice a year. The library, like poverty itself, was always with them. It was their most constant pleasure during the peacetime depression, and when the war brought unaccustomed prosperity they remained faithful to its serviceable cloth bindings and penny fines for each week that a borrowed book was overdue.

So even in the days of comparative affluence the library remained our constant joy. It was part of our lives, a home from home housed in what had once been a mansion owned by a local worthy who (at least according to folklore) had named most of the nearby roads after the numerous daughters on whom he spent his jerry-built fortune.

When we detoured down Dorothy Road to catch the tram at one stop nearer to the city centre than the Middlewood terminus, we thought of the lucky young ladies who had been brought up in the library at Hillsborough Park. It had become a classic northern civic amenity. Part of it – simply designed to amaze and delight all who beheld its beauties – was immaculate acres of lawn into which careful flowerbeds had been cut. The rest was intended for active recreation – tennis, rowing, bowls played with eccentric precision on the gently convex 'crown' green, and kicking balls about on the vast expanse of bare brown soil where athletic feet had worn the grass away. We approached the library from the ornamental end of the park. The lawns were shaved every summer's day by an apprentice with hand-shears who knelt all working-day for the creation of – and in tribute to – perfect grass.

When the red shale paths that crossed the formal gardens turned, the angles of grass across which the anti-social pedestrian might have been tempted to walk were protected from the damaging tread by foot-high wire fences which deterred trespassers but did not obscure the view. The plants in the round, oval and star-shaped beds which were sculpted into the otherwise inviolate sward were all carefully matched for colour and size. What little glimpses of earth were allowed between the leaves that never turned brown and the petals that never wilted was perfect sifted sand; as smooth as the flour in a proper Yorkshire pudding. The only hint of untidiness came from a mulberry tree that stood just outside the library door and persisted in shedding its leaves and fruit in clear defiance of the park-keeper's wishes. My mother told me that if I ate the fallen berries I would die. But I knew that her counterfeit concern was just another deterrent to keep me off the grass.

The children's library beyond the mulberry bush was a single-storey extension, built onto the old mansion but only connected to it by mysteriously private doors which were out of bounds to the library's quaintly-named 'subscribers'. At first my mother accompanied me into the 'junior section' and selected my books with a ruthless disregard of my own preferences. Then I was sent in through the junior library's door to choose my own books whilst my parents performed a similar adult task next door. Left alone, I invariably behaved badly, a course of conduct which I irrationally blamed on the library rules. Each junior 'subscriber' had three tickets. But only two of them could be used for novels. The City Father who set the rules believed that truth was more educative than fiction. At the age of eight I was never quite sure of how to use the yellow ticket that entitled me to borrow nature studies, pictorial biographies and hobbies hardbacks. But I was obsessively determined to use my two fiction tickets to maximum advantage. And I had no doubt what maximum advantage was. Success was measured in William books or Biggles stories. To return home with one of each or even a matching pair was a literary triumph. Several times I was ordered out of the library for pursuing my favourites too enthusiastically. I developed the habit of stalking the young ladies who replaced recently-returned books to their shelves. If I saw the object of my desire on their trolleys I would pounce before it was back in its proper place. When my behaviour broke the bounds of propriety I was exiled to the outside of the adult library, where I waited for the reappearance of my parents in the company of the dogs that were tethered to the nearby railings.

II

The Broken Circle

—

Richmal Crompton was the enthusiasm of my seventh and eighth years. Captain W. E. Johns was my favourite author during my ninth and tenth. When I was old enough to put away such childish things I was judged big enough to take up cycling. In the little shed that had been bought to protect deck chairs and garden tools from the snow of winter, two elderly bicycles were slowly rotting away. They were the only portable property of any value that George or Syd possessed when they left home. In the mid-Thirties they had been at the centre of my uncles' lives, carrying them to work on weekdays and on trips to the nearby country in the summer. By the beginning of the following decade, the cycles were riddled with rust from front mudguard to back fork. I rubbed at the diseased places with emery paper for weeks on end. But although I disturbed the brown excretion that had formed like a scab on the once shiny surfaces, I never fully freed the pitted steel from the infection, which could be painted over but not destroyed. A bike, once rusted, cannot be restored to anything like its first glory. Silver paint is a poor substitute for chromium plate. And the black enamel that comes out of tins never shines like the black enamel that has been sprayed and baked in a factory oven. But although the two old bicycles had lost their shine for ever, the inner tubes were still air-tight and the pedals still turned. One of them was a Raleigh, the 'all steel bicycle'. It had, my father told me, been made in the Nottingham factory where once my grandfather polished spokes. It was the one I chose. On it I learnt how to move steadily forward without losing my balance – tricks that proved invaluable in later life.

Naturally I was not allowed to learn by climbing on and falling off. I was taken onto flat pieces of straight road by my father – each one of us pushing, rather than riding, our crudely repainted cycles. I straddled the cross-bar with ungainly difficulty, braced myself and pedalled forward with my father holding me and the bicycle in an uprighted position. After a few preliminary lessons, I could remain erect and moving with no more assistance than a paternal hand under the saddle. As I grew more proficient, my father gladly broke first into a trot then into a run. My father did not tell me I had learned to keep my balance, and for some days still ran behind, simulating holding me upright.

My father always took his own bicycle on these training sessions. He could not ride it to the place picked out for practice, for he was walking with me. He had to leave it carefully propped up with a pedal jammed against the pavement-edge whilst he put me through the paces, and push it back home after the lesson had been learned. I suppose that he was anticipating the rides we would have together when I could be trusted not to wobble under every passing milk-cart and bread van.

When we did ride together I was, at first, required to keep to the pavement side of the road whilst my father protected me from traffic like an outrider in a convoy. We had to avoid all roads on which trams ran. Trams occupying the middle of roads was a terrible hazard to tyro cyclists, and tram-lines were said to be an even greater danger. According to folklore, cycle wheels slid into their shiny grooves and bike and rider were propelled along the track unable to deviate to left or right, risking the terrible fate of being flattened from the back by the juggernaut that was supposed to use the lines. Roads that were free of tramcars often had gradients that were too steep for my old machine and young lungs. In fact there were only two 'rides' that we ever went in in those days – Worral and back, and Bradfield and back.

Bradfield and back was our favourite. Bradfield itself was a proper English village with an ancient church high above it on the hillside and a village green on a flat acre of land in the curve of the river at the valley bottom. The 'bottom way' to Bradfield was a route that ran beside the Loxley dams, part of the series of interlinked reservoirs that collected Pennine water for Sheffield taps. From Loxley and Bradfield brambles intertwined with hawthorn in the hedgerows, and in the autumn my father and I would collect blackberries which – no matter how squashed by the time we got them home – were always incorporated into what would otherwise have only been an apple pie.

The blackberries which grew in Wadsley Churchyard were nothing like as sweet. For they were picked in what I regarded as my own backyard, not gathered from foreign fields and distant pastures. For years I roamed the churchyard, picking dandelions for my rabbit, holly for Christmas decorations and sticks for catapults, quarter-staffs, bows and arrows. I never thought of the cemetery as being a sad or a morbid place. I never thought of death and desolation until the year we lost both my grandmother and Uncle George.

My grandmother died, as for six years she had lived, huddled and immobile in her little bed under the living room window. I knew that she was dying. First I was kept out of the back room for days on end. Then I was sent to the 'phone box in Dykes Hall Road to call Uncle Ern in his Retford woodyard and ask him to send one of the aunts to our urgent rescue. I pressed 'button A' at the wrong time and lost the one and ninepence that the trunk call cost. Angry though she was, my mother was less angry than I anticipated. I realised that other things were on her mind. Then the doctor began to call every day and I could hear urgent footsteps and the filling of kettles in the middle of the night. When the door of the doctor's car slammed long after the street lights had gone out I knew that, right below me, my grandmother was at the point of death.

Next morning, both my mother and father came into my bedroom. My mother actually got into bed beside me before she told me what I already knew. My response was reasonable but unforgivable. During the previous fortnight, I had heard so many people talk of death as a 'merciful relief' that I had begun to believe their platitude without fully understanding it. The cliché seemed the only comfort that I could offer. So I mechanically told her that it was all for the best. It was. For my grandmother had endured a week of unremitting and incurable agony. But it was not what my mother wanted me to say. Crying after she had left the bedroom made no amends.

I behaved barely better at the funeral. 'Cut flowers' were abominated by my grandmother, who believed that plants should be left to grow in peace and freedom. Bought 'cut flowers' were thought of as both extravagant and artificial. But something was needed for the top of the coffin that Uncle Ern had sent from Retford. So on the morning of the burial, I set off to Wadsley Common to pick (as distinct from cut) a wild tribute. Unfortunately, Wadsley Common was neither the Derbyshire hedgerows nor Trent-side pasture. It was south Yorkshire scrubland. And on it only moorland bushes bloomed. Scorning cuts and scratches, I brought home a great yellow sheaf of broom. But I knew that in my mother's mind was a picture of fields of dog daisies, buttercups and celandines that I had not bothered to find.

Of course, I was obliged to see the body before the coffin lid was put in place and, of course, I was terrified. At the news of my grandmother's death I was over-rational. At the moment of our final parting I was irrational to the point of trauma. As we walked out to the car I was told, in tones of genuine despair, that I must stop grinning. If I appeared to smile it was the result of suppressed hysteria. I sat with teeth clenched all the way to Steetley, the last resting place of the House of Skinner where both my grandmother's parents were buried.

After the service was over, and the dust had been returned to dust, I noticed my father allow himself a half-smile. Uncle Ern – chief mourner, major domo and undertaking consultant – was forming up the mourners for the return journey. As we waited for the car that would take us home to Wadsley he lit his pipe. Noticing the aunts' disapproval at this profanity, he explained (with apparent conviction) that since he was leaning on the churchyard gate, his feet were on consecrated ground but his briar was on the King's highway. The aunts seemed satisfied by his casuistry. My father, with greater experience in these matters, was obviously less than convinced.

George's passing was, in its way, even more dramatic. In the Ordnance Corps he had risen to the rank of 'Senior Conductor', a very superior sort of NCO who wore the 'Tate and Lyle' badge of a Regimental Sergeant Major on his sleeve. He had also – unbeknown to us – married the manageress of the NAAFI store where he was stationed. His marriage at least explained his disappointing refusal to be considered for a commission. For promotion would have required him to leave his recently acquired home and hearth. His reluctance to tell the joyous news to his brother and sister-in-law can only be understood in terms of the complicated family relationship. Eventually – with my cousin's expected arrival imminent and obvious – the belated bride was brought to Airedale Road.

The real cause of the arguments that followed, I have never understood. Two facts only are clear. Inevitably, my father began the afternoon anxious to avoid trouble. Equally inevitably he ended it giving my mother his full support – root and branch, neck and crop, heart and soul, body and mind. In my absence, things were said that could not lightly be forgiven. George and his wife Vera left before afternoon school was over. Indeed, to my astonishment, I saw them waiting at the Worrall bus stop as I hurried home for more stories of army life. Once again Airedale Road was filled with grief and regret.

With Syd still in the Western Desert, the Hattersley family had shrunk to three. We did not see George again for six years.

Only the strange emotions that bound the former fugitives together could have produced such a cataclysm. In normal families, the marriage of a brother-in-law is usually the cause of momentary pleasure or passing disapproval. But until that moment, we were not an ordinary family. We were all bound together by the bonds of previous secret vicissitudes. My grandmother's death and George's going began to break the spell. Into 'double figures' at last, I began to feel the influence of world, flesh and devil. Freed from my grandmother's prophecies of death and abduction, my mother even allowed me to enjoy some of the pleasures I had long been denied.

Going to see a real football match seemed to me as grown-up and as daring as smoking or wearing long trousers – neither of which adult habit I had acquired. Indeed, as a result of that first visit to the Hillsborough ground of the Sheffield Wednesday Football Club, I have still to experience what I assume to be the repulsive taste of a first cigarette. For from the moment that my father and I took our seat in the wooden 'Old Stand', I knew that God had called me to play left-half for 'the Owls' and when other little boys puffed away surreptitiously behind scout huts and in school lavatories, I never risked my health and respiration. I kept myself pure for Sheffield Wednesday.

Inevitably the first game I saw was against Nottingham Forest. Indeed, I suspect the decision that I was old enough and big enough to be jostled by the crowd was partly influenced by my father's desire to take me to see his team. It was concern for my safety that prompted the extravagance of tickets and seats. In later years, we always stood on Spion Kop, exposed to weather and the pressure of the thousand tightly packed football supporters. But on the first day I was in comfort and under cover, only in danger as we were swept in and out of the ground at the start and after the end of the game. My father guided me through the crush with his arm over my shoulders in a way which was supposed to protect me but caused something approaching strangulation. I knew he was trying to be helpful and felt unable to beg him to release the pressure on my windpipe.

I was enchanted by the game. It ended in a goalless draw and was, so my father later assured me, unexceptional in every way. But I think that I recognised what J. B. Priestley called the combination of

'conflict and art'. It was the beginning of a lifetime of eager anticipation of winter Saturday afternoons, climaxing in the hour after four
forty-five being filled by the triumph of victory, the despair of defeat,
or the cold consolation of a draw and a single point. I know that I
should have grown out of such infantile passion. But becoming a
prejudiced football partisan was, for me, part of the onset of age,
wisdom and maturity – the discovery of one of the wonders of the
world.

The formal recognition of impending puberty was my graduation
from cubs to scouts. I had actually joined a few weeks before my
grandmother's death – lying about my age and relying on my size to
allow me to move on into the senior branch a year before I was
technically entitled to join. My 'tenderfoot' weeks coincided with
some sort of Scouting Festival, and my father faithfully attended all
the displays and camp-fire nights, leaving my mother at home to
attend to 'Mrs Brackenbury's' final fatal illness. I found the scouts far
more congenial than the cubs. In the scouts there was no obligation
to perform forward rolls or skip backwards. The scouts encouraged
worthwhile pastimes like learning morse code, building rope bridges
across Wadsley Common's little ravines and recognising the difference between stoats and weasels. The scouts also offered the prospect
of 'national service' – war work performed in what used to be
Wadsley Asylum and had become Wharncliffe Military Hospital.
After fifty hours national service scouts were awarded a red badge
with a gold crown embroidered upon it. I set to work winning that
distinction in Ward 13b, the refuge of shell-shocked survivors from
the Normandy landing. There was no blood in the psychiatric wards.
Occasionally, a patient would shout or jibber and be led away. But
the blood-stained dressings about which other scouts would talk
with a mixture of horror and pride were, for me, mercifully absent. I
posted letters, bought toothpaste, read newspapers aloud and
listened to old soldiers' stories. Then one day an officious doctor said
that a ward crammed with mentally unstable soldiers was no place
for a boy of eleven to spend his spare time.

Sister Wragg – whose weekend joint I collected from the butcher
each Saturday she was on duty – promised to find me another place. I
was moved downstairs in the old Victorian hospital block to a more
acceptable surgical ward and handed over to Sister Hall, a large lady
with owl-like spectacles and an upper-class accent of a sort I had
previously never heard. On the first Saturday of my revised duties I

worked away until a little before one o'clock when, as was scouting practice in the ward above, I took my place in the queue that had formed in front of the lunch trolley and awaited my dollop of meat and mashed potatoes. Sister Hall was scandalised. Dragging me into her office, she delivered a lecture on the vice of scrounging. Mortified by the humiliation, I cycled home as instructed, too embarrassed ever to return.

Three weeks later our scoutmaster, Mr Bull, received a report about one of his troop who had lost interest in 'national service' after the discovery that free meals were not included. Although he later denied it, we also suspected that Sister Hall's calumny was the reason that my 'national service' badge was not presented when the other Wadsley Scout awards were made. Having completed my fifty hours of endeavour it was mine by right. So my mother went round to see Mr Bull – who lived in the next street – and told him where his duty lay. Her eloquence was so successful that I was both awarded the badge and promoted to 'second' in the Otter Patrol. Harold Wool-house was the Patrol Leader. Although a strict disciplinarian, I always felt that he was slightly overawed by my hat. Other scouts had rather skimpy headgear – the product of the wartime felt famine; I was crowned by a cross between a stetson and a sombrero. It had been the possession of Jack Hancock, our new neighbour, who in the peaceful pre-war years had been some sort of super-scout. He sold it us for some nominal sum and I wore it with a mixture of pride and shame. I was still deeply confused about the need to be the same and the necessity, sometimes, to be different.

To me, scouting was also irrevocably associated with knives, and before my days in the Otter Patrol were done I had assembled a formidable collection. I possessed the standard jack-knife that every scout carried clipped to his belt ready to remove stones from limping horses' feet. Uncle Ern gave me a buck-horn-handled penknife with five blades and a corkscrew. I broke the large blade digging for horse-radish on a nearby building site. Why I wanted to unearth the bitter tasting roots, I no longer remember. But I do recall how hard I worked to keep news of the damage from my mother. The destruc-tion of the Bowie knife that she bought me for Christmas could not be concealed, for its plastic handle shattered with a terrible noise when I threw it at the dart board in my bedroom. The two knives given me by soldiers in Wharncliffe Hospital proved more durable. I covered their sheaths with fur from rabbits we had eaten for dinner and used both of them for their proper purpose – carving my initials on trees.

One day, whilst rashly hacking at the bark of a silver birch in the part of Wadsley Churchyard which was exposed to the road, I was reproved by a figure well known, and much revered, in our suburb. He was Councillor James Gill, Chairman of the Schools Sub-Committee of the Education Committee, Methodist lay preacher, retired headmaster, and nurse and companion to the second Mrs Gill. Malicious neighbours claimed that the bearded and dapper 'Jimmy Gill' had, on the death of his first wife, set out with non-conformist zeal to find himself a sturdy single teacher who would care for him in old age. An apparently suitable quarry was run to ground. But no sooner was the ceremony over than it was discovered that the unfortunate bride suffered from Parkinson's disease. Councillor Gill passed his declining years pushing a wheel-chair. He was thus occupied when he caught me vandalising the silver birch. It turned out to be a fortunate apprehension. Having marched off up Airedale Road with no more amicable intention than reporting me to my parents, he began a conversation with my mother and father which turned him into their friend. He had strong views about my education, particularly the necessity of liberating me from Hillsborough High School.

The school door at which he pushed was ready to swing open. Miss Roberts had, by error or design, failed to enter me for 'the scholarship', the test by which the Council's Educational Committee chose ten per cent of the city's pupils for places in grammar schools. Thanks to my mother's eloquence and energy (reinforced by Dr Stephen's certificates confirming my asthmatic condition), I was soon to sit the 'over-age examination', the safety net designed to catch deserving candidates who had been sick on the day or who had failed to qualify for an academic education by a margin of error so small that they deserved a second chance. But everyone knew that despite the theoretical reprieve, I was doomed. The 'over-age' was doctored to take account of the maturity of the entrants and was therefore composed of questions beyond human comprehension. And the original failure even to enter for the examination hung over the whole family like an omen and an augury. The municipal grammar schools were not for me.

I faced up to the pointless ordeal of the 'over-age' in the Hillsborough Special School. It had been cleared of its educationally subnormal pupils whilst the older than eleven-plus children sat the first part of the two morning examinations. I had never been under the supervision of male teachers, and I found the habit of punctuating every sentence with several 'sirs' a strange embarrassment. But I learned a great deal from the other entrants during the mid-morning break. When the ten-minute respite was over I could make matches explode in the sliding tops of the ink wells without being nauseated by the smell and I could construct, out of a marble and a milk bottle top, a tortoise and tank hybrid that rolled down the sloping surface of my desk. I completed the test which was supposed to measure my ability and aptitude with very little interest and no hope. In such a spirit of calm despair was I caught etching my initials in churchyard trees.

The friendship carved out by my penknife took me often to James Gill's dark and book-lined house. He told me tales of Don Bradman, whom he had seen during the tour of 1938, and urged me to follow the manly virtues – especially modesty. I remember the shocking story of a primary school speech day where the headmaster had boasted that his pupils were 'also paramount at football'. I was suitably disgusted and accepted with gratitude the oblong blotter that he gave me as a reminder of the importance of neatness.

James Gill agreed that there was no chance of my winning a grammar school place. But he still urged immediate removal from Hillsborough High School and my enrolment at Wisewood Senior where I could compete for a place at the Junior Technical School. The 'tech' was essentially second-best, but boys had been known to leap from its metalwork classes to the sixth forms of more academically inclined institutions. In any case, it was designed for teenage boys, not simpering adolescent girls and infants. Mr Gill was persuasive in his advocacy of Wisewood now, tomorrow the 'tech', and eventually the world.

With an enlightenment unusual in those distant days, my mother asked me my opinion. And with an effrontery rare even in the emergent working classes, we went to reconnoitre the school of which James Gill spoke so highly. Perhaps the Chairman of the Schools Sub-Committee warned them that his friends were coming. At the time I just assumed that they were all naturally friendly. I was to learn better as the weeks went by, but as I met Mr Linfoot (the headmaster), Mr Wood (his deputy), Mr Drake (woodwork), I contrasted their joviality with Miss Roberts's sour assertion that the standard of my work in class inspired no confidence in my suitability for grammar school education. I chose Wisewood without the slightest hesitation and, after the Easter holidays, began what I suppose was the most important term in my whole twelve years at school.

12
Chance of a Lifetime

—

For the rest of the world, the really important event had taken place several weeks earlier. The war in Europe was over. It had gone out with the bang of flying bombs extending their range from London and the south-east coast to industrial targets in the north. I remember listening to the sound of every passing aeroplane certain that it was a rocket. I waited, breathless with fear, for the moment when the engine cut out and the whole explosive apparatus plunged onto the city below. My father, still a Police War Reserve, confessed that he always took cover in shop doorways when such terrors occurred during his periods of constabulary duty. He accepted that there was an obvious absurdity in seeking refuge in a cubicle of plate glass. But he found a psychological comfort in being under some sort of shelter.

By VE Day, even the war in the cemetery had taken on a more realistic aspect. The dressing up and the charades were over. For The Boys' Own Army had at last been touched by real conflict. Old Fred Guest had retired and been replaced by Bob, his son, who intended in turn to pass the inheritance on to the third generation – young Fred, who had begun his working life in a forge, where he spent his time dreaming of motor cycles. But his job and his fantasies were both interrupted by conscription. Wounded in Normandy, he came home for rest and recuperation and sat in the winter sunshine of the churchyard talking to us like Old Caspar about battles. When he recovered he returned to France and died crossing the Rhine. Having known a real soldier killed in action we abandoned the silliness of childhood, and started to make a serious contribution to the war effort.

On the day that Germany surrendered, we all went to the bonfire in nearby Walders Avenue, rejoicing to realise that it was no longer illegal to light up the sky, and that the golden glow that shone all over Sheffield were signs of allied rejoicing not enemy activity. Mrs Hemmingway – one of the unqualified Hillsborough High School teachers – confronted us in the glow of victory. Was I really being 'taken away?' My mother confirmed our decision – 'based on Councillor Gill's recommendation'.

I imagined that I was about to emerge from the protective chrysallis of Hillsborough High School as a fully-fledged, and aggressively male, butterfly – doing dazzling wordwork, swooping into the cricket team and alighting elegantly on every branch of masculine society. It all turned out rather differently. I was enormously relieved to leave the genteel respectability of the Dr Barnardo's collecting boxes (tastefully made in papier-maché and shaped like one of the cottages in which the foundlings lived) and the end of term concerts where we all sang 'Bless this House' and the stars of the elocution classes recited 'Admirals All' and 'If'. But I was not ready for the fights in the playgrounds, the physical education lessons in the hall or the rigorous enthusiasm for basic learning. There was no French at Wisewood, but a lot of spelling and arithmetic.

Being part of Sheffield's non-conformist working-class tradition, Wisewood Secondary worshipped local gods. Part of its spiritual inheritance was the election of a school 'queen'. The senior royalty in the annual ritual were selected by chapels, and on Whit Sunday they paraded through the city in convoys of decorated coal lorries and milk floats which had been dressed over-all, like men-of-war in a regatta. The Hattersleys were deeply contemptuous of such pagan rites and although I did not comprehend the real reason for their disapproval, I shared it. At Wisewood, I was required to participate in a 'ceremony' which had as its climax the school's May Queen crowned with a chaplet of roses and daffodils.

I played only a passive part, sitting cross-legged on the assembly hall floor and humming 'To A Wild Rose' as the chosen virgin paraded in, looking like a cross between Queen Mab and a bridesmaid at a grinder's wedding. Once the spirit of spring was appointed, we reverted to rousing chapel community hymn singing. I gave forth at the top of my voice, particularly enjoying the line – 'the song of sacred joy, it never seems to cloy'. Mr Wood, the deputy headmaster, explained to us what cloy meant – 'I like chocolates but if I ate a boxful, they would cloy'. In the ration-book world in which we lived it was an unlikely image. But I had learned a new word.

Of course, such passing pleasures did not make up for the humiliation of attempting to perform the feats of athleticism that were called physical education. I could not vault the wooden horse, balance on beams, somersault over the padded top of the 'box' or even climb the rope. My incapacities incurred the open contempt of my classmates, and my shame was in no way reduced by various teachers demanding that I be shown the sympathy appropriate to one who had only recently escaped from Hillsborough High School. A similar indignity was inflicted upon me in woodwork where I was not allowed to make the stool that demonstrated the mortice and tenon joint, for I was unfamiliar with the potentially lethal chisels. Instead, I was required to renew the white paint on the two school flagpoles that had been temporarily removed from the roof to be put in a state of pristine preparedness for victory in the east.

But before Hiroshima and Nagasaki were devastated, I was to experience the seminal event of my young life – the General Election of 1945. The part of the campaign which I remember most vividly was preceded by the second leg of the eleven plus examination. In those days the 'scholarship' was taken in two parts and for me the twin terrors fell either side of my change from private to public education. Although by then at Wisewood Secondary Modern, I went to the old 'daft school' in Hillsborough for the second part of my torment, completed it with no great interest or enthusiasm, and walked from the bottom of the Don Valley up Wadsley Lane (past our old house which I suspected to be still throbbing with diptheria microbes) and Laird Road (with Hillsborough High School standing deserted and reproachful) and on to my new school. I was not expected. Nobody went back to school on the afternoon of the 'examination'.

So I went home. My father – still a sort of policeman – was working the early turn and arrived shortly after me. He suggested a trip to the museum in Western Park. My mother agreed – as long as we could pause on the way to deliver leaflets in the Labour Party's cause. I remember (or imagine that I remember) every minute of the afternoon which followed – the tram to Hillsborough and my first visit to the old hut behind the co-op grocery that was A. V. Alexander's Committee Room; the second tram ride to Shalesmoor, which I was one day to represent on the Sheffield City Council; my meeting with Albert Ballard, alderman and agent; and the daring delight of pushing pieces of paper through peoples' doors.

Shalesmoor did not boast letter-boxes. Its rows of dilapidated, terraced houses had been hurriedly built a hundred years before to accommodate the cheap labour that flooded in from the dales to work the wheels of Sheffield's new factories. There were no steps to

95

climb or paths to trudge, for the front door opened out onto the pavements and to that convenience was added the advantage of wood so warped by a century of damp cold wind that between the bottom of the door and the step there was often a half-inch gap through which a piece of propaganda could be flipped with an easy flick of the wrist. The only moment of concern in the whole afternoon was when we ran out of our original choice of leaflet and had to change to a new variety, brought to reinforce us by a butcher's boy from the co-op.

On one side of our new weapon in the propaganda war there was a strip cartoon featuring 'Jane', the famous *Daily Mirror* pin-up girl who had, in a more innocent age, improved the armed forces' morale. Jane was inclined to behave in a provocative way – cycling with her skirts above her knees, tearing her dresses on protruding nails and being caught wearing nothing more than three layers of underclothes. Such debauchery did not seem to Mr Ballard proper for dissemination by one of my tender years. But my mother took a more broad-minded view and we finished the delivery together.

The work completed, we toiled up Oxford Street and Addy Street to Weston Park. Behind the mock-classical City Museum, the red brick of Sheffield University's main building stood between us and the Derbyshire skyline. 'Today,' my mother announced dramatically, 'you have taken your first step towards there' – and she waved her hand airily towards the local seat of learning. I had no real idea what she meant. But I did realise the prospect she dangled in front of me was in some way dependent on eleven plus success. So I put it out of my mind.

There were, however, other academic prospects offered to me by enrolment at Wisewood. I sat the special examination for the Art School and failed hopelessly. The tulip (which I was 'required' to draw) looked like a poppy and the 'composition of my own choice' was ruined by what I now suppose was nerves. I chose to draw a market cross – a complicated little exercise, involving careful respect for the rules of perspective, which Syd had led me through a hundred times. Normally I could make the steps look genuinely three-dimensional. But on the day, the cross itself leaned drunkenly forward and the steps were all front and no top. When the invigilator asked me what my picture was supposed to be, I realised that the Art School was not for me.

Of the Junior Technical School, I was more hopeful. The arithmetic test seemed simple. The comprehension paper was easy. More important, the examination involved an interview and I sustained a serious conversation with the Headmaster who asked me about my real interests. A more calculating child might have answered 'metal work' or 'technical drawing', but I confessed 'cricket' and 'reading'. I had just read *Prester John* (my first recognition that half the world was as black as the two Jamaican boy scouts who had fascinated me in the stalls of a pre-war pantomime) and I rambled on about John Buchan in general. 'You ought to go to the grammar school' the Head told me. But he added encouragingly that I would probably end up with him.

I have no recollection of waiting for or worrying about the results of the examinations. But sometime between the Junior Tech interview and the day when the news was delivered, I attended my first political meeting. It was held in the great black Primitive Methodist Chapel on Langsett Road and was, of course, addressed by our local M.P. and hero, Mr A. V. Alexander, First Lord of the Admiralty. Mr Alexander had served with Attlee, Bevin and Morrison as the Labour members of Winston Churchill's coalition government. He was a survivor from Ramsey McDonald's second Administration, and behaved like what he was, a great man from Labour's neolithic period.

A. V. Alexander wore a stiff-winged collar (improperly described by my father as a 'come to Jesus' because of its association with non-conformist lay preachers), a waistcoat with watch-chain and a set of fascinatingly obvious false teeth. In later years, more cynical senior members of the Labour League of Youth would claim that they had seen the formidable dentures pop out in mid-plosive, and that without an interruption in his sentence 'A.V.' had caught them in full flight and returned them to their proper place in a single eloquent gesture. I certainly saw the spittle flying. But it did nothing to reduce the fascination. I was entranced by politics.

It was, of course, a tribal attraction, based on the enthusiasm that my mother obviously felt and enhanced by the rough romanticism of battles that I always realised spilt real blood. I knew that it was not just a game, not least because of a constant source of trivial friction between my parents. Apparently, in 1935 my father had attended a meeting at which Jimmy Thomas had spoken in support of Gurney Braithwaite, the Conservative Candidate for Hillsborough. Jimmy Thomas was a hate figure to all loyal colliers' daughters. Not only had he joined the National Government. He had led the railway union at the time it had 'deserted the miners' during the General Strike of 1926. Mr Thomas announced that if the socialists won he would send his son to Australia to escape growing up under Mr Attlee's totalitarian yoke. My father, it was claimed, had been so influenced by this statement of paternal affection that he decided to protect his own offspring's future by voting Tory. He always denied it. But my mother was never quite convinced. In 1964, when the Thomas child was an elderly Conservative M.P., I used to see him sitting opposite me in the House of Commons and think of the trouble he had caused in our family twenty years before.

Wisewood School was closed on polling day and I recall nothing of the tensions and the triumphs of that historic moment. I do however remember the following morning when Mr Linfoot, the Headmaster, sent for me and a couple of classmates to tell us that we had won places at the Junior Tech. When I got home with the joyous news we all rushed to tell James Gill that his judgement had been vindicated. He was about to witness the declaration that my father had to sign as a formal commitment that I would stay in school until I was sixteen, when his Methodist conscience made him pause, pen in hand. What, he asked, if I *had* won a Grammar School place? When the news arrived the following week I would be promised to the 'tech' and my father would be forced, in honour, to keep his word. We had three days in which to return the forms – the period allowed to working-class families for an assessment of the obligations they were assuming. Councillor Gill promised to spend the seventy-two hours fruit fully.

I remember four-thirty on the following afternoon more vividly than any other moment during the decade. I was walking home up Airedale Road when I saw my father pretending to dig the front garden. I remember his exact words when I reached the gate – 'You've got five years at the City Grammar School'. James Gill had exercised his rights as ex-Chairman of the Secondary Sub-Committee and looked at the pass list. 'Hattersley R. S. G.' was there.

Next day at Wisewood, Mr Linfoot came into our class-room to pursue me and two other malingerers, whose irresponsible parents had failed to make the fateful Junior Tech decision. The boy who sat next to me claimed, quite correctly, that I had boasted of winning a place at the City Grammar. Sworn to secrecy until the official announcement was published, I denied having made any such claim. Linfoot, assuming that I had been fantasising, asked a scathing question about being offered a place at Oxford (of which I had never heard) and urged me to bring a message about my future the following day. I prayed that by then the big buff envelope would have arrived.

Next morning at a quarter to eight there was a knock on the front door. Unfortunately, it was not a registered letter but Gordon Woolhouse bearing the news that he was bound for Firth Park, a grammar school in a northern suburb. Had I, he enquired, heard anything? My mother answered firmly that we had not, and I began to lose faith in James Gill's infallibility. I suppose by then Mr Linfoot had learned the truth, for he pursued my technical intentions no further before, on the following day, the glad tidings were delivered. We read with wonder of the obligation to buy school uniform, the duty to attend regularly, the prohibition of part-time jobs and the meeting with staff before term began. It had all really happened.

I took the letter to Wisewood in triumph, careless of any recrimination about previous deceptions. But before my bragging began Mr Linfoot visited us again with news of the recent internal examination that we had all taken. I was nearer the bottom than the top. How is it, asked the Headmaster, that this boy has done so badly but won two scholarships? My form teacher confessed her bewilderment. The only possible explanation was that I read all the time; an unhealthy preoccupation only slightly mitigated by my growing passion for cricket. I sat at the back of the class learning that nothing ever turns out to be as good as we expected.

13
Home is the Hero

—

I was neither promised nor given a bicycle as a reward for my scholarship success. I think my mother genuinely disapproved of dangling the prospect of glittering prizes in front of my eyes. In any case, the price of a bicycle was more than we could afford. So as neighbour after neighbour reported the conditional offer of Raleigh and Rudge, Hercules and Humber, my mother increased her denunciation of materialism's corrupting effect. Would these misguided parents – she enquired of nobody in particular – really refuse a trip to Robinson's Cycle Shop, if the bribe failed and son or daughter did not pass? Did they – she asked herself out loud – really imagine that the promise of spokes and wheels would encourage candidates to concentrate harder? These forays into moral philosophy were interspersed with calculations about the cost of school uniform. After much weekly counting of coppers we acquired the obligatory items piece by piece and set them out in triumphant display on the battered old Victorian chest of drawers which furnished my bedroom.

In these comprehensive days of all-embracing jeans, it is hard to recall the social cachet which was attached to grammar school uniform. Thanks to caps and scarves the difference between 'passing' and 'failing' was visible to every neighbour. Green, maroon and navy blazers were the raiment of success. Second-hand jackets handed down from elder brothers and sweaters hastily knitted by grandma were the apparel of defeat. The lucky parents regarded the weeks of outfitting as a period of public rejoicing. They announced the dates of their visits to the recommended outfitters as if they were events in the social calendar. Close relatives were invited to attend the scene of the actual purchase as if it were a wedding or christening. Naturally enough, 'Worksop' became my sartorial godparents. Indeed, there was a terrible moment when I feared that they would offer to tailor-make everything themselves in the 'Worksop' showroom. But the danger passed and Aunt Annie accompanied my mother to Cole Brothers and paid for a blazer with crumpled old pound notes. Uncle

Ern sent me five shillings wrapped up in a letter of congratulation which referred to me several times as 'the Prof'. The two half crowns were dropped into my National Savings money box and kept safe behind the two rows of teeth that prevented knife-assisted pilfering.

To my profound disappointment I was not allowed to deck myself out in the red and green before the first day of the new term. My mother wanted me to keep the livery free from dirt and stain until the great day actually arrived. And she believed that immediately parading the streets in the manifestation of my new glory would do nothing to encourage the reticent character which she regarded as essential to my future profession. For she had already decided that I should go to university and eventually become a history master at a grammar school – preferably one further up the ladder of parental preference than the one which I was about to attend.

To reinforce her strictures on the need for modesty she held before me the awful example of a boy from nearby Grove Avenue. This unfortunate youth was unlucky enough to possess parents who anticipated his enrolment at King Edward's – the city's most prestigious grammar school – by purchasing and allowing him to wear all the regalia of that institution even before the scholarship results were published. He was actually playing in the street, fully robed, when the postman brought the awful news that, far from passing for King Edward's, he had failed altogether. As a result of his parents' presumption he was required to enrol at some secondary modern dressed in the uniform of his hopes from which the insignia had been cut like chevrons torn from the tunic of a courtmartialled sergeant major. Despite the episode's total irrelevance to my condition, I was remarkably chastened by the story. For I had already begun to suspect that providence punished wrongdoers. And I had a vision of the awful retribution fate might exact from any act of presumption. It would take the form of a note from the Education Office saying that their previous letter was a mistake and I should report in September to Wisewood Secondary.

I began to experience an anguish that I had not suffered since the Christmas Eves of my real childhood – the growing certainty that the great and long-awaited day would never arrive. There seemed no real hope that I would live until September. I would first be bored sick by visits to Hillsborough Library and then killed off by recurrent visits to 'Worksop', with whom we had exchanged roles. Each week my mother carried large quantities of cooked food to them. And during the holidays I was required to accompany her. I sat on the horse-hair sofa and stared at the beehive clock listening to its intolerably lethargic tick and awaiting death by a thousand frustrations.

'Worksop' had amalgamated. The aunts had sold Newcastle Avenue and moved in with Uncle Ern at Overend Road. The trio remained the enemies of progress, rejecting food cooked by gas (as they would taste the poisonous fumes in whatever had been baked or boiled by the lethal energy) and refusing to install electricity. In the bedroom – where I was occasionally required to sleep – candles were the only illumination. On the ground floor the gas was at least used to give a flickering light. One concession had, however, been made to modernity. Just above the black-leaded stove that heated the room and water as well as the oven a brown box protruded from the wall. It was a 'radio rental' – a sort of loudspeaker connected to some mysterious distribution centre in downtown Worksop which retailed two BBC radio stations and the private enterprise broadcasts from Luxembourg.

One day, during the interminably uneventful summer of 1945, my father clicked the little knob in pursuit of one of his few obsessions – listening to the news. The announcer informed us in a matter of fact voice that the Americans had dropped a new sort of bomb on Japan. I do not know if he described its unique properties or if he estimated the number of dead and the scale of destruction that the single explosion caused. But something that he said moved my father to speak with a didactic authority which he rarely commanded or employed. 'They have' my father told us, 'spoilt the world'. And that being generally agreed, my mother packed up the pots and pans in which 'Worksop's' supplies of pies and puddings had made the bumpy journey from Sheffield and we all walked to the end of the road to catch the bus home. 'If Japan gives in', my mother said, 'Syd will be able to come home.' My father put down the copy of the *Star* which he was reading in order to ponder the idea without distraction, I noticed the back page headlines, 'Australians at Bramall Lane'. I had something to live for during the summer.

In fact Syd had set out for Europe and home before the war in the East had ended, and he finished his westward journey sometime between Hiroshima and the beginning of the autumn term. The news of his embarkation in Nairobi was kept secret from us. But somehow the message that he was on his way got through and we were sufficiently certain about the day of his arrival to iron the cheap print Red Ensign (which had lain for crumpled years on the bicycle-shed floor) and nail it to an old broom handle. Together with the Southern Cross emblazoned flag of Australia (which had been the standard of the now disbanded Boys' Own Army) it was hung out of the front bedroom window. A couple of friendly and patriotic neighbours followed suit. But his actual arrival naturally took us all by surprise. Those were the days before the likes of us owned telephones, and any power that we might have had to calculate the moment of his coming was destroyed by the agony of waiting. Even when we heard the bang on the back door, we did not recognise the knuckles as his.

The hero had lost his key somewhere in Africa. So he had to knock like the milkman. He had been baked to a deep shade of desert brown and he carried a sun-bleached kit-bag on the shoulder that had been rubbed raw by the sacks of sand which he had humped home from Wadsley Common to my play pit. His first words were incredulous gratitude. The conductress on the Bramall bus had noticed the ribbon of the Africa Star which was badly sewn to his tunic. Recognising him as a returning warrior, she had refused to accept his fare. He showed us the two pennies which she had told him to keep as if we needed proof of the extraordinary event.

The kit-bag was almost immediately tipped open on the living room floor in the space under the window which had once been occupied by my grandmother's bed. In between the spare uniform and the dirty laundry were the relics of four years' campaigning. A solid brass obelisk which I instantly recognised as Cleopatra's needle. A string of beads strung from shells collected on the shores of the Sea of Galilee. Three little pyramids which fitted into each other like the set of stacking tables that our modern neighbours bought for their lounges. A real Arab head-dress, which was my special gift. A camel train carved out of sandalwood. A New Testament bound inside cedar wood covers and, most wondrous of all, three hand-blocked ledgers which had once held Air Force inventories. They had become Syd's scrap books, the records of his journeys half way round the world.

These were the pictures of RAF football teams and airmen in fezzes posing on leave outside Cairo hotels. The snapshots of the Sphinx and the Nile cataracts (sold to a new sort of tourist by an ancient style hawker) were attached to the pages by home-made mountings which, on closer inspection, turned out to be corners cut from OHMS sticky labels. Coins from each of the countries that Syd had visited were held in rigid place by strands of thread which lashed them to the page with a taut St Andrew's cross. Cigarette packets, which at first glance looked like ordinary Woodbine wrappers, were discovered to bear Arabic inscriptions. Grass from the hill of Golgotha was pressed and gummed in place alongside a faded flower from the foothills of Kilimanjaro.

There was sand from Sinai in a little cellophane packet and a menu for Christmas dinner eaten under canvas. The second volume was dedicated to my grandmother's memory; for it was begun shortly after her death. But inside the cover of part one there was an inscription of a bolder sort. In Syd's careful upright hand four lines of verse had been painstakingly written.

> Ship me somewhere east of Suez
> where the best is like the worst
> where there ain't no Ten Commandments
> and a man can raise a thirst.

A careful note followed, 'we were' it explained 'just west of Suez in Egypt. But the rules about the Commandments and drinking were much the same.' For reasons which at the time I did not understand, my mother took great exception to the poetry. She turned from it to the photograph of WAAFs playing tennis and said, 'Here we are worrying about you and there you were learning all the answers.' Syd was too happy at being home to mind.

After a week of what was supposed to be rest and recreation, Syd set off to Padgate to be demobilised in proper style and to decide what to do with his free suit, his gratuity and the rest of his life. The suit was a double breasted grey chalk-stripe with shoulders of which Victor Mature would have been proud. It did not come into my possession for a further three years. But part of the gratuity was passed on to me at once. Syd bought me a bicycle. It was not the model which I wanted. My own choice would have been a lightweight racer with drop handlebars that almost touched the ground, a mauve enamelled frame and a high, hard saddle. I saw it in Redgate's window, but was warned at once against agitating for it. Instead my mother chose a 'touring model' with three speed, hub dynamo and a tin chain-guard that was clearly designed to protect curate's turn-ups from oil as they pedalled between one parishioner and another. I pretended to be pleased.

The feeling of guilt which Syd engendered in me was wholly sincere. Sometime during the war I had started to sleep in the large back bedroom which, in the early years of our Airedale Road occupancy, had been called 'Syd and George's'. Despite Syd's return, I remained in my new spacious surroundings whilst he squeezed into the box room at the front of the house. I am sure that I made some token offer of removal and redress. But there was never any chance of my mother agreeing to her son's demotion. How Syd hung his suits or where he kept his shirts is now a mystery to me – his storage arrangements having been blocked out of my mind by a combination of remorse and embarrassment. But in that cramped little room Syd slept for the next seven years, resitting examinations he had first taken twenty years before, entering Brincliffe College under the 'emergency teachers training scheme', and becoming an assistant master at a series of city primary schools. He lived with us as part of us and found most of his pleasures in our company. Indeed when he spent time 'away from home' he always found it necessary to explain and justify his desertion from the circle. He and I grew very close, but we were never boys together. His affection was partly the feeling uncles often have for nephews. But it was also, at least in part, the product of his abandoned calling. He felt a clear duty to improve me.

I suspect that he, like my mother and father, was against my going to camp with the scouts. But that summer Baden Powell's call was irresistible. The idea of sleeping under canvas was profoundly unattractive. So was the thought of digging my own lavatory in the Derbyshire countryside. But the leader of the 150th (Wadsley Church) Troop was Geoffrey Kirkby, a sixteen-year-old who was about to enter the sixth form of the City Grammar school, and an athlete who played both cricket and football for the school and was expected to enter Loughborough College of Physical Education the following autumn. Geoff Kirkby was the City Grammar School made flesh. If that squat hairy youth was going to scout camp, I was going to scout camp. And off I set on the tramcar that bore us on the first stage of all our journeys.

Harold Woolhouse – whose botanical inclinations made him a much more successful scout than me – was part of the camping party. A year senior to me, he should have been happily contemplating his second grammar school year. But the place his ability justified had been denied him by a combination of farce and fate. During the first morning of his scholarship examination a desk had, somehow, been dropped on one of his toes. So, instead of completing his paper, he had been sent off to the Royal Infirmary to have his fracture set. On the strength of the second morning's test, he was offered a place at Marcliffe Intermediate, one of the strange hybrid establishments that bridged the gap between grammar school success and secondary modern failure. Harold would have to wait in his demi-monde until his school certificate results demonstrated that he was destined for somewhere better. In the meantime, he found quiet consolation in nature. The scout camp (bringing him into close proximity with plants and shrubs) was a great consolation.

I tried to be equally enthusiastic and to live down the reputation which I feared had been created by my mother describing my asthmatic history to Geoff Kirkby and insisting that I be subject to no test of skill and courage or required to perform any initiation rite that might 'take my breath away'. On the first night under canvas, another scout troop was found camping in a nearby field and a game of 'flag raiding' was arranged. I volunteered to take part, not suspecting for a moment that I would tiptoe through the dark and snatch our opponent's pennant from its reef-knot-reinforced flagpole, but anxious to be so tired at the end of my first night away from home that I would sleep despite the hard ground and the proximity of twelve other pairs of feet all fighting for space at the centre of the bell tent. At first neither Kirkby or his second-in-command, 'Podge' Rogerson, wanted me to take part. But, impressed by my apparent enthusiasm, they eventually allowed me to join the select band. I raced through a number of recently mown fields with no idea of how I might steal the enemy's ensign or protect our own. Then the whistle blew to signal that hostilities were over and we came together in the quartermaster's tent and ate lumps of unbuttered bread and spoonsful of cold beans. It was one of the happiest moments of my life.

For the rest of the week it rained, and the warnings of Syd and my parents grew increasingly indisputable. One wet afternoon two City Grammar School girls came to visit Kirkby and Rogerson, and I was shocked to recognise them as erstwhile friends of soldiers in Wharncliffe Hospital. On official visiting day my mother and father brought my dart board in response to a sodden letter of request which they had received that morning. One boy immediately threw a dart in the sole of a helpful compatriot who was lying on his back holding a board between his feet. Blood trickled first on to his ground sheet and then onto the mud on which the ground sheet was floating. Mud was everywhere.

Unfortunately when my parents returned home, my father chose to describe the camp by an image from the wrong war. Flanders might have been an appropriate metaphor. Belsen certainly was not – at least as long as the beans and bacon held out. Somehow the slighting description got back to Kirkby and Rogerson, and naturally enough the sins of the father were paid for by the son. The requirements of my asthmatic condition were rigidly respected. Not once was I thrown in the stagnant duck pond – a constant experience for other junior scouts. But my protected status was openly, and contemptuously, discussed. The taste of the bread and beans vanished. I could not wait for Saturday and home.

The Saturday was, by chance, the first day of the three-day cricket match for which Sheffield had been waiting for six years. First-class cricket – or something very like it – had returned to Bramall Lane in the form of the English XI (captained by Walter Hammond) versus the Australian Combined Services (led by Linsday Hassett). I had started to agitate about getting a ticket as soon as the fixture was announced in May. By August my prayers and pleas must have become so intolerable that my week's absence with the scouts should have provided temporary respite from my two obsessions. It was, I insisted, a 'real' Test Match, whatever my father said to the contrary, and I demanded the right to see it. The first question which I asked my parents – as they walked into camp on visiting day – was whether or not they had got me a ticket. The moment I arrived home, the urgent request was renewed.

The idea of my going alone was ruled out immediately. My father could not take me on the following Monday, for he would be at work. Syd actually began, that very day, a temporary teaching job in the summer 'open air school' which Sheffield had founded in the Twenties to pump oxygen into the lungs of the tubercular poor. Only my mother was free to take me and she was deeply reluctant to spend time or (more important) money on a certain fiasco. I would, she had no doubt, be bored before the lunch interval. But by Sunday evening I had worn her down, and off we went the following morning and took our place in the queue for the cheapest tickets. Thanks to

A Yorkshire Boyhood

anxiety, I got stuck in the turnstile. But eventually the Hattersleys
and their lettuce and tomato sandwiches found their way onto the
concrete terraces of what became Spion Kop when Sheffield United
played football at Bramall Lane in the winter. There were still bomb
holes in the corrugated iron roof, and we spread our raincoats at a
spot which caught a shaft of jagged-edged sunlight. When I stood up
to applaud Keith Miller's century I cracked my head on one of the
steel barriers that had saved many a Saturday afternoon crowd from
plunging goalward to its own destruction. It was the only unhappy
moment of the day. Of course, my mother was right in her prediction
that I would 'whittle'. But my question was not, 'Can we go home?'. I
repeated again and again, 'Can we come back tomorrow?'.

Permission was sternly refused and I steeled myself to live out the
last few weeks before I ascended into the glory that was situated at
the corner of Orchard Street and the Education Offices. The location
was important. On the other side of the block was the 'Junior Tech'
from which I had escaped. Both schools had been created in the
1920s and housed in the rejected premises of the 'old central school'
which had been moved out (under the new name of High Storrs) into
a salubrious southern suburb. The City Grammar School, if it had
any antecedents at all, was the lineal descendant of the Pupil Teacher
Centre where once elementary school masters had served a sort of
apprenticeship. That quaint institution had occupied an adjacent
building facing onto Holly Street. And as the unfashionable and
insecure City Grammar School attempted to invent tradition, holly
became one of the symbols around which our myths were woven.

Not surprisingly, all the completed genealogy was unknown to my
father. One day, in the ever-faithful Hillsborough Library, he discovered a volume called *All Right on the Night*, the history of the
dramatic society in a school in Orchard Lane which had a holly leaf
as its emblem. Naturally enough, he believed it to be of an account of
the City Grammar's glorious ancestry, and it was brought home as a
contribution to my insipient *esprit de corps*. The title baffled me (the
inadequacy of my spelling, leading me to believe that it was concerned in some way with chivalry) but I felt suitably proud about
attending an institution that had its exploits immortalised between
hard covers. Indeed, when Geoff Kirkby (forgiven by my mother for
the mud, but not by me for the exposé of my 'weak chest') led me off
towards the tram stop I took the book with me. Perhaps my arrival
carrying a book about a different school should have been taken as

an omen or augury. But even if I had recognised the error, it would have done nothing to depress my spirits. I was determined to enjoy every minute of the next five — indeed, if I was lucky and clever, the next seven — years.

14
At the Deep End

—

All the new first years were required to report to the Chemistry Lecture Theatre, a steeply sloping auditorium which I quickly came to call 'CL' with all the familiarity of an established science student. I can remember only two of the sixty-one girls who took their nervous places on the same morning. One was Cath Carter, who became everybody's sister. And the other was called Linda Emett, who demonstrated style and flair initially by possessing a name which I associated with the history of Yorkshire cricket, and eventually by getting a job in the cosmetics department at Boots. The boys – known to the staff, and therefore to their classmates, by surnames alone – I remember more distinctly. They seemed to hunt in pairs. Lindley and Longley were two obvious rogues who invented romantic stories about themselves. One day they claimed joint ownership of a fish and chip shop. On the next they announced that they were bound apprentice to a merchant captain who would bear them off to sea before they could sit the school certificate examination. Bower and Bowler were large youths who expressed their affection for Sheffield United by tearing up my crude cartoons of Wednesday players. Newman and Betts were obvious athletes. And Cressy and Shepherd – red-faced but undernourished – proclaimed their poverty even to insensitive twelve-year-olds. Both wore the cheap blazers which were supplied to the sons of the unemployed, and both lacked the extra items of equipment which, though not compulsory, were essential to grammar school life.

As little boys are more interested in their elders than their contemporaries, I can still recall the names of the four teachers who stood before us that first morning. Mr Drake was so tall that he could sit on the edge of the science theatre work-bench, as if it were a shooting stick, and still seem to be standing up. Miss Tate and Miss Dixon were relics of an earlier age. Both wore skirts that swept the ground and both had their hair drawn up in tight buns. Miss Dixon represented the gentle school of old fashioned teaching; Miss Tate, the hard. Miss Forster was a large – indeed fat – lady, with white frizzy hair. In the years which followed, she often described herself to her pupils as 'a jolly sort of person', and I came to think of her walking, gloved but unloved through the fields. She lived with her sister. Her fiancé had been killed in the First World War. She had been trained at Homerton College which she claimed was part of Cambridge 'varsity'. She took command of our initiation. It was an wholly unjustified assumption of authority which was consistent with her character. The text of her speech of welcome was the slightly irrelevant 'history teaches us to be fair'. It was her homily for every occasion. During the next five years I heard it every week, during the forty minute ramble around Miss Forster's life and work which was described on the official timetable as 'religious instruction'.

Mr Drake was in charge of the real business. The first-year pupils of the City Grammar School had to be divided into forms. Numerically we amounted to four classes. But a simple quartering of the nervous multitude would have blurred differences which had to be emphasised. Half the new pupils were 'over-age' entrants who had been prevented from sitting the 'scholarship' at the proper time or had failed to be awarded a grammar school place by a marginal fraction of a mark. Several hundred 'over-age candidates' took or retook the examination each year, and sixty-four of them were lucky at their second attempt. There was no reason why 'over-age entrants' should not have been integrated with their junior contemporaries. But the elderly scholars were all sent to the City Grammar School, and even there they were confined within a distinct and discrete community.

Within the City Grammar they became Forms 1x and 1y. Choosing letters from the end of the alphabet (scholars of normal age became 1p and 1q) was a subtlety of which the school was very proud. Had classes been called 1a, 1b and 1c the secrets of selection and streaming might well have been revealed. But as 1945 was the age of 'parity of esteem', the idea of relative superiority had to be kept from us. In a limited way, the scheme worked. It took me forty-eight hours to discover that 1x was superior to 1y. On Wednesday morning Miss Tate revealed the classification to us. She was uncompromisingly explicit. Had we been up to true grammar school standard we would have passed the examination first time. But allocation to 1x suggested that we were slightly less unworthy of the education which we were about to receive than were the 1y intruders. I was not sure if I should feel moderately proud or deeply ashamed.

But that was only the beginning of the complicated division. Although the City Grammar was co-educational in formal constitution, great trouble was taken to ensure that the two sexes met as little as possible. We were taught in mixed classes, with boys on one side of the room and girls on the other. But the register was marked, milk money collected, dinners eaten and leisure time spent in rigid segregation. For administrative (as distinct from academic) purposes I was a member of 'Form 1xy (boys)'. But when I went to learn French with Miss Cole or English with Miss Dixon I became 1x and was joined in my studies by half of 'Form 1xy (girls)'. Mr Drake explained the facts of our complicated existence in a way which he hoped would minimise our bewilderment. I liked the elderly and avuncular Mr Drake from the first sound of his Yorkshire vowels, and I was delighted when he told us that he was the form master of 1xy (boys). But of course, the good news was qualified. He warned us 'not to get used to him'. For he was only the woodwork master 'for the duration'. Too old for military service, he had been drafted in from an elementary school to fill the place of the permanent incumbent, Mr Shields, who at the moment of my arrival was Captain Shields RA. The captain was on his way home from the war to reclaim his kingdom of mortice and tenon-joints, raffia-topped stools and gate-legged tables.

Mr Drake was not the only temporary member of staff. Games were technically under the control of a Mr Smith, who presided over our physical education while the established master was keeping the RAF fit in India. Mr Smith, it was whispered, had retired early from full-time teaching after a motor cycle crash. We all speculated about the physical shape in which the accident had left him, assuming that he never took off his double-breasted, belted, Crombie overcoat or lifted his trilby hat because their removal would have revealed some terrible deformity. We hoped that the Capstan Full Strength he always smoked eased his pain. I only ever saw him attired in what we charitably supposed to be medically prescribed clothes and puffing on the pain-killer of our imagination. Thus dressed, he sat in class rooms, stood in gymnasiums, loitered on the edges of swimming baths. But the hat and coat were not familiar sights on the football pitch, for Mr Smith never ventured on the football field at all. One afternoon each fortnight he accompanied us on the bus that travelled

to our storm-lashed playing fields. We pulled on whatever items of
football kit we possessed and kicked a ball about for almost a full
hour. Occasionally we would notice a trilby-surmounted head peer-
ing out from one of the condensation covered windows of the
changing hut.

The City Grammar – situated as its name suggests in the centre of
Sheffield – had few of the facilities that the suburban schools
enjoyed. The bus ride to our playing fields cut a valuable quarter of
an hour from the beginning and end of each games afternoon and,
since we had no gymnasium or swimming baths of our own, the time
spent on every sort of healthy activity was hedged about, restricted
and reduced by the need to travel to and fro from the premises we
borrowed and rented. We hired gymnasium time from the YM and
the YMCA, each of the sexes in every class marching off towards the
appropriate initials once every week. With the passing of the Butler
Education Act, and the incorporation of King Edward VII School
into the municipal system, the City Education Committee acquired
swimming baths of its very own. For King Edward's – having once
been that sort of school – had financed the building of baths by
parental donation. After a major argument which split the controll-
ing Labour Group on the Council and filled the local papers, it was
decided that less well-endowed grammar schools should be allowed
the occasional plunge in the once-exclusive water. On the first Friday
of my grammar school career it was Mr Smith's turn to teach the
crawl and the butterfly.

Of course I did not swim myself. At the time my health was in an
ambivalent state. I was said to be 'growing out' of asthma and the
susceptibility to colds had certainly decreased. But the hay-fever
continued. I ran, kicked, shoved and climbed with the same ferocity
as other little boys. But sometimes I suddenly lost my breath. With
such a complicated medical history to exploit, neither my mother nor
I could resist the temptation to manipulate life around my irregularly
delicate condition. Her prohibitions on cycling into the centre of the
city were reinforced with the prophecy that I would have a sudden
'wheezing fit' and fall under a tram-car. I, on the other hand, always
detected the onset of breathlessness when there were unattractive
duties to avoid. I was genuinely terrified that total immersion would
produce instant asphyxiation. And the idea of being submerged in
water fouled by sixty little boys was deeply repugnant to me. So I
predicted asthma. Syd and my father (both in their day enthusiastic

swimmers) expressed mild regret. But my mother produced the necessary note.

Godfrey Fenton, a King Edward's pupil who lived nearby, accompanied me to the baths, complaining all the way about my intrusion into the school's territory. We arrived at the time of his convenience and I stood about the school yard fascinated by a relic of the independent system beginning its day with the ringing of bells and a calling of rolls that might have been based on a Frank Richards Greyfriars story. The rest of the City Grammar party waited at a proper place outside the gate until Mr Smith appeared and announced that anyone who arrived later than him was late. By the time I reached the changing room everyone (except Mr Smith) was stark naked. As soon as I was in range he struck me a flat-handed blow across the back of my head. My mother's note – which I held silently in his direction – provoked two more attacks, once before it was read and once after. I was marked out, he assured me, for the ranks of 'the sick, lame and lazy'. Suitably chastened, I began to watch an extraordinary ritual.

Boys without trunks (Cressy and Shepherd, of course included) were the first to be punished. Second in line for discipline were boys with dirty feet. Third were boys who had arrived clean but had washed themselves inadequately during the pre-entry showering that the regulations required. Other culprits were denounced for other offences. And all the miscreants were forbidden to enter the pool. In fact, not a single boy took the plunge. I cowered, fully clothed, behind clouds of chlorine-impregnated steam and began to fear that (as my feet were clean, my bathing methodical and my trunks available as the rules required even for the sick, lame and lazy) I would have become a lonely swimmer, had it not been for my mother's note. All such speculation was driven from my mind by the awful sight of the punishment which every defaulter received. Each one was required to lie face down on the wooden bench which ran along the back of the changing room. Then Mr Smith – complete with hat, coat and Capstan Full Strength – leaned over each miscreant in turn and pressed his thumbs into the tender thigh muscles until his victim begged for mercy. When I described the scene to my mother that evening, she forbade me to invent such 'fairy stories'.

For the next month Mr Smith did not speak to me again. Each week I marched to the YMCA, put on my shorts and plimsolls, and failed to climb ropes or leapfrog over vaulting horses. But I did it all inconspicuously. Then I made a terrible mistake. One morning, after my weekly exertions were ended, I struggled back into shirt and blazer with such speed that I was the first boy ready for the return journey. So I led the crocodile that weaved its way back to school through a downpour of October rain, towards the Boys' Entrance, the stone vestibule and the ground floor corridors and classrooms which lay beyond that exclusively male entrance to our 'mixed' school. No doubt Mr Smith was particularly susceptible to the autumn cold. For as my mother could have told him, wearing his outdoor clothes in school meant that he 'would not feel the benefit when it was needed'. From the back of the crocodile he shouted 'Go straight in'. And straight in I went – through the Boys' entrance, through the vestibule, through the ground-floor corridor and into the form room of 1xy (boys) where Miss Tate was teaching a group of girls. The sheep of the first form followed.

Miss Tate was deeply affronted. Mr Smith made as gallant an apology as the retention of his trilby hat allowed and explained that the intrusion was entirely my fault. We shuffled out, shamefaced, into the vestibule where an enquiry was held. My answers to his questions concerning my wilful decision to disturb Miss Tate proved either evasive or unsatisfactory so, seizing an ear in each hand, he began to beat my head, rhythmically, against the stone wall. Later that night, I told my mother that I collapsed unconscious. That was untrue. Geoffrey Kirkby – who hung about PT classes in preparation for his entry into Loughborough – intervened long before my mind went blank in the way that I pretended. In fact, I continued the school day as if nothing had happened – other than my becoming a temporary hero. But when I described the incident to my mother later that day, asthma set in at once. My mother announced that she would visit the City Grammar School next day.

To this day I do not know the outcome of the interview which she had with the headmaster, the improbably named Mr Northeast. My suspicion is that she was told some pathetic story about Mr Smith's physical condition and reminded that he was soon to leave the City Grammar for ever. At any rate the spectacular denunciation of my brutal assailant, which I hoped would be performed in front of the whole school, never took place and Mr Smith's final days passed off uneventfully. After Christmas there were three new arrivals. Two of them had a considerable – and wholly beneficial – influence on my next five years.

The exception was, paradoxically, my new form master, Mr Shields. At first I was captivated by him. He still wore his captain's trenchcoat, and he maintained his military bearing even in the essentially un-military atmosphere of the woodwork room. He threw small pieces of wood at boys who talked in what they imagined to be the safety of distant work-benches, and when his missiles landed on target he proclaimed that he had not been a gunner for nothing. I prided myself that I was one of his favourites. Bower was elected form captain with Bowler as his deputy. They collected dinner and milk money respectively. But I was sent off each morning with a huge bunch of keys which I proudly used to open all the tool cupboards and the woodwork room.

One Monday duties were reallocated. I kept the keys, but new tasks had to be found for Bowler. Milk was henceforth to be free. How many boys, Mr Shields asked, would want milk that day? Twenty-two hands pointed to heaven. How many boys, he inquired of Bowler, had drunk milk the previous week? Twenty, said Bowler, looking pointedly at Shepherd and Cressy. 'Disgraceful', our form master said. Two of his boys were having milk simply because it was free. I hated Mr Shields for that. My anger was not the product of prodigious political commitment or incipient concern for the poor. It was the result of a special sort of class consciousness. I had a fellow feeling for Shepherd and Cressy. None of us ever had the equipment that we needed. They had never been bought set-squares and rough notebooks, mine were always lost, mislaid or left at home. We were the form borrowers and scroungers. If they were near to tears, I was near to tears. But fortunately in twelve-year-olds such emotions do not last for long.

Shepherd grew gradually to hate the City Grammar. For much of his first year he ran home in the middle of each morning, and throughout the five years which we spent in the same form his only consolation was the conviction that he would one day be a professional footballer. That ambition was gently discouraged by the second of the returning servicemen, Mr Walker – a real games master, as his white flannels and white polo-neck sweater proclaimed. Without the laundry facilities that were no doubt available to the RAF in India, Mr Walker's 'whites' only withstood a couple of weeks in the dusty YMCA gymnasium. But then he assumed a tracksuit, the first I had ever seen. And even on the freezing Gleadless playing fields (the highest land, he assured us, between Sheffield and the Urals) he wore the navy shorts and blazer of a football referee. Mr Walker attempted to teach us football skills and tactics. One snowy day, when even he dared not venture outside the changing room, he tested our knowledge of the way in which the game ought to be played. 'What' he asked 'is the answer to "first time passing"?' Without waiting to put up my hand or feel embarrassed, I called out 'close marking'. Instead of reproving me for my rashness, he said 'Quite right' and repeated my answer. Even now I feel a glow when I remember the incident. For the next few years one of the chief objects of my existence was to convince Mr Walker that although I was rotten at PT, I could bat and I could keep goal.

My other preoccupation actually concerned three of the subjects on my timetable – French, English and History. My attitude to French is easily described. I simply wanted to block its existence out of my mind. Perhaps the terror I had felt in the presence of Mme Wortilier and the traumas I had experienced during the endless detention of Hillsborough High School were still boring their way into my brain. But whatever the reason, I could not and would not learn the vocabulary, master the grammar or make even a possible imitation of the pronunciation. Miss Cole, who tried to teach me, was kind in a stern sort of way. But in French I was beyond instruction. History and English excited quite the opposite passion. I loved every minute of each lesson.

I loved history despite being taught by Miss Forster in the time she had left over from 'religious instruction'. And I loved English, initially under the guidance of the benign Miss Dixon, despite her quaint teaching methods and the absurd set books which were thought appropriate for twelve-year-olds. Miss Dixon was a great believer in standing-up-out-of-respect. When she arrived in the classroom, when she left and when another teacher came to call, she expected us all to leap to our feet and the boys to give a half salute. I put such aberrations down to her age, and I assumed her obligation to take us through *A Midsummer Night's Dream* was imposed from above. I thought then, as I think now, that Thesius, Titania and Oberon were extremely foolish people and that both Puck and Bottom were, in their different ways, extremely unamusing. But I read the parts which I was allocated in class as convincingly as I could as a concession to my less literate contemporaries. The only moment of near revolt came when I was required to comment on a slim volume called *Dotheboys Hall.* It was a simplified extract from

Nicholas Nickleby, a book which I had read, in its original entirety, a year earlier. I knew that I could not proclaim my superiority. But I seethed at the indignity which I was forced to accept.

Before the end of the year, Miss Dixon faded into the background of the timetable. For a third returning hero, Mr Etchells, entered our lives as a student fulfilling his 'teaching practice' before he became qualified to minister alone. Mr Etchells came from Easington, in what was to me a foreign country called County Durham. He was (though I did not hear of it until long after I left school) an ex-fighter pilot with a DFM and DFC who had almost finished his degree before the war. Like so many returning servicemen, he was being rushed through the final stages of his education as I was beginning mine. Mr Etchells shared my enthusiasm for the good things in life — football, cricket, the Labour Party and poems short enough to be read in the lavatory. He read *Manchester Guardian* cricket and football reports in class as if they were literature. And he laughed a lot — a quality which I had not previously associated with teachers.

Towards the end of the year there were hints and hopes that Mr Etchells might take the job that Miss Dixon's retirement would soon leave vacant. And during the last week of the summer term, the good news was confirmed. Indeed, Mr Etchells took a premature place in the staff team that played the school at cricket on the Wednesday afternoon before we broke up. Mr Drake returned to make a guest appearance and Mr Smith briefly left the sanatorium in which I supposed he lived to umpire, pulling on a white coat over his double-breasted and belted Crombie. On the morning of the match, Mr Shields told us to be sure not to walk behind the bowler's arm and predicted a victory for the staff. And so it turned out. Fate being what it is, I had the agony of seeing Walker, Etchells and Drake all getting out for next to nothing. Then Shields saved his side by knocking Geoff Kirkby all over the field.

The following day, my depression deepened. For the annual internal examination results were published. I came near the top in English and History and near the bottom in everything else. In French, I was last of all, scoring seventeen marks out of a hundred. From the whole first year, I was one hundred and twenty-fourth out of a hundred and thirty-two. One doom was already irrevocably sealed. I would take the five years to make my way to School Certificate; neither catching up the year I had lost at Hillsborough High School, nor making room for an extra 'scholarship year' in the sixth form. The report repeated time after time (and only partially correctly) that I 'could do better if tried harder'. Even my father was stern with me; threatening (for the first, though by no means the last, time) early removal and junior employment in the linoleum department of the Brightside and Carbrook Co-Operative Society. Why the linoleum department was chosen as the scene of my humiliation, I never quite understood. Nor could I fully understand my own inability even to attempt an explanation of what had gone wrong. The City Grammar School was a strange as well as wonderful world. I needed time to adjust from the sheltered world of 'Worksop', Grandma and Hillsborough High School. But I could not bring myself to admit it.

15

Inside the Stockade

—

My results must have been cruelly disappointing to parents who wished and worked for their son's success with unremitting determination. My enthusiasm for the City Grammar School had been at its greatest when the school was a distant prospect rather than a daily experience. But my mother and father were able to maintain their interest and commitment through all the vicissitudes of reality. Their relationship with the school had not begun well. At the meeting arranged for the parents of new entrants, a sample school uniform had been displayed. Unfortunately, at the end of the evening a tie was found to be missing from the exhibition, and the novitiates in the immediate vicinity of the display were asked to turn their pockets out. Undeterred, my mother and father put the humiliation behind them and turned out to every City Grammar School function at which visitors were welcomed or tolerated.

I accompanied my parents to the school dramatic society's production of *Arms and the Man* and pointed out, with immense pride, the pieces of cardboard Balkan castle wall which I had painted under the supervision of Mr Drake. We went together to the Sheffield Philharmonic Society's concert performance of *Merrie England*, an evening's entertainment largely chosen because the conductor was one E. L. Taylor, the music master at the City Grammar School. While an apprentice at the Teacher's Training Centre he had composed the music of a student song. Words had been added by one of his contemporaries, A. W. Goodfellow. By the time I arrived at the City Grammar, Mr Goodfellow had become a senior master, an immaculately gowned figure of awe-inspiring eminence. The names A. W. Goodfellow and E. L. Taylor were printed on the bottom of each of the song sheets that new pupils were given. Thanks to their talents as composer and librettist, they were the two teachers whose initials were known to me. Indeed, the idea that other members of the staff possessed Christian names never entered my mind. If someone had suggested such a possibility, I would have regarded the notion as no less fanciful than the proposition that they had homes and families and lived on after the bell rang at four o'clock.

The words of the Goodfellow—Taylor number were based on the assumption that everyone who sang it would go on to become a teacher. They also leant heavily on the names of roads in the vicinity of our building — Holly Street in particular. It began,

> The oak, the ash, the bonny ivy tree
> Are known in story famed in song,
> But we who know thee certain are,
> That search the woodlands near or far,
> We ne'er will find, though seek we long,
> A bush so well renowned in history
> As Centre's holly, evergreen.

It had a Latin verse which, to me at least, confirmed its class. I looked with contempt upon less elegant school songs — like that of Wath Grammar School, for instance, which set to the 'Dwarf's March' from Walt Disney's *Snow White* a remarkable verse beginning 'As we march, march, march through the valley of the Dearne'.

We sang *Semper Discamus* at every possible opportunity and at several which were, to say the least, improbable. We even sang it at the end of a wet sports day on the City of Sheffield Police Recreation Ground — an occasion which my mother attended even though I had not qualified for any of the finals. They took place during the last week of my first summer term and my mother and I walked home together and discussed the report card which I had to return (bearing the signature of parent or guardian) the following day. She blamed my disappointing performance entirely on the Wadsley Church Youth Club.

The Wadsley Church Youth Club met in what was left of a First World War army hut that had been erected in the yard of the church school. On Tuesday evening it provided table tennis and shuffling about to Glen Miller records. True to the rules of Christian charity on which it was organised, the club required its members to play table tennis with whoever was next in line for a bash at one of the over-worked balls. Waiting to take on swift-footed, sharp-eyed competitive friends was forbidden. I usually found myself drawn against youths in pebble glasses who held their bats as if they were fountain pens and giggled whenever my smash flew over their shoulders. And while I was waiting for what my opponents inevitably called ping-pong, the 'club leaders' (thought by my mother to be recruited for the specific purpose of keeping the sexes apart) always urged me to do the military two-step with some giggling girl in ankle socks and page-boy haircut.

On Sundays, however – when uplifting talks on social and spiritual matters were offered up after evensong – the youth club was mine to command. Only when the Reverend Alfred Jowett of the Marriage Guidance Council came to give us a talk on 'love and responsibility' was my dominance in doubt. On other Sundays, I either knew a little more than anyone else, or was prepared to risk the question which others feared would expose ignorance but I knew would demonstrate interest. After the visit of a curate from a neighbouring high church parish my supremacy was unchallengeable. He had chosen as his lecture subject 'Nicholas Breakespeare, the English Pope'. When the title was announced the previous week, I already knew that we were to learn about Hadrian VI. For I had a Vatican stamp in my collection with his picture – and both names – on it. My father told me that he had 'put the interdict on Rome' and explained the audacity of preventing mass being said in the Holy City. At the end of the talk, I repeated my father's comment word for word and became the undisputed champion of Sunday nights.

Fears that the youth club was leading me into a life of juvenile debauchery were wholly unfounded. But I did have an ulterior motive in joining and persisting in my membership on both Tuesdays and Sundays. Like so many of my ideas in those early years, it concerned cricket. I had known from the moment that the summer term began that I was going to have a most unsuccessful season at the City Grammar School. We had no 'Under Fourteen' team that played in competition with other schools. And Mr Walker – despite all his virtues – seemed to think of batting as a privilege to be earned rather than as a sacred duty to be performed with relentless regularity. Boys were only allowed to buckle on pads when they had qualified for the honour by passing a number of tests involving running and jumping – all of which were beyond me. So there I was, certainly the best batsman in the whole year, denied my destiny. I did not intend to waste the summer of the next year without competitive cricket. So I decided to become a person of authority in the youth club – no matter how many palais glides I was required to perform. My intention was to use the power thus acquired to organise a cricket team which would play in the Norton League (Under-Sixteen Division). What is more, I meant to be captain.

I was triumphantly successful in both endeavours. Indeed had not my father offered to become our regular umpire (to 'keep an eye on things', as I heard my mother say in the hall as she instructed him to volunteer) the Wadsley Church Youth Club CC might have launched my longed-for professional cricket career. My father was desperate for me to succeed as a boy cricketer. But he also regarded it as his duty to compensate for his natural bias in my favour by giving me out in response to every appeal. His attitude did more for his reputation as a man of honour than it did for me as a batsman. In the end my place in the side was only saved by an injury he sustained as the result of a wild attempt at a run-out hitting him on the foot. His ankle was too swollen to support him through two innings, so his place was taken by a Mr Stringfellow, the virtually blind father of our wicket-keeper. Mr Stringfellow was less inhibited in his attitude towards his son. And the only way in which he could be sure of never dismissing the object of his paternal loyalty was the cry 'not out' in response to an appeal against all the shadowy figures at the far end of the wicket.

But while I waited for the formation of the WCYCC as the vehicle of my ambition, I had to prepare to face my destiny. Walks of Wadsley Common with Harold Woolhouse helped to keep me fit. Harold caught lizards and took them home in his pocket and I threw stones at trees pretending that I was fielding at Bramall Lane and running out the enemies of Yorkshire. The walks always ended with a detour through the long grass that marked the boundary of the Hillsborough Golf Club, where we shuffled our feet in the hope of finding golf balls. We usually succeeded – often before they were lost.

Golf balls were not allowed in the Hattersley house, for they choked dogs to death. When the cover of a golf ball is nibbled away by innocent canine teeth a terrible web of lethal rubber is exposed. Many a much-loved mongrel had to be 'put out of its misery' because of its owner's irresponsible attachment to such loathsome objects. Golf balls also possessed a second undesirable characteristic. Dropped on or thrown at hard surfaces they bounced with unexpected velocity and could be relied on to break windows and black eyes. So when, on one lucky walk, I collected three in a single afternoon I was required to give them away at once. The recipients were Mr Brown and his son Cyril, who would use them in the proper place. I calculated that the gift was worth over five shillings.

On the evening of my enforced generosity I was playing cricket in the road on a pitch that ran from pavement to pavement with gateposts acting as wickets. Eric Gill floated me a full slow toss which I rashly drove in the air. The tennis ball hit – but did not break – the Browns' front bedroom window. It then fell into the maze of cement crazy paving with which that family had covered the front garden. By unlucky chance, it hit one of the sharp concrete edges which were constructed to counterfeit separate pieces of stone. From there, it ricocheted past the side of the house and into the mess of weeds that flourished by the side of their prefabricated garage. Such a crisis always required a strategic decision. One alternative was to creep stealthily up the drive and snatch back the missing ball. The other involved a polite knock on the door, a gracious apology and a courteous request. Harold Woolhouse – who said everything would be all right because Mr Brown and his father were both in the same Masons' lodge – volunteered to execute the second option. Sitting across the road on Barry Constable's wall (with Barry himself endlessly repeating that the rule was clear and a drive into Brown's was 'six and out') we watched Harold's tentative taps. The thunderclap of the door slamming in his face reached us before we realised that our request had been refused.

Naturally enough we were outraged. We held a council of war in our garden. Only that morning, I unnecessarily reminded Harold, I had given three golf balls to the offending family. He agreed, adding that he had always known that my generosity was misplaced. We concentrated so hard on our moralising that we did not notice Mrs Brown standing barely three feet away from us on the other side of the privet hedge which separated the two gardens. We only realised that she was within listening distance when she expressed her displeasure with one of the sharp intakes of breath in which middle-aged ladies used to specialise. To our relief, instead of the oxygen thus collected to denounce us, she hurried away into the house – 'retired hurt' as one of us called it.

But not for long. As soon as she had found the gifts of the morning, she returned to the garden and methodically threw them at me one by one. Fortunately, Mrs Brown was nothing of a fielder, and the missiles flew to uninhabited corners of the garden. But we were so shaken by the assault that despite our determination to keep the affray secret, my mother recognised the symptoms of barely suppressed hysteria. After a few pointless denials I told her the whole story. To my astonishment, I was treated more like a victim than a culprit. Next day, Mrs Brown was accosted as she was hanging the washing out to dry and given a full list of the injuries which her violence might have caused. Diplomatic relations were cut off and Syd, still waiting for the beginning of his teacher training course, offered to build a more substantial fence between the feuding families. Unfortunately the offer was accepted by my mother who was determined that when she walked out of her back door she would never again have to set eyes on her son's would-be assassin.

Syd was not one of nature's carpenters. But he was enthusiastic in his defence of family honour and he set out for a local wood-yard early the next morning. The passion for bargains was less pronounced in him than in his brother George. But the offer of a load of 'surplus timber' for a few shillings was irresistible. By early afternoon he was hammering together a stockade sturdy enough to repel the most determined Indian assault. In his eagerness, he had not realised that two of the pieces of his palisades had once been doors. And he did not notice that when they had swung on hinges, it had been thought expedient to stencil on them descriptions of what lay beyond their dark brown panels. Thanks to all this naivety, Mr Brown came home to find his wife lying in a darkened room awaiting a nervous breakdown. Leading him into the kitchen she pointed at what she could not bring herself to describe. Six feet away from her kitchen window was the fence which Syd had erected in a single afternoon. His posts and beams – none of which met each other at right-angles – were all exposed on the Browns' side of the construction, and on the flat boards which had been crudely nailed to the rickety framework two faded words remained distinct enough to read – 'Ladies' and 'Gents'.

The Browns believed the entire edifice to be a complicated and wholly calculated insult. Too proud to ask for Syd's unworldliness to be taken into consideration, we responded to the receipt of a dreaded 'solicitor's letter' with the confident assertion that the fence was not intrinsically objectionable and that all complaints against it were malicious. The next legal assault asked secondary questions about how the wood from which it was made had been obtained. So we decided to obtain legal advice of our own. It was absolutely unequivocal. The erection of any fence would have been a breach of the lease. The erection of a fence that leaned and swayed, bristled with bent and rusty nails and was decorated with words which were both indecent and indicative of the wood's dubious origins was an offence so grave that immediate demolition was essential. So we pulled it down. But we did not forgive the Browns for twenty years.

The Hattersleys were psychologically ill-equipped for street fighting. Rowing with the neighbours was not a respectable activity, and the class of person who admitted that they were 'not speaking' to the family next door was not the class of person to which we wanted to belong. Indeed I was constantly enjoined to model myself on acquaintances of superior habits and position – James Gill, headmaster, lay preacher and councillor; the Rhinds, both of them Scottish doctors and therefore doubly respectable. The idea of those paragons becoming embroiled in such a squalid altercation was inconceivable. I could not fully understand why being denied the right to discuss wash-day weather with Mrs Brown caused my mother so much distress, or my father's regret at being spared Mr Brown's silly Sunday morning banter. But although they both suffered in silence I, at least, noticed their suffering and hazily understood its cause. I suppose that I should have felt guilty. But I never did. Nor, as far as I could detect, did my parents expect it of me.

Because their complicated and complementary characters were so different, my parents did not respond to the semi-detached siege in the same way. My mother never condescended to avoid the Browns. If one of them was on the road, in the garden or actually standing on the drive which ran parallel to ours she swept past without a glance in their direction. My father, however, preferred complicated detours to the risks of face-to-face meeting. And if he heard talking in the neighbours' back yard, he would postpone his departure from the house until the Browns had gone. If my mother was ever tempted to behave with similar timidity she certainly suppressed the feeling. But, alien though it was to her own personality, she admired my father's reticence. Indeed – despite occasional moments of irritation when he failed to assert himself on her behalf – she actively encouraged the quieter side of his character. For she knew that it did not spring from any fear or feeling of inferiority. It was the result of the sublime contentment that had engulfed him since the moment of his marriage. All he really wanted to do was live in peace with my mother.

He hurried home from football matches distressed by two hours of unnecessary separation. When she was out of the house for longer than expected he always feared that 'something had happened'. He took her side in every dispute. He always deferred to her opinion. He invariably supported her judgement, and after its result was known always claimed that she was vindicated. If my mother was ever either embarrassed or irritated by her husband's undisguised idolatry she never showed it. Though it was a passion that brought its own problems. The burden of responsibility was never fully shared. And since all my father's enthusiasm was spent on hearth and home, he had no energy left over to drive him onward at work.

Of course he was a loyal and faithful provider – working whatever overtime was available and handing over his pay packet at the end of the week. But he only worked in order to support his wife, his son (who enjoyed the inestimable privilege of being his wife's son) and the household of which Enid was undisputed head. There was no independent ambition or compulsion to get on. Before the war, when he first became 'permanent' with the Council's 'Local Assistance Committee', he had taken the Relieving Officer's examination as a preliminary step to promotion. He always attributed his failure to inadequate work. Whilst his competitors spent their evenings in well-organised study, he was cutting the grass or giving my grandmother one of her constant 'lifts'.

But the abilities which took him into and out the other side of the English College in Rome should have seen him through the Relieving Officer's examination, however inadequate his preparation. The truth was that he had no interest in any success other than the constant achievement of being married to Enid. For him, life was a vast jigsaw puzzle, and his destiny was the provision of pieces which fitted whatever complicated shape my mother chose to lay on the table. He never wanted to engage in any activity which distracted him from his demanding life's work. Professional progress might have deflected attention from the principal object of his existence. So he hurried home each evening to triumph at what he most enjoyed – basking in the light of what had replaced his earlier notion of the Beatific Vision.

But pagan achievement was expected from me. Success was an obligation which my mother – and therefore my father – insisted that I accepted: a duty as certain and imperative as showing proper respect to 'Worksop', being kind to insects, having a hot meal before I left home in the morning and making regular visits to Hillsborough Public Library. I have no idea whether or not they expected, as well as hoped for, better results during my second year. No doubt realising that my performance could not be any worse, they gave thanks that the horrors of form one were behind us and rekindled hope of the history degree and the grammar school staff-room. Perhaps that is what my mother used to talk to my father about in bed at night. I could hear her voice through the wall. But as I could only catch the occasional word 'Roy', I was never sure whether it was praise or blame to which my father added an occasional grunt of sleepy agreement.

1. Enid Hattersley with her parents.

Enid Hattersley and her mother.

4. Great-uncle Ern, *c.* 1950.

3. Enid Hattersley at about the time of her marriage in 1928.

5. Great-aunt Lot, *c.* 1938.

6. Uncle George. 7. Uncle Syd.

8. Syd and George leaving for a bicycling holiday; the author on the bike.

9. The author and his father: Bridlington, 1936.

10. Family holiday: Bridlington, 1937.

11. Wadsley Church Scout troop.

12. Form 1 xy (boys), Sheffield City Grammar School, 1945. Mr Shields is in the centre of the front row.

Wadsley Church Scouts football team, 1948.

14. Lower VI (boys), Sheffield City Grammar School, 1951.
A. W. Goodfellow is third from the right in the front row.

15. Sheffield City Grammar School's First Eleven, 1951.
Mr Walker is on the left.

16

Winter Sports

—

The second year passed uneventfully. I abandoned woodwork and, since my lowly position in the end of term examinations disqualified me from a study of the classics, I had 'extra science' written into my timetable. For a week or two I was in thrall to the smells that came out of the fume cupboards, the liquids that bubbled in the test-tubes, and the variegated flames that spluttered from the bunsen burners. Indeed, I was as captivated by the equipment as I was by the so-called experiments and I saved up my pocket money to buy glass beakers and litmus paper of my own. But, like most infatuations, the passion was brief. One night, whilst boiling some noxious liquid, I knocked the flask from the kitchen table and smashed it on the floor. Although almost thirteen years old, I cried. I wept partly at the destruction of my prized possession and partly at the knowledge that science and I were about to go separate ways. I knew that next week I would want to spend my pocket money on something quite different.

I am not sure of either how much spending money I was given or how it was usually spent. Syd, I recall, added two shillings for whatever my parents provided. But I still received something below the local going rate. Two of my new school friends – Melbourne and Makin – were particularly affluent. Both had taken the 'eleven plus' at the normal age, but in the second year segregation according to age, like the pretence at parity, had been abandoned. Melbourne and Makin were, like me, in the bottom class, 2s, and like me they were considerable disappointments to their hopeful parents. They were well-groomed and well-dressed boys from Sheffield's southern suburbs who – also like me – still found pleasure in the company of their families. Though, in their cases, the fact that they went to the pictures each week with their relations was not thought of as justification for cutting down their personal incomes.

I went to the cinema almost every Saturday evening with my mother, my father and Syd. Often we booked for the front row of the balcony, the best seats in the house. My father was particularly

129

addicted to Movietone News – which he called in his old-fashioned way 'Current Events'. And the films which we enjoyed most of all were screen versions of the classics – Vivien Leigh as Anna Karenina, John Mills in *Great Expectations*, even Errol Flynn as Soames Forsyte. Each of those films gently weaned me onto the books from which they were adapted and mercifully truncated my period of enthusiasm for imperial literature. The John Buchan contagion began towards the end of the war. It started with *Prester John* and spread to the Richard Hannay Stories. Then it was Rudyard Kipling – not the poetry but the tales of the Raj. Nothing that happened in the fantasy world of Hentzau or Monte Cristo could hold my interest like stories of the veldt and of the Hindu Kush. Gainsborough Pictures and Ealing Studios came just in time. Had they not pointed me in the direction of *Vanity Fair* and *Wuthering Heights*, imperialist literature and socialist politics might have met in head-on collision. For I was beginning to grow up in the Labour Party.

The adult reading matter at Airedale Road was rather different from the books over which I was persuaded to pore. Every visit to the library involved me being elbowed in the direction of the classics. And there was always much appetite-whetting conversation about the passages which were thought most likely to attract and hold my attention – Thackeray's account of the battle of Waterloo, and the Brontë sisters' lyrical description of Yorkshire moors, which were expected to tally with the parts of Wadsley Common on which I ran, jumped and fell down. But my parents read biographies and the five hundred-page novels of the period – *The Crowthers of Bank Dam*, *London Belongs to Me*, *So Well Remembered* and *Fame is the Spur*. I read *Fame is the Spur* myself, and I recognised within it the real excitement of elective politics. My mother shook her head and said that the principal character (he could hardly be called the hero) was really Ramsay Macdonald, a thoroughly bad lot. And she quoted a couple of lines from Browning to reinforce her condemnation – 'Just for a handful of silver he left us/Just for a ribbon to pin on his coat'. Ramsay was the great traitor, the arch-villain, the lost leader. I must remain true to the theology of the Socialist Sunday School which met in the old cobbler's shop of the Brightside and Carbrook Co-op under the theological supervision of Alderman Bingham JP. 'When wilt though save the people: Oh God of mercy when?/The people Lord, the people: not crowns and thrones but men' we sang at the opening of every prayer meeting. But we ended with the last verse of the Red Flag: 'With heads uncovered swear we all to bear it unaware till we fall'. Ramsay broke faith with the vow. It was the ultimate heresy. Worse than being rude to 'Worksop', worse than kicking dogs, worse than writing in library books, worse even than wasting money.

Little poetic quotations – not all of them as relevant as the opening lines from 'The Lost Leader' – were one of my mother's self-indulgences. She was particularly strong on Browning, Tennyson and Keats. For my father's first present to her had been four little leather volumes – the three poets and Palgrave's *Golden Treasury*. Occasionally she invaded the wilder shores of verse, Edward Carpenter and Ella Wheeler Wilcox. But it all resulted in me being brought up within the sound of poetry.

I was also brought up within the sound of the Sheffield Wednesday football ground. In Wadsley Lane, the noise of every near miss had reverberated through the house. But at Airedale Road, only the exultation of actual goals ricocheted through the walls. By 1947, I was at the ground in person to witness the triumphs and tragedies. Judged big enough to stand the Spion Kop, I took my place with Syd and my father on the shale terraces at about two o'clock on alternate winter Saturday afternoons. When Wednesday played away from home we agonised between watching the reserve team and making the journey to Bramall Lane and Sheffield United. George – my father used to tell me in order to keep the memory green – was a Unitedite. And much as I disapproved of that affiliation, I used to scan the terraces in the hope of sighting the long-lost uncle. I suspect that Syd had secret meetings with his brother – secret even from my father. For my father's anxious loyalty would not allow him to parley with anyone who was in dispute with my mother. I have no doubt that he longed to see George. But he disapproved of – and suppressed – the longing, because he felt it was disloyal to his wife.

So the three of us stood on the Spion Kop together. At Bramall Lane we were protected from the rain by a corrugated iron roof, but for me at least there was not the warmth and shelter of being at home on the exposed slope of Sheffield Wednesday's uncovered terraces. I spent most of the afternoon staring anxiously at the 'results board' that had been erected in front of the pavilion. The halftime scores of all the major matches were hung from its iron frame, and the latest score in the game that Sheffield Wednesday was playing away to some far-flung and exotic opponent like Luton Town or Cardiff City was exhibited at fifteen-minute intervals. I was really at Sheffield United's ground to chart the quarter-hourly progress of Sheffield Wednesday, to cheer in company with other Wednesdayites when we were ahead, to groan in unison with my desolate co-religionists when we were behind, and to live in agonised anticipation of the revised score when a draw was displayed.

At Bramall Lane we existed vicariously. But at the Wednesday ground we lived life to the full, experiencing every emotion known to man, boy or beast. For me it was fantasy time. I really did expect the crackling tannoy system to splutter into life with an announcement that Goodfellow, Norton or Mackintosh (the delusion survived several generations of goalkeepers) were injured and a request for Roy Hattersley to make his way to the players' entrance complete with football boots and jersey. Even when the game started without me, I felt that I was down there on the pitch tackling the opposing forwards with Swift and Westlake, nodding crosses clear with Packard and Turton, and creating all manner of openings and opportunities with the hero of those early adolescent writers, Jackie Robinson. When Robinson swung at the ball the man in front of me felt the kick on the back of his legs.

Jackie Robinson was the last relic of Sheffield Wednesday's pre-war Cup-winning team. In fact, he had not played at Wembley. But Wednesday fans claimed for him the esoteric record of being 'the youngest man ever to play in a semi-final'. And starting from such juvenile distinction he had gone from personal strength to strength as the team he served declined into the second division. He played a couple of times for England and in the mid-Forties was north Sheffield's answer to Jimmy Hagan, the city's other international inside-forward who played in the south for United. Robinson was my winter hero. Even after he left Wednesday for Sunderland I looked anxiously at the *Green 'Un* each Saturday night in the hope that he had scored. But if Sunderland had ever played Wednesday there would have been no problem of divided allegiance. I always wanted Wednesday to win. Unfortunately, during the early years of my fervent enthusiasm, they rarely played such elevated opposition.

When Wednesday were in the second division the great clubs only came to Hillsborough for Cup ties. And then only for what, in those ancient days, was called the 'third round proper'. For that was the round when Wednesday entered the competition, and the round when they left it. But on the first Saturday after Christmas we were

Winter Sports

sometimes given a tantalising glimpse of greatness. In 1947 we were drawn against Arsenal – the team of the Comptons, Joe Mercer, Logie and Lishman – who had beaten Grimsby ten–nil at the end of the previous season. My father and I looked forward to the game for weeks.

In those pre-floodlight days, winter football matches began at two o'clock to make sure that they ended before the wintry sunlight faded into early evening darkness. If a fixture was postponed because of snow or ice, the game was played on some subsequent weekday working afternoon. The long-awaited Arsenal match – planned for the third Saturday in January 1947 – had been scheduled for the beginning of the worst winter of the century. At the time of the intended kick-off, the pitch was a foot deep in snow. Volunteers had dug away at the edges of the avalanche, but the following week rumour insisted that the amateur groundsmen had merely pressed the soft flakes into hard pack ice and prejudiced the real reclamation work that the groundsman began when the blizzard ended on Sunday morning. By mid-week, assiduous sweeping and shovelling had made the field fit for play, but the ground was still covered by a thin layer of compact snow and the pitch was marked on it with blue paint. There were great mounds of snow piled along the touch-lines, and the steps of uncleared terraces were obliterated under a sheet of ice which made the fans feel as secure in their foothold as if they were attempting to balance on a steeply sloping glacier. I can describe every detail because, despite the problems involved in a Wednesday afternoon game, I was there.

I cannot remember if I left for school that morning with the calculated intention of playing truant, or if I had a sudden fit of madness during the morning. But the evidence suggests premeditated irresponsibility, for I took with me when I left home in the morning, the hand-made rosette which I had secretly constructed from two lengths of blue and white plastic ribbon which I had bought from a Hillsborough haberdasher. I pinned it on my blazer as soon as I was out of sight of City Grammar and travelled by bus to Wisewood with an acquaintance whose mother was out at work and whose house was therefore available for a surreptitious sandwich and an under-cover cup of tea. Wisewood is at the summit of a higher hill than Wadsley. But both villages are the source of roads that run down into the Don Valley like tributary streams. On match days the Wednes-dayites flowed down those roads towards Hillsborough. On the day of the re-arranged Arsenal match my father and I met at the confluence of Fair Lane and Mardcliffe Road. I think that his embarrassment was far greater than mine.

To this day I cannot be absolutely certain that my father was also a truant. It seemed inconceivable then, and it seems inconceivable still, that he had filled in an official leave form and agreed to an official half-day's holiday being recorded against his name. But since he was proceeding to the match from the direction of Airedale Road it seemed as if my mother knew of his afternoon's intention. Indeed, I could not have imagined him taking time off work without using some of it to bask in the pleasure of her company. It was clearly my mother's tacit approval of his brief and unusual irresponsibility that confused my father about our relative culpability. Neither of us should have been at the match. But I had committed the added sin of being absent from school without my mother's knowledge. We walked together to the ground in mutual guilt and common confusion. 'You must', he said, 'tell your mother'; desperate lest it became his duty to turn Enid's Evidence. After Arsenal had won their anticipated victory and I had walked back up the hill to home, I made my confession. The recriminations were as predictable as Wednesday's defeat. At school the next day, the headmaster spoke to me for the first time. It was obvious, he said, that I had been to the football match. Did my parents know that I had taken the afternoon off school? With absolute conviction I answered 'Yes'. For the next three years I was branded a bad lot, with character deficiencies compounded by uncaring parents.

For most of my boyhood, the snow seemed to remain in greying piles until half-way through March. The crocuses in the herbaceous borders were already in bloom when, one year, my mother forgot the chip pan bubbling on the kitchen gas-ring and the whole mass of boiling fat caught fire. Without thinking for long enough to be afraid she grasped the handle and (with the flames a foot in front of her hands) marched through the open back door into the yard where she tipped the whole conflagration onto a heap of snow.

Vivid though that memory remains, it is not what first comes to mind when I think of those Yorkshire winters. It is 'bedtime' that I recall most clearly; the half-hour between bread and dripping and falling to sleep, the time when I took off my clothes in the unheated bedroom and the moments in the bone-chilling bed before I grew warm enough to fall asleep. Over the years I developed a sophisti-

cated technique for undressing at such a speed that no part of my
body was exposed to the sub-zero air for more than a few seconds.
Walking barefoot across the freezing linoleum was to court frost-
bite. Indeed, I often leapt into bed with socks still protecting my
atrophying feet. Once under the covers, I curled up into a shivering
ball until the heat from my body bounced back from the layers of
insulation which I pulled over me. Only good luck can have saved
generations of south Yorkshire children from being crushed to death
during those post-war winters, for we passed our nights under the
immense weight of sheet, thread-bare blankets, home-made eider-
down and coats carried up from the wardrobe at the bottom of the
stairs to add the final strata of warmth and comfort. Reading in bed
was impossible. Exposed hands would have been too numb to hold a
book.

Despite all these privations, I loved the winter. Each January
morning I peered out of my bedroom window, through the thin film
of ice which had been formed from condensation on the inside of the
pane, in the hope that the snow had come and that it was 'lying'. For
firm snow in Wadsley meant sledging – tearing downhill on home-
made toboggans as we used the public highways as our Cresta Run.
In the Forties, there were few motor-cars in Wadsley. And the few
that there were – belonging to local doctors, farmers, part-time
milkmen and half-a-dozen inspiringly senior works managers – were
off the road by dusk on a foggy night. So we assembled after school
encased in home knitted balaclava helmets, gumboots and old socks,
worn on our hands so that the one pair of gloves which we each
possessed would be kept in Sunday School or Bible-class condition.
Thus armoured, we raced our sledges down the incline as far as their
iron runners would carry them. Sometimes we sat upright with our
legs stuck out each side so that heels deftly ground into the snow
could be used as brakes or rudders. The bolder spirits lay face
downwards, pointing the crown of their exposed heads down the hill
and seeing nothing except the dirty ice racing away beneath them. As
I recall, nobody was killed.

I had learned my sledging during the war on the twenty-foot gently
sloping drive at Airedale Road. Mr Wheatley had sold us a patent
sledge with high curved steel blades and a fancy seat made from red
and yellow lathes. When other drives had been shovelled clear of
snow, ours had been beaten flat and hard with the back of our garden
spade and I had then made brief and sedate descents from kitchen

door to front gate. Inevitably the Wheatley Special had disintegrated during its first winter. But my father unscrewed the runners from the shattered fusilage and fitted them to a cruder but tougher contraption made from some of the planks left over from Syd's many attempts at a new fence. I suppose I raced that sledge down Vainor Road for three or four winters – at first sitting up straight and nervous with my heels slowing me down for most of the journey, then turning over on my stomach and skimming the slippery slope to the very bottom of the road, there to end my journey with a spectacular roll from the still flying sledge. During my last season of winter sports, I developed a habit of always carrying out the final feat of daring in front of a group of girls. My mother's worst fears about the youth club were coming true.

17
End of Innocence

The end of innocence came, as my mother had always feared and long expected, in the Garden of Eden which assembled every Sunday and Tuesday under the roof of an old army hut in the yard of an almost-abandoned primary school. The Wadsley Church Youth Club was the natural – indeed, the inevitable – place in which to experience the social agonies of adolescence. It was the magnet to which my complex-ridden and acne-conscious contemporaries were all drawn. Even without the cricket which I had grafted onto its constitution, the club, with its record-player and mixed company, would eventually have emitted a tribal call that could neither be ignored nor denied. In fact it was no more than chance that my enthusiasm for the club coincided with the Hattersleys' brief period of Anglican enthusiasm.

The Reformation arrived at Number 101 Airedale Road almost exactly four hundred years late. I do not know whether it came because my father felt a sudden need for some sort of spiritual outlet or if, no longer confined to the house by the needs of Mrs Brackenbury, my mother thought of the church as the obvious place to begin a long-retarded social life. Certainly she never believed in any of the theology. Indeed, we rarely went to church without her telling the story of the atheist funeral she had attended in Shirebrook. As she repeated her account of one Owen Ford arriving on his bicycle to read a passage from Karl Marx over the communist grave, I always felt that I detected a yearning for the days of dialectic certainty and simple faith.

But, notwithstanding the agnostic nostalgia, both my mother and father became temporarily enmeshed in the church's life and work. They became candidates for the parochial council, and my father's election the only example I can recall of his worldly triumph being greater than hers. They attended the 'adult club', and stayed out until half-past ten on Thursday nights. The vicar, Canon George Cherry Weaver M.A. (Oxon) rarely left the vicarage, but his curates – Mr

Gough and subsequently Mr Fox and Mr Hunt – were regular visitors. I was dragged into the religious, as well as the social, life of the parish.

I joined the 'Bible class', a sort of postgraduate Sunday School for those who had passed through confirmation. Canon Weaver took the confirmation class and half-a-dozen initiates sat in his study each Wednesday evening and heard arcane explanations of obscure passages from the Old Testament. Canon Weaver was – or had been – a Hebrew scholar. The actual confirmation was performed by a suffragan bishop, which I regarded as something of an indignity. I retaliated by giggling when Jack Pinder (an associate from scout and youth club) was bidden to reaffirm his faith in the name of John.

A whole new cast of parochial characters came into our lives. There was Mr Nicholson, an immaculately-dressed church warden who was also an incorrigible conjuror ('every magician needs a little mystic and here's m'stick') and his son, the organist/choirmaster. Despite the urgings of Dick Martin (who performed the seminal duty of explaining to me the facts of life), I never joined the choir. Any doubts which I might have had about my decision to remain in the body of the church were dispelled one day at a Sheffield Wednesday football match when the tannoy system broadcast a message for our musician: would he return home at once, as his wife needed him. I could not have borne to be conducted by anyone who had been so publicly humiliated.

The lay Christians I recall most clearly are those who took temporary, and usually disastrous, command of the youth club. Mr Haigh, an architect, contracted polio. When he recovered from the first crisis, he persuaded me to enter for an amateur house-design competition. Although he coached me from his wheelchair to the point of actually drawing the lines himself, I lost. Mr Burton (father of Geoffrey, who was my fellow opening batsman in the cricket team and therefore my major rival) accused me of spoiling one of his Christmasses. When the youth club carol singers were invited into his living room for tea and mince-pies, I hid the fire-tongs under my coat and bore them off. Later that evening I returned with them wrapped in festive paper. Mr Burton promised 'not to open the present from the youth club until Christmas morning'. He must have risen early on the joyous morn, for he was indignantly knocking on our front door before the chicken was in the oven. I still believe that the verb 'to steal' was a wholly inappropriate description of what happened.

The club leader who stayed the longest remains the clearest in my memory. Peggy Stringfield, the most durable of all my mentors, had dropped in and out of my life since I had attended the infants' Sunday School before the war. A large, bony lady with sensible hair and firm stride, she later became leader *pro tem* of the Wadsley Wolf Cubs. Although only of Bagheera status, she assumed command while Akela (Miss Weaver from the vicarage) saw service with the W.R.N.S. After the war, when the Canon's daughter returned, Peggy Stringfield enrolled at Brincliffe Emergency Teachers Training College, where she and my Uncle Syd became friends. The nature of their friendship was never certain, though it was claimed by one of my associates that they had been seen walking to Worrall hand-in-hand. I told my mother of the story, and she used the secret intelligence against Syd in retaliation when he, one day, complained about dinner being late.

Mr Hunt (about whom I used to spread rumours concerning Miss Stringfield to protect Syd's reputation) was the unlikely star of one of the youth club's fringe activities – school-yard football. At least in appearance, he did not come within the category of Sporting Parson. He was pale and thin, and he wore delicate spectacles on the bridge of his extended but elegant nose. He played the violin, wanted to form a church orchestra and pronounced 'God' as if the Almighty spelt his name G-A-W-D. He was also the most ferocious participant in the mob violence which we perpetrated in the school-yard by chasing a balding tennis ball and called football.

The game we played must have been very like the activity which Henry VIII forbade because it was becoming more popular than archery and endangering the lives and limbs of his young nobles. Often so many players took part that it was impossible to take a kick at the ball without inadvertently injuring half-a-dozen other eager participants. The ruthlessly committed players did almost as much physical harm to friend as to foe, and the *aficionados* always played in gloves, to protect the palms and knuckles against the abrasions and bruises which came from the tarmac onto which they were constantly thrown, pushed, tripped, pitched and flung. Fortunately I had progressed into long trousers a year before my first game of school-yard football, having been taken by my mother (and accompanied by my father, who she insisted was an essential participant in the historic event) to Parkins Outfitters in Hillsborough and bought a dark grey herringbone. By the time I was first hacked to the ground, half the epoch-making new suit had deteriorated into school trousers. So my knees were protected by cloth that I could damage without risk of retribution. They were most in need of protection when Mr Hunt bore down upon me. Once he had removed his coat, folded it with the spectacles safe inside its innermost recesses and placed the bundle like a clerical grey nest in the lower branches of a churchyard tree, he charged about – stock flying out of his waistcoat – as if he was trying to despatch us all to heaven.

The school-yard in which this always violent (but never vicious) activity took place began to play an increasingly important part in my life as I moved into the social exhibitionist phase of adolescence. When girls were hanging about the yard's perimeter, we played our football with an unusually flamboyant violence. And when girls were within range of ear or eye we behaved in a similarly foolish way within the school-yard hut in which the youth club met. We played table tennis with an extra forehand flourish, replied to the anxious questions of our adult guardians with extra impertinence and refused to perform the military two-step with extra vehemence. The refusal to learn to dance was an extremely important symbol of our masculinity. Females had to be treated with open contempt. If every form of life began at puberty with the sexual aggression we displayed, young birds would be pecked unconscious and adolescent bees would be stung almost beyond recovery.

When we matured into actually speaking to girls we rarely made the gracious gesture in the formality of the club itself. Inside the old army hut, the battle of the sexes took the form of bitter arguments about the gramophone. They wanted foxtrots and waltzes as accompaniment to the complicated steps that they taught each other, often with the aid of Victor Sylvester diagrams from the *Radio Times* which plotted feet positions like the Zulu tracks illustrated in the Boy Scout manuals. We wanted nonsense music, played as loud as Miss Stringfield or Mr Hunt would allow. Some of the records were not intended to be 'novelties'. I now realise that Ted Heath's 'Opus One' was a serious contribution to big band jazz. But at the time, I put it in the same category as Doctor Crack and his Crack Pots, the drunken version of 'Cocktails for Two' and 'Tuli-Tuli-Tuli-Tuli-Tulip Time'. Not for me Doris Day and 'You Go to my Head' or Frank Sinatra's 'I Fall in Love Too Easily'. The nearest I would go to romance was Harry James and 'Carnival in Venice'.

The real point of sexual contact was the wall which divided the school yard from Worrall Road. It was where we rested after an hour or two of shoving and hacking in pursuit of the balding tennis ball, and the refuge that we found after a piece of particularly gross impertinence had resulted in our expulsion from the old army hut. We lolled against its low stone parapet under the shade or shelter of massive horse-chestnut trees which had taken root in the churchyard over a century before but which, by the time I stood under their branches, had spread their shadow far beyond consecrated ground. The wall was the first community of equals into which I was admitted. But the society held a ruthlessly competitive view of equality. Everyone was allowed to compete for attention, esteem, influence and domination. The clever and strong were respected and revered. The weak and stupid were constantly humiliated. Anyone suspected of cowardice was mercilessly persecuted. I was usually on the losing side.

I had no stomach for – and could see little sense in – the constant tests of courage and physical strength in which most of the youths engaged, swaying about enmeshed in head-grips and stumbling to the ground in arm-locks and half-nelsons. And although I often invented brilliant lines of repartee, I could never speak the words; I was too afraid that, once outside my head, the joke would fall flat. I was also obsessively conscious of the whole range of physical deformities which I imagined impaired my speech as well as rendering my appearance ridiculous.

The deformities were all nasal and aural. Whilst other adolescents were worrying about the size of their ears and the unnatural shape of their Adam's apples, I worked myself into a neurotic frenzy about my larynx and my epiglottis. Some of the paranoia was, I suppose, connected with the sleepless asthmatic nights of my recent childhood. But one part of the complex – like the most debilitating ingredients of every trauma – grew out of a grain of truth. Once, during a school dental inspection, I was distracted from my usual terror of extraction and filling by a comment concerning the roof of my mouth. According to the dentist, it had an 'unusually high roof'. Instead of rejoicing in the possession of a Gothic orifice, I assumed that I was afflicted by a terrible deformity. I began to hear words rumbling around my cavernous interior like the echo of thunder in a mountain cave. Combined with my real or imagined difficulty in breathing through my nose (which forced me to keep my mouth open like a self-conscious village idiot) the palate, which I imagined was

141

about to become cleft, kept me in a state of constant embarrassment. I shielded myself from the cruel world by holding my hand in front of my face. Thus inhibited, I observed but rarely took part in the social intercourse of the school-yard wall.

The stars of our social circle were Jack Camplin and Alex Siddall, two older youths approaching their late teens who – although united in their affection for football and dirty songs – were destined to go different ways. Siddall (who was in the lower sixth form at King Edward's) was bound for Oxford. Camplin was already at work, harbouring a soon-to-be-fulfilled ambition to join the Merchant Navy. Both called me 'Pudding'; Siddall with a patronising affection, and Camplin with a contempt that bordered on hatred.

Usually the hatred was silently reciprocated. But once Camplin's behaviour inspired both awe and admiration. On the day of the first broadcast of *Dick Barton – Special Agent*, he ascended Worrall Road (with Siddall, like Snowy, at his side) in hot pursuit of a haulier who propelled his overloaded cart up the steep hill by the simple expedient of beating his bony horse with a huge whip. Camplin seized the scourge and broke it, dramatically, across his knee. To me, in my grandstand seat on the wall, it was like *Tom Brown's Schooldays* coming to life – an extraordinary confluence of the animal fetish with which I had been reared and the new vulgar recklessness to which I vaguely (though hopelessly) aspired. Even Camplin turned from Flashman into Dr Arnold. I longed to stand beside him, comforting the horse if not chastising its tormentor. But when we were playing neither football nor cricket my role was to sit and stare.

My life was, in a strange way, a vindication of the playing-fields-of-Eton view of life. I don't claim for a moment that games made a man of me. But, when I was wearing the heavy boots which were fashionable for football in those days, the huge rug-wool hand-knitted sweater which was never fashionable for cricket at any time, or the old kid gloves which I kept for my bruising encounters with Mr Hunt in the school yard, I at least counterfeited the manly virtues. I bumped and bored when I was on the blind side of the referee, appealed for catches which I had not taken cleanly and rejoiced as my school-yard opponents crashed to the ground.

In early adolescence, manliness is easily confused with uncouth brutality, and most of the males in the school-yard wall gang sought to demonstrate their manhood by exhibitions of spectacularly boorish behaviour. We were all particularly unpleasant to a girl called Doreen Glossop for the simple, if perverse, reason that we especially liked her. And we made spectacular trouble Tuesday after Tuesday in the youth club – at least until the arrival of the new vicar, the Reverend Reginald David Morgan Hughes.

Initially Mr Hughes and I got on. For some reason, I visited the vicarage early in his incumbency and noticed an elderly cricket bat in his umbrella stand. Not only did he confess to being a cricketer; he agreed to turn out for the Parents XI in their historic match against the youth club – a Wadsley tradition which I had invented the previous year. He was also complimentary about my tie – a bright yellow creation which my mother had tried to take back to Parkin's shop. Mr Hughes said I should be in Chelsea, an allusion, he explained, to the frequency of Bohemian artists in that London borough, rather than the home for army pensioners, which was located in the same area. I had been in trouble about my liking for yellow when his predecessor enjoyed the benefice. Mr Hughes's higher level of aesthetic appreciation, combined with his enthusiasm for cricket, marked him out as a good man.

The earlier trouble had occurred when the Wadsley scouts were given a room inside the almost derelict school building, provided that the good-deed-a-day brigade carried out the long-overdue cleaning and painting. We scrubbed floorboards encrusted with inch-thick grime and rubbed the walls with a damp cloth until the dirt of ages ran down the filthy paper in grey streaks, rather than covering it in a uniform film of black mire. Then Harold Woolhouse and I were persuaded to paint the woodwork with the promise that we could decorate it in the colour of our choice. We chose primrose. When our artistic excess was discovered, the scout troop's tenancy of the room was cancelled. But for years a single yellow window-frame smiled down on the school yard from the grey stone of the old school building. Harold Woolhouse and I thought of it as a sort of memorial.

Mr Hughes, I was initially convinced, was exactly the sort of man who would have congratulated rather than castigated me for my avant-garde selection of colours. And my faith in his libertarianism was slightly, if sentimentally, confirmed by the discovery that he rode a motor bicycle and kept pigs. I once saw him scratching the pigs' backs with a piece of wood, an indication of affection which I took at face value until the morning we heard their death-squeals as the man from the abattoir performed his lethal duties. The doubts which I began to have about Mr Hughes early that day were reinforced by his first involvement in the youth club. My fears were confirmed by his later behaviour.

The youth club was inadequately heated by the same cast-iron coke stove which had failed to warm its military occupants during the winters of the First World War. It stood, occasionally red-hot and always irrelevant, in the middle of the room. We charged it with old wood scavenged from the deserted school and neglected country churchyard, rather than with expensive coke which had to be bought from the Brightside and Carbrooke Co-operative Society. One day, Harold Woolhouse and I were instructed to feed it with a couple of old table-legs. As the legs were longer than the cast cylinder itself, they had either to be broken into pieces or left protruding from the open top of the stove. As the open stove belched noxious fumes into the youth club, we determined to break up the mock-Jacobean fuel. Pushing half a leg inside the stove, and levering wood against cast-iron would have been an admirable expedient if the wood had given way before the cast-iron. When quite the opposite happened, a sequence of events began with burning coke spreading across the youth club floor. It ended with the Fire Brigade flooding the entire hut. We believed that Mr Hughes was wrong to describe our behaviour as 'wanton vandalism and destruction'. And closing the club for a month was unforgivable.

At least there was still the scout troop in which to find refuge. It was my last year of smiling and whistling under all difficulties, but a new organisation – the Senior Scouts – added a little adult entertainment to the knot-tying and first aid. A camp-fire concert was arranged on Wadsley Common to celebrate the holiday return of Geoff Kirkby from Loughborough College. Geoff was in great form and led us in endless campfire songs. By the time out titular Group Leader – the Reverend Hughes – arrived, we were half way into an interminable number in which every verse began, 'If I were not a Boy Scout . . .' and continued with speculation about the appropriate jobs for local notables. Kirkby, to whom Mr Hughes was an unknown if respected figure, asked advice about how he should celebrate the great man's arrival. 'If I were not a Boy Scout, a Vicar I would be' was an easy enough beginning. I suggested he ended the verse with 'keeping prize pigs, closing youth clubs every happy day'. Geoff performed beautifully. The scouts were closed for a month.

Of course both the social institutions in my life rose from the dead. The youth club was suitably chastened, and spent more of its time on discussions. It was during such a cerebral evening that Jack Camplin persisted in pushing his knees into the small of my back, thus testing my courage in front of a girl called Joy Lax whom I had begun to walk home to Macliffe Road after the club was over. I hit him with a chair. Mr Hunt, showing his yard football bravado, stopped Camplin from killing me and ushered me home.

The club's Corinthian solution was that Camplin and I should settle our differences in a boxing match, and for some bizarre reason Mr Hughes was consulted. The vicar said it was an unequal match as four years divided us. Camplin argued that 'on the scales' I would qualify for a more senior division than the one in which he boxed at the Hillsborough Boys' Club. Our spiritual adviser did not enjoy his judgment being questioned. If he heard that we had boxed (and he certainly would hear if we did) he would give a good hiding to whoever was the winner, a comment he accompanied with a hard look at Jack Camplin. He closed the youth club for a month. Next day he came around to Airedale Road to offer me a lift to Bradford on the back of his motorbike; England were playing the Rest at Park Avenue and he had two tickets. I was too ashamed at being rescued to accept.

18
Could Do Better

Gradually the centre of my social life moved away from Wadsley Church, its youth club and its school-yard wall. For several summers I still played cricket with the old cronies. But we changed our name to Wadsley Church Youth, believing that by removing the 'club' we became the nursery for Wadsley Church CC, a wholly secular institution which occasionally called upon our better players to make up the numbers of the second team. I still saw Harold Woolhouse at weekends. But each of us was becoming more and more absorbed in the school which provided more and more pleasure as well as demanding more and more time. When we met, we swapped school stories; not tales of heroes on football or cricket fields, but accounts of his latest dissection and my most recent essay on the Corn Laws. But, at best, my feelings towards the City Grammar were an emotional confusion. I was often bored, occasionally elated and sometimes frightened. I was afraid of failing in the subjects at which I usually performed well, and of being humiliated in those at which I normally did badly. Life was hard for a naturally competitive boy, living in a highly competitive society and constantly losing the competition. At the end of my second year an incident involving my annual report card reinforced the ambivalence of my attitude.

My first year examination results had been a disaster. I was almost bottom of my class, and no better placed in the merit list made up of all one hundred and sixty new pupils. But at the end of my second summer the placings on the report card were quite different. I was second in Form 2s, and third or fourth out of the sixty-odd pupils who had been consigned to the long five-year route to School Certificate. Of course, I was no longer competing against the cream. The most talented of my contemporaries were on the four-year course. But there were real signs of a genuine improvement in effort and attitude. The threat of academic exile in the linoleum department of the Co-op had proved a deterrent to sloth, and I was beginning to adjust to the once-unaccustomed life in a bustling city centre school. I began to feel occasionally relaxed, if not yet quite at home. It was, I suspect, a combination of the new confidence and old hysteria which caused me to make a fuss about the second year examination results.

It seemed to me that, together with whoever had come top, I should be promoted from the five- to the four-year course. I put the idea to Miss Laycock, my form mistress – a bony spinster with a bun and a weakness for dictating in such detail that she specified the sort of underlining which should emphasise her headings, sub-headings and inset titles. She explained that the enviable members of 2a and 2b had completed a full year of Latin and 'special science', and that there would be no hope of my catching them up even if I had the innate ability to absorb those taxing subjects. I accepted her judgment without argument. I had no wish to spend another year in hopeless pursuit of fellow pupils who enjoyed a year's advantage. I consoled myself with the thought that I would find much pleasure in taking home my obviously complimentary report card.

When it was handed to me at the end of term, I ignored the instruction that the package must be delivered intact to parent or guardian and tore the envelope open – anticipating the joy with which it would be handed over. The columns of 'Results Obtained' and 'Position in Form' were exactly as I expected. With the exception of French, which I quickly passed over, the percentage was always over seventy and the place was always first, second or third. But the comments alongside the figures bore no relationship to my achievements. They were just the same as the year before when I had been near to the bottom of almost anything. The judgments lacked originality as well as relevance – 'could do better if tried' . . . 'must work harder' . . . 'greater effort needed'. Ignoring the consequences of admitting that I had opened the envelope, I rushed towards the Ladies' Staff Room and Miss Laycock. The bell for the end of mid-morning break rang as I was halfway down the upper corridor and Miss Laycock conveniently emerged just as my courage began to run out. I suspect that, had the door not opened with Feydeau farce timing, my nerve would have failed and I would have slunk off back to my form-room, silently to reflect on the injustices of the world. But the sight of Miss Laycock – who had underwritten every libel with her 'form teacher's signature' at the bottom of the card – topped up the righteous anger, and I waved the torn envelope in the air like Mr Chamberlain's 'piece of paper' on his return from Munich. Miss

Laycock, who had been in the business for almost forty years, recognised a juvenile hysteric at first sight. Before I said a word, she issued a warning which was supposed to transfix me: 'If you're not careful, you'll have to see Mr Northeast.'

The headmaster was a remote figure. I had only met him once but I saw him on the podium during the school assemblies which were held on Wednesdays and Thursdays. He was also the one member of staff legally empowered to administer corporal punishment. I knew very well that 'seeing Mr Northeast' was a euphemism for being hit across the bottom several times with a leather belt. But I did not care. Indeed, I decided to take the battle to the enemy. After all, underneath Miss Laycock's endorsement of the subject-teacher's prejudiced rubbish was the signature of the headmaster himself. Instead of striking out the libels on my year's industrious progress, he had lamely added his name in confirmation of the calumny. Miss Laycock suddenly became too insignificant an object for my wrath. I performed a clumsy manoeuvre which I thought of as 'swivelling on his heel', and marched off into the school office, reckless enough to demand audience, but not in such a state of abandoned self-destruction that I barged straight into 'the Study', unbidden and unannounced.

An elegant figure sat immaculate and cross-ankled amongst the piles of old textbooks, form registers, boxes of chalk and rolls of school dinner tickets. It was A. W. Goodfellow – senior master, head of the history department, sometime Commandant of the Sheffield Air Training Corps, President of the Local History Association and man of general cultivation and refinement, temporarily on leave of absence from the school to perform the duties of Lecturer in Education at the Brincliffe Emergency Training College. His year with Uncle Syd and Peggy Stringfield had not dimmed the schoolmaster's eye. He too could tell when a boy was about to go berserk. 'What's the matter, old man?' he asked in a consciously gentle voice which was disturbingly out of keeping with the way in which he snatched the report card and torn envelope from my hand.

I looked at him – gleaming shoes, pinstripe suit into which no crease would ever dare to intrude, stiff white collar and clipped moustache – and I explained. I think that the phrase 'not fair' was repeated half a dozen times in a single spoken paragraph. 'These,' he said, 'are extremely good results,' pausing to allow his emollient message to sink in. 'But you can hardly expect the comments simply to make the same point. If the results and comment columns said the same thing, the comment column would be wholly unnecessary. Take the two things together – top in English and History but could do better still.' He emphasised the 'still' as if the word actually appeared on the offending report card. 'I would,' he concluded, 'be proud to take that report home.' To this day, I do not know if I walked out of the school office a more rational human being or the victim of a confidence trick.

It was the beginning of my friendship with Alan Goodfellow. For the next three years, I never met him again, for either he was at Brincliffe or my history was taught by someone else. But when I reached the sixth form and he had returned, I remembered with gratitude the report card incident. I felt indebted, not because of the way in which he had dismissed the disgrace of the teachers' comments, but because of what I slowly realised he must have done after I had left the school office. As my head began to clear, I feared that Miss Laycock's retribution would be terrible if not swift. For days I waited for some awful punishment to be imposed upon me. But nothing happened. At first, I thought that she had forgotten. Then I realised that Alan Goodfellow had, like his namesake, carried a message concerning an ass. Miss Laycock, a most unlikely Titania, had been made oblivious to my sudden insubordination.

So I passed into the third year of the City Grammar School part-disgruntled and part-encouraged. Of the winter and spring terms I remember nothing. But the summer term began with a never-to-be-forgotten moment of glory. On the first Saturday I turned up at the pre-cricket season nets – the opportunity for any boy in the school to demonstrate his claim to a place in one of the school teams. The following week, when the lists were pinned up on the notice board outside the classroom of the upper sixth, I was selected to open the batting for the second XI. Had the season gone well, I might have begun to feel unequivocally part of the school, ensconced in the establishment of a games-playing blood-brotherhood. But I only opened three innings. My scores were adequate if not exceptional – certainly good enough to keep me in the team. But in June I caught a cold which seemed to develop into the bronchial asthma which I was supposed to have 'grown out of'. Dr Stephen was sent for. I had pneumonia. Although in that dawn of antibiotic treatment I was dosed with M&B tablets (which would, we were assured, reduce temperatures and restore health), my mother applied an

Antiflagistine poultice front and back to 'avoid congestion of the lungs'. The rest of the summer was spent in bed listening to the radio. It was a good summer for radio cricketers. The Australians were on tour.

I lay for days in the back bedroom drinking home-made beef tea, reading the textbook histories which were my temporary passion and waiting for the next broadcast from Lords or Manchester, Nottingham or wherever the tourists were thrashing a county side. In those days, there were no continuous commentaries. So I had impatiently to wait for Rex Alston's urbanity and John Arlott's (then still novel) genius for setting the game out in front of his listeners. 'The Dream of Olwen' was the popular tune of the year and I must have heard it a hundred times as I dozed over the copy of G. M. Trevelyan's *History of England* that Syd had bought me the previous Christmas. Then there would be that sudden flash of Arlott lightning. He counterfeited difficulty in choosing the right word to describe Don Tallon, the Australian wicket-keeper. Then he had it – 'prehensile, all talons are prehensile'. I banged on the bedroom floor, and when my mother arrived flustered and frightened at the thought that I had been overcome by a sudden fit of 'wheezing', I demanded that she bring me that old Chambers Encyclopaedia from the living-room.

When the tourists came to Sheffield, I was well enough to make a delicate and brief visit to the game. I had become a junior member of Sheffield United Cricket Club, a status which entitled me to a seat in the Bramall Lane pavilion as well as a weekly lesson at the nets behind the Spion Kop of the football ground. My mother ruled that, despite my recovery, I could not make the journey across Sheffield without her, and for a moment it looked as though Bradman would have to bat without me. But James Gill – the retired headmaster and sometime City Councillor who added an element of middle-class distinction to our lives – came to my rescue. He was a Yorkshire member, and his membership ticket included an entry permit for 'lady or youth under fourteen years of age – transferable'. James Gill (on his ticket), my mother (as his transferable lady) and I would all go together in a taxi. And so we did. The ground was so crowded that all the pavilion seats were taken by the time that we arrived. A commissionaire was bribed to find a chair on which I sat, embarrassed, in a gangway. There is no pleasure for a fifteen-year-old boy in sitting at a cricket match whilst his mother and a bearded octogenarian stand behind him. I feared that instead of watching Len Hutton (who scored very few runs) and Arthur Morriss (who scored a very large number), the whole crowd concentrated its attention on the whey-faced, ill-mannered, tubby Lord Fauntieroy. I rarely felt the 'spoilt only one', although my mother constantly told me that I enjoyed that status. But that day at Bramall Lane I imagined that every robust youth within the ground looked at me with contemptuous loathing. My embarrassment was compounded by the gift that Councillor Gill had given me to celebrate my recovery. As I was the one member of our party with a seat, convenience as well as courtesy required me to keep it on my knee all day. It was an ebony blotter of the kind much favoured by Victorian clerks – a black half-moon of wood around which the blotting-paper was stretched, and an ornate handle for rocking the absorbent strip backwards and forwards along the lines of wet longhand. Suffer though I did, it was not the greatest humiliation of the summer.

That came in August, after two days at the Leeds Test Match – courtesy of Mr Stringfield, the myopic umpire and father of Chris, a surviving member of the youth cricket team. We travelled together by train to Leeds, clutching our tickets for the Old Bowling Green Stand and anxious to arrive in time to see the Australian giants set out for Headingley from The Queens Hotel. Bradman came out of the swing doors, carrying a pair of flannels over his arm as if he had just taken them from under his mattress. Disappointed as I was to discover that he did not own a proper cricket bag, I was even more depressed by the sight of young Neil Harvey, who was playing his first Test Match that day. He left for the game wearing a maroon suit. I still harboured the belief that cricket was a game for gentlemen. C. B. Fry would not have been seen dead in a maroon suit.

But my spirits did not sag for long. On Monday we were all off on a holiday to London, my first visit to the capital. Syd, for some reason, would only be with us for a couple of days, but we would all set off together, bright and early on the first weekday train. Rooms had been booked in a little hotel off Russell Square, and I had been encouraged to prepare for our numerous outings by reading potted histories of the Tower and Hampton Court. Thanks to my upbringing in the Wadsley churchyard, I retained my morbid interest in graves and *mementi mori*; I particularly looked forward to the crypt at St Paul's. My mother told me about Poets' Corner in Westminster Abbey – a whole Palgrave of monuments and commemorative plaques. I was genuinely enthusiastic about the holiday which lay ahead.

We spent Sunday morning packing, the first time I can recall performing that fascinating activity. I thought then – as I think now – that there is something particularly satisfying about neatly folding clothes and carefully arranging them, along with treasured possessions, within a portable container. I cannot account for the pleasure that packing provides; it may be attributable to the jackdaw's desire to hoard, or to the prisoner's need to simulate escape. Whatever the reason, I first felt the joy on that Sunday morning as I listened to *Family Favourites* – 'Tunes you have asked us to play' – on the radio, and arranged what passed for my wardrobe in neat piles. Syd's demob suit was still going strong. It had become my second long-trousered suit, and it was augmented by a brown bird's-eye that had been sent by distant relatives of Aunt Lot who lived in Cleveland, Ohio and thought that all the Brits were starving. The American suit possessed two pairs of pants, each of which was equipped with a zip fastener rather than a buttoned fly. I thought the whole outfit was the acme of sophistication and I wore it with a pair of fawn crêpe-soled shoes which I had persuaded my mother to buy me in one of her sentimental moments of rejoicing over my recovery from pneumonia. We men of the world in the Wadsley Church Youth cricket team called them 'brothel-creepers' without being exactly sure what a brothel was.

Neither the brothel-creepers nor the Yankee suit went into the old pressed-cardboard suitcase (still bearing the faded labels of journeys to Rome) which I had been allocated. They were my travelling clothes, and they were also the uniform of incipient manhood which I was to wear at evensong on the night before my journey. Together with Kenneth Hardwick from Walden Avenue and the Junior Tech, I regularly sat at the back of the church, hoping that girls would occupy the row in front, and that vicar's warden Nicholson would not move us to a more exposed part of the nave. Once the choir had progressed past us we began our *sotto voce* banter, anxious so to impress with our wit that the girls (who heard, but did not turn) would walk with us on Wadsley Common after the final responses had echoed out of the vestry.

On that lucky night before the London holiday, Doreen Glossop – the most desired and desirable of the youth club girls – agreed to perform the ritual with Ken Hardwick and me. We strolled out into the August night, Ken and I occasionally offering Doreen a furtive hand which she held for a minute to the joyous embarrassment of the lucky youth and the contempt and envy of his momentary rival. I do not think that we walked further than usual or that we stopped along our way. The whole evening's entertainment was over by nine o'clock, and we were back at the top of Vaino Road, Ken turning to the right into his cul-de-sac and me preparing my sad farewell to 'Dot' Glossop before I turned to the left towards the suitcase with the crushed corners and the prospect of Piccadilly Circus. We stopped at the corner of Airedale Road for a final word. It was long before the peck-on-the-cheek phase. I suppose that I was boasting about the adult pleasures of the week ahead when I saw my mother bearing down upon us.

She 'wanted to have a word with the young lady'. But that young lady had more sense than to wait for the word that my mother had for her. I was left alone and humiliated to be marched off to bed like a child, and reminded that we were leaving for London at six o'clock the next morning. We left as planned at eight; my mother obviously unrepentant, and I still suffering from the awful experience of the previous night. There followed six days of tube trains and peaches bought from street barrows, *Oklahoma!* and tiring trips to the top of the Monument and down the Mall to see the Changing of the Guard, suppers in Lyons Corner House and boat-rides to Kew and Greenwich. I returned home with most of the wounds healed.

19
Lost and Found

—

My year in the fourth form was twelve months of unremitting humiliation. Now, most of the disasters seem to have been no more than the routine embarrassments of adolescence. But at the time I thought that doom had stretched out its hand and clutched me in its awful grip. And each little crisis was accentuated by the underlying shame of being in the fourth form at all. I felt that I lived in failure in the way that some people (as I had recently discovered) lived in sin; it was all around me, pervasive and inescapable. The degradation of the five-year course was, in truth, equally spread over the whole elongated march from eleven-plus to School Certificate. But in the fourth form it was much more visible. Clever pupils missed the fourth form altogether. So there was no question about rank or position which I could answer without revealing my awful status as a second-class student. The mark of my shame was written on my exercise books, stencilled on my classroom door and appended to my name whenever it appeared on a school notice. I hated every symbol of the fourth year as intensely as I hated the fourth year itself.

So I mounted my own feeble little rebellion. I did nothing daring or dangerous. There were no mysterious fires in cloakrooms or paint-daubed walls. The lavatories remained undefiled, the windows were un-smashed and not a single page was torn from a library book. I just turned my energy and attention away from school. I chose to spend my time on activities which were really diversions. I needed to devote my days to interests which could become enthusiasms. And I was incapable of becoming enthusiastic about a race in which I had already been declared an also-ran. Outside the City Grammar School, life proved full of opportunities for the creative waste of time. It took only a modicum of ingenuity to fill my days with absorbing absurdities.

Some of them had the bogus appearance of serious study. Uncle Syd bought me a huge drawing board for Christmas — a six-feet-square expanse of laminated wood about which my father warned me in early Advent so that I would be able to counterfeit gratitude on the shining morn. I used it occasionally for the landscapes and watercolours for which it was intended. But I spent far more time on a reversion to the list-making obsession which had begun five years before with the careful compilation of every detail about my army of lead soldiers. I stretched the cartridge paper tight between its drawing pins and drew carefully parallel columns. Then I decided what information I could collate. The most successful exercise tabulated all of Napoleon's battles. We owned an old copy of H. A. L. Fisher's brief biography, and I borrowed Belloc's and A. C. MacDonald's portraits of the Marshal from the Hillsborough Public Library. I can still half-remember the details that I entered on the page in an ugly longhand – the Ligurian Campaign; 'lightning from the hills'; Lodi, Rivoli, Castiglione; Augereau, an ex-waiter whose later sins were constantly forgiven by the Emperor because 'he saved us at Lodi' (or was it Rivoli?). I was also much amused by the description of the hook-nosed cavalryman as an 'Alsatian'. For I had not grown up. Had I been anything like as adult as my complicated and pointless charts could make me feel, I would have devoted my time to more serious pursuits.

The infantile obsession of the spring was a Pageant of Cricket. The idea was not, in itself, original. Sheffield had organised a Festival of Steel, and the cultural highlight of the celebration was a pageant written and produced by L. du Garde Peach, the author of a hundred *Children's Hour* broadcasts on Castles of Britain and How Things Began. Inspired by my memories of these childhood pleasures (and slightly envious of a classmate called Olga Bennett, who basked in the glory of tap-dancing at the bottom end of the festival programme in an entertainment called *Starlets of Steelopolis*), I decided to write and direct a pageant of my own. Of course it would be produced by the Wadsley Youth Cricket team in collaboration with the Wadsley Church Youth Club. It was to star the Woolhouse brothers, Harold and Gordon; Dick Martin (youth club, cricket club and amateur dramatic society) and Chris Stringfield (wicket-keeper and owner of a motor-cycle). I did not want to take part; I was the writer.

The script consisted of linking passages of my own and huge, unattributed, extracts from borrowed cricket books. A boy in dyed cottonwool whiskers (representing W. G. Grace) recited pages from Neville Cardus, and a youth in a joke-shop moustache (C. B. Fry) repeated stolen passages from an anthology called *Bat and Ball*. It was a work of nostalgia – partly because the author was nostalgic by temperament and cricket is a nostalgic game, and partly because I took the view that our historical sweep should end before the 'bodyline' tour of 1932. None of us had the effrontery to represent contemporary heroes. To appear on stage pretending to be Don Bradman or Len Hutton would have been to risk being struck down by a thunderbolt.

The pageant was actually produced. We borrowed straw boaters from local residents who retained the symbols of their roaring twenties youth, made cardboard top-hats, and wore collarless shirts with our cricket flannels. Thus attired we trod the boards in the youth club hut, performing on the little stage at the farthest end from the draughty door on the very spot where, during the previous years, I had done nothing more constructive than argue about which record would be played on the wind-up gramophone. At the last moment, Dick Martin dropped out, afraid that a confusion of lines would spoil his performance in *Dear Octopus* the following week. Naturally enough, I stepped into his place. My mother – never lacking in either initiative or nerve – asked Henry Hall (local resident and welter-weight champion of Great Britain) to perform a sort of opening ceremony. He made a brief speech and distributed postcard pictures of himself in fighting pose, wearing the Lonsdale Belt which he never won outright. He did not stay for the performance.

Neville Cardus, the real star of the show, was unwittingly the cause of my further alienation from the City Grammar School. We were taught English by Mrs Potter, the myopic wife of the professor of history in our home town university, who was known to us as 'Pansy'. For those were innocent days, and a comic carried a cartoon concerning *Pansy Potter the Strong Man's Daughter*. She was gentle, literate, of mildly Fabian opinions and completely out of touch with the life and times of teenage working-class boys. We discussed with disbelief her aside about 'dinner not usually consisting of four courses these days'. We realised that what we called dinner she called lunch. But how what we called tea could consist of four separate items was wholly beyond our imaginations. Tea was what the luckiest amongst us had shortly after getting home from school. It was poached eggs, or cauliflower cheese, or pressed meat, and it kept us going right up to the few minutes before bedtime when we had bread and dripping, or bread and lard. We took dripping and lard very seriously at Airedale Road. Indeed, it was all part of the fetish –

part concerned with cost and part a passion for purity – for the 'home-made'. Lard (since we rarely cooked a Sunday joint of pork) had to be bought from a shop. But the indignity of that was mitigated by insistence (at the point of consumption if not the point of purchase) that it was 'home-rendered'. I was never sure in whose home the rendering took place. But for a whole adolescence of winter evenings I sprinkled salt on the fat my mother had spread on her home-made bread, and listened to the same assurance of its domestic quality. Mrs Potter was part of a different culinary culture.

Mrs Potter was also part of a different theatrical tradition. We had begun to go in school parties to the local repertory company – and even to the Lyceum when the production was suitable. During the three years which followed I saw Donald Wolfit (touring in *King Lear*), some unknown Hamlet (interrupting his third soliloquy to invite the audience to choose between its own conversation and Shakespeare's poetry) and a rare whole performance of *The Dynasts*. Thomas Hardy's epic of the First Empire was produced by the Little Theatre on a six-foot stage, and we all sat in complete silence as the Grande Armée, the Austrians at Austerlitz and the multitudes proclaiming Napoleon's coronation were successively depicted by the same half-dozen actors. In the fourth form we began to enjoy the theatre, but we did not understand Mrs Potter's casual attitude towards an evening in stalls or circle. She could not understand our view that the theatre was essentially the entertainment of the respectable middle classes; the climax of an outing which began with a bath, and required both best suit and best behaviour. 'The pictures', on the other hand, was the relaxed escape of our own kind and class. Watching Clark Gable and John Wayne, we could eat sweets and slump in our seats. We were astonished that Mrs Potter was too obtuse to tell the difference.

Mrs Potter was similarly perplexed by our ignorance of both literature and life. She particularly antagonised me by the allegation that my essays were not my own work, justifying the unjustifiable with the nonsensical notion that it was impossible simultaneously to get all the grammar right and all the spelling wrong. I was also caused deep distress by a passing reference that she made to Neville Cardus. Beginning with the offensive assumption that none of us had ever heard of the *Manchester Guardian*, she went on to imply that the greatest of all writers about the greatest of all games dashed off his summer reports as a poor substitute for winter music criticisms.

There was also a dispute about *More Essays by Modern Masters* – a collection of contemporary pieces by Robert Lynd, Hilaire Belloc, G. K. Chesterton, A. A. Milne, E. V. Lucas and, above all, J. B. Priestley which I believed (despite Mrs Potter's disparaging dismissal) were a joy to read. The final act of alienation concerned Shakespeare. We were acting a scene from *Macbeth* and Melbourne, Makin and I were three of the numerous apparitions which so discomforted the King of Scotland from time to time. The stage directions required us to have 'glasses in our hands'. The idea that we were supposed to walk about looking into mirrors was a concept beyond our vocabulary. To us, glasses were used for drinking when visitors came and cups seemed the wrong receptacles for lemonade. So we walked across the front of the classroom bearing empty ink-bottles, from which we took the occasional imaginary sip, swig or gulp. Mrs Potter lost her temper. I lost my patience. We were not reconciled until the eve of School Certificate.

Indeed, our antagonism intensified during the spring term. I was regularly and recklessly neglecting my homework. Sometimes, I rushed through the minimum requirement early in the evening before I turned to making lists of every cricketer to play for Yorkshire, or writing pageants. Often I scrawled out a few lines in the back-bay of the tramcar on my way to school. On the occasions when my homework was not done at all I made transparent excuses and stoically endured the detention which followed. Only history essays were conscientiously prepared and carefully written. Mrs Potter's grammatical exercises were parsed and analysed with variable enthusiasm. But pages of continuous prose became more and more difficult to prepare for her, for I knew that at some point in the second paragraph a spelling error would provoke Mrs Potter into reading no more. A red line would cross out the entire page and the 'A' which I confidently expected would be denied me once again.

However, no matter how great the provocation, a grammar-school boy of fifteen cannot survive indefinitely without at least attempting his English essays. And what I knew to be breaking point came one Monday morning. As usual the books, in which the work should have been done, were piled on our form teacher's table. With care and cunning, I hid them in an empty desk. When their loss was reported to Mrs Potter, she accepted it with remarkable calm. They must, she said, be *somewhere*. All we had to do was find them. Her choice of me to lead the search was one of the practical jokes which fate plays from time to time. I carried out my task with mock thoroughness until, two days after the loss was first detected, one of my classmates reported that he had seen a now-nameless girl hurrying home with her raincoat wrapped round a suspicious parcel. It was more fear than chivalry which made me confess. I was terrified of what might happen if the subterfuge ran on, and foolishly optimistic that the honourable exoneration of an innocent suspect would be regarded as a sort of King's Evidence, absolving me from blame and protecting me from punishment. I was wrong. I was removed from the production of John Galsworthy's *The Little Man* (in which I wore Uncle Syd's demob suit and played the part of the bumptious American) and sent 'to see Mr Northeast'. The headmaster made me bend over the back of a chair with my palms touching its wooden seat whilst he struck me six not very hard blows with a leather belt. I was also warned that next time he would 'send for my parents'. The threat to send for a pupil's parents was another of the school's euphemisms. In translation it meant 'arrange to be expelled'. Fortunately, Mr Northeast proved a merciful man.

His opportunity to show clemency came during the summer term. In those distant days Yorkshire still played cricket at Bramall Lane, and two of the season's matches always began on a Wednesday. On the morning of the mid-week game with Worcester, I simply sat fast while the tramcar clanged to a halt outside the Town Hall, claiming that the foot infection which was to keep me out of the weekend's cricket match required me to visit a distant doctor. Three stops later, I was within half a mile of the pavilion. I was so early that there was no gateman to examine my Lady or Youth Member's Ticket (non-transferable). By the time that the City Grammar assembly began I was sitting on the front row of the balcony. I suppose the pickets of groundsmen who rolled the pitch and mowed the outfield noticed the solitary schoolboy figure sitting in the most sought-after place on the ground. And no doubt they guessed why I was there so early. But they left me undisturbed as I carefully composed and laboriously copied out the counterfeit sick note which I planned to take to school next day.

Of course the excursion ended in tragedy. Worcestershire beat Yorkshire for the first time in cricket history (although Len Hutton carried his bat through the second innings), and I was seen – flagrant in my truancy – by Mrs Hemmings, City Grammar School's biology teacher who, inconsiderately, chose to spend her lunch-time at

Bramall Lane. What was worse, I saw her and knew that she had seen me. So the sick note lost whatever power to deceive that it had ever possessed. On the second day of the match, I turned up at the ground not so much as a spectator as a displaced person. By the third day I was a refugee. Fortunately, Yorkshire played their next match at Hove. If my ticket had taken me into any ground north of the Trent, I would certainly not have gone to school on the following Monday. Indeed, I might not have returned to my desk until after the Scarborough Festival in September. But, as I had nowhere else to go, I turned up in class at the start of the next week and waited for the blow to fall.

It fell just before lunch. Until then, Miss Taylor – my form teacher – never even mentioned my truancy. But just before the five-past-twelve bell began to ring, the school secretary came to say that Mr Northeast wanted to see me. Cowed by the almost morning-long suspense, I tottered off to the headmaster's room, fearful that my shaking legs would fold up like a delinquent deckchair before I reached his door. I was, of course, prepared for the strap. But a beating was neither threatened nor administered. Instead, I was handed an envelope addressed to my father and instructed to take it home at once. I was so frightened that I arrived at Airedale Road with the letter still intact. My mother, having recovered from her initial assumption that I was ill or injured, tore it open. The suspense was to continue for another twenty-four hours. My father was bidden to see the headmaster the following day.

Inevitably, it was my mother who went. No doubt she made excuses about difficulties in taking time off from work. But the real reason was quite different. The family was in crisis, and crisis management was her job. Of course, she succeeded in putting things right. From a subsequent conversation I had with Mr Northeast, I got the vague impression that she had made byzantine excuses and given precise promises. But she never reported any part of the confrontation to me. There were no recriminations nor reproofs, no calls for future good behaviour nor assurances of serious application. All she said was that the headmaster was worried about my French. Without French I would not win a place at a university. In some way the discussion had been switched from my imminent expulsion to my distant prospect of higher education. It had been agreed that I would spend each Wednesday evening with a Miss Parsons who, before her retirement, had taught modern languages at the City Grammar.

My mother visited Miss Parsons the same day and judged her 'nice'
– a tribute to her vaguely bookish respectability and a quality of
which my mother spoke with approval without explaining how it
had been discovered. The old lady was, apparently, 'fond of animals'. On the strength of these qualifications, a bargain was struck and
it was agreed that I would begin my cramming the following day. I
made my way to the front door of Miss Parson's bungalow with
unqualified enthusiasm. I had occasionally seen her on the Worrall
bus and felt that there was something forbidding about her ankle-
length tweed coat and old cloche hat. But her character was far less
important than her vocation. 'Extra French' made me special again.
Inside her dilapidated front door lay the path to a university place, a
destination to which I was now apparently travelling with the full
agreement of Mr Northeast.

My first impression of Chez Parsons is still imprinted on my
memory. It was not the chintz furniture nor the shelves of books, the
roaring fire nor the school photographs on the living-room walls. It
was the smell. Or – to be both fair to Miss Parsons and scientifically
accurate – the whole atmosphere. For I was assaulted not by smell
alone, but by the full aura of cat. The essence of cat seemed to hang in
the air as if particles of whiskers and hair had been atomised and
blown about the bungalow by some feline fan. Of course, nothing so
mysterious or mechanical had happened. Miss Parsons possessed
twelve cats, and in their invisible presence I broke down into
uncontrollable tears, sobbing to the disconcerted old lady that what
she witnessed was allergy rather than emotion. I coughed my way
through a few irregular verbs and wept over an unseen passage. But
even with the window open the dictation was beyond me. When I got
home I reported that everything had gone splendidly. The night air
had blown away all medical evidence except for the vestiges of red
rims around my eyes. And that symptom was not noticed by parents
more interested – at least at that moment – in a healthy mind
than a healthy body. The following week, instead of becoming
de-sensitised to the allergy, the affliction became more intense. On
the third Wednesday, I was so ill that I had to leave before my
paid-for-in-advance hour was over. To my surprise, both my parents
were standing under the lamp outside Miss Parsons's gate. They were
arm-in-arm like a courting couple, but their mission was essentially
un-, indeed anti-, romantic. They had heard that I was meeting a girl
from the youth club after my lesson was over. In fact, Joy Lax and I

had met in the churchyard before the hour of oral French and orificial irritation began. All that my mother and father therefore noticed were the tears streaming down my face. The extra French lessons were over.

It did not matter, for the hope which had been rekindled by our contract with Miss Parsons had been extinguished the day after I had spent my first hour *avec les chats de Mademoiselle sur la table, sur les chaises, et sur tout*. For when the second cricket team was selected on the Thursday of that eventful week, I was not included. At first I feared that I had been left out because of the verruca that had caused me to miss the match during the week in which Worcester beat Yorkshire. So I made my way to the men's staff-room door to explain to Mr Walker that my foot was healed. Mr Etchells answered my knock, a breezy figure just visible in the haze of lunchtime tobacco smoke. He demanded to know why the games master was to be disturbed. I told him. His instruction that I should return to my classroom at once perforated even my naïveté. I had been dropped as a punishment for the previous week's truancy, and I felt special no longer.

20
Sporting Life

—

The summer of my suspension began – like most grammar-school summers – barely halfway through spring. Cricket started at the City Grammar eight days after Good Friday, no matter how early in the year Easter had come to rest. Whilst the Cup Final was being played at Wembley, I was batting on some bumpy pitch belonging to Firth Park or High Storrs GSCC. Sometimes I had started to oil my bat and whiten my pads before the semi-finals were over. Whitening the pads was a strange mixture of pleasure and pain, for the pads were both a triumph and a mistake. I had saved up months of pocket-money to buy them, and I proudly walked home with the brown-paper parcel under my arm during a January snowstorm. But the possession of personal pads was undeniably pretentious – an announcement that I regarded myself as a special cricketer; the owner of equipment which my colleagues did not own because I was, in some way, different from them. Owning pads was wonderful when I scored twenty or more runs. When I was out for a duck, they simply heightened the humiliation. I never enjoyed summer Friday nights, for I looked forward to the next day's game with a fear of failure which totally drove hope of pleasure out of my mind. The pads became a symbol of the tension and the trauma of my cricketing years.

In most of those years, the Saturday of the football semi-final was the point at which my cricket bag was pulled from under the bed. One of the semi-finals was almost invariably played at Hillsborough, a match which became the highlight of the Sheffield football purists' year. For the partisan, no game could compare with a confrontation in which one of the local favourites took part. What I wanted to see was Sheffield Wednesday winning. But once a year I looked forward to the more relaxed pleasure of Derby County versus Manchester United or Newcastle against Wolves. Indeed, like my father, I was so keen on enjoying an uncommitted ninety minutes that I rose at half-past six on the Sunday when the tickets were sold. By seven we were in the queue, waiting with anxious calm for noon and the moment when the sale actually started. By one o'clock we had reached a turnstile and were about to take possession of the two tickets which each frozen enthusiast was allowed. By half-past one we were back home, having missed *Family Favourites* and the *Billy Cotton Band Show*, but the proud possessors of the ability to take our place on Spion Kop on the next Saturday.

I could of course have gone on my own to buy the two tickets that my father and I needed. The extra tickets which we always bought were less of a boon than a burden. We never even thought of selling them at a profit, and there was always much embarrassed confusion about who should buy them at face value. Indeed, there were times when – for all their scarcity – we were almost left with the valuable property on our hands. We bought them because the offer seemed too good to refuse, and the idea of queuing all those hours and then taking only half the number of tickets we were offered seemed self-evidently ridiculous. Of course, one of us could have stayed in bed whilst the other made the early morning expedition. But football was for my father and me a joint enterprise. We stood on Spion Kop, eating our Mintoes together. And together we queued for the tickets.

On the day of the big game we took our places on the red shale terraces two hours before the time of the kick-off. We always stood in front of one of the steel barriers on which less experienced spectators leaned their elbows. With the Spion Kop crowd packed so tight that it was impossible to take a handkerchief out of a topcoat pocket there was a special danger in standing there behind the goal. At every sudden shot and calculated corner, twenty thousand necks craned forward and twenty thousand chests pressed, with increasing force, against twenty thousand backs. For many of the spectactors, the result was a cumulative pressure that lurched them down half a dozen steps, packing sections of the crowd more tightly than seemed possible and lifting grown men off their feet with an irresistible and infuriating force. But anyone wise enough to find a place *in front* of a barrier was protected from the human avalanche. So we arrived at the ground two hours before the teams ran out onto the pitch. Queuing combined with waiting for the kick-off lasted four times as long as the match itself. But the game was always worth it, and there were diversions to help us pass the time.

There was, of course, the local Steelworks Band, playing martial music in a wholly un-military way – which was entirely consistent with their wholly un-military appearance. And there was the crowd itself – Blackpool fans walking with an orange-ribboned duck along the touchline; wandering Wolverhamptonites passing a black-and-white coffin over their heads in preparation for the slaughter of Newcastle United, and the whole panoply and pageant of coloured hats and supporters club songs. And that was all before the match began.

After the first whistle blew, there were Stan Mortensen of Blackpool and Billy Wright of Wolves, and for two marvellous consecutive years the magpies of Newcastle who won at Hillsborough and went on to win the Cup – Jackie Milburne, Bobby Mitchell, Joe Harvey and the Robledo brothers from South America. It was a short walk home, but our feet always dragged with the sad anti-climax that swallows up the football fan at twenty minutes to five.

After the semi-final of my fourth form year, I turned my mind to two summer sports. Cricket, as always, had first call on my time and imagination. I practised all the time I could persuade anyone to bowl to me and I fantasised about hurrying up the Headingley pavilion steps – bat under arm and cap in hand – anxious not to milk the polite applause that had greeted my century. But tennis, if not a real competitor for my affection, had captured a little corner of my interest. I had played tennis of a sort for years, travelling by bus with my mother and father to a little West Riding village called Oughtibridge and playing with them in the seclusion of a weed-covered court in a park called Glen Howe. All that tennis meant to me then was sitting on the rotting steps of the old wooden pavilion and watching my mother and father re-live their brief and furtive courtship. They played with the heavy wooden rackets that had smashed and volleyed in Shirebrook twenty years before and, as in the good old days, my mother always won. Indeed, if my father won a point, he always apologised as if it were a mistake. Sometimes I joined in. But what I really enjoyed about Glen How was the lemonade. It was sold in old-fashioned glass bottles that had glass marbles in their necks. Instead of unscrewing bakelite stoppers or pulling out tin-topped corks, the thirsty owner pushed the marble down from the place where it blocked the escape route of even the smallest bubble of sparkle and fizz. Pushing down the marble produced an explosion of carbon dioxide which I found just as satisfying as the sound of racket on ball.

But when I was fifteen I pushed away such childish things. Tennis itself began to excite me. It was the age of the crew-cut and the cannonball serve and Max Robertson commentating on the radio from Wimbledon. Kramer and Sedgman seemed to play in a way that bore little resemblance to the girlish game which I had seen played at Hillsborough High School. And Uncle Syd, despite his cricketing talents, was beginning to take tennis very seriously. At the Teachers' Training College he had failed to win a place in the cricket team. So he had switched summer sports and bought himself a brand-new Dunlop racket. My mother held it in awe. The woodwork (off which I was to fluke so many future volleys) was covered in white plastic and the strings, instead of being made of catgut, were synthesised from some man-made material. It said 'All Weather' on the handle and Syd assured us that the wooden press with butterfly bolts at each corner which had kept my mother's racket in shape for almost twenty years was a superfluous adjunct to such a modern device.

Syd played in parks with his recently-made friends from Brincliffe College and gradually persuaded my mother and father to join him for a game on Hillsborough's municipal courts. Park tennis in post-war Sheffield was segregated. There were courts on which only 'the club' were allowed to play and benches on which only club members were allowed to sit – at least on Saturday afternoons and specified weekday evenings. On Sunday, of course, no one was allowed to play or sit on anything at all. Club members (who paid £1 a year membership fees) were easily distinguished from the ordinary riff-raff who played the occasional game with hired rackets and no visible skill. Club members wore white shorts and blancoed tennis-shoes; the ordinary riff-raff took off their jackets and pullovers and changed into black plimsolls or 'pumps', but otherwise looked much the same as when they were working in office or factory. Club members played in knockout competitions, and the winners were formed into teams which travelled to other parks to take part in the municipal tennis league; ordinary riff-raff felt very inferior if, during a quick dash to the tap in the wooden pavilion, they crossed the path of a club member on his or her way to one of the dressing-rooms. My father inevitably called the club members 'professionals', a term which caused my mother much annoyance. For we were the ordinary riff-raff, and that come-down was, in itself, hard enough to bear without affording the cause of her discomfiture a status to which it was clearly not entitled. 'Enid,' Syd assured his brother, 'could have beaten any of them fifteen years ago.' Enid herself did not disagree.

Her husband insisted that he meant no offence, but continued to refer to the bank clerks and school teachers who played on the grey concrete court by a title which they did not deserve.

I, of course, determined to become one of the élite. Syd bought me a tennis racket – a Slazenger of lighter weight than his own, with conventional cat-gut rather than nylon strings. 'Worksop' – believing tennis to be a gentleman's game – had actually made an earlier offer. Indeed, Aunt Annie had made a real effort to encourage my interest in the game by taking me, during one of my frequent afternoons at Overend Road, on an expedition to a shop where she had seen 'just the thing'. I was led into a junk-shop that claimed to sell antiques, and shown a Victorian fish-tail racket. Its huge handle (ending in the fins from which the style derived its name) looked as if it had been chiselled out of solid mahogany by a carpenter who normally carved pews and pulpits for neo-gothic churches. Miraculously, the strings – though hairy with age – were still intact. I counterfeited delight. Aunt Annie paid whatever price would have been asked from the curator of the National Tennis Museum. And I carried my gift home through the streets of Worksop feeling that my prospects of being the first Englishman to win at Wimbledon since Fred Perry had taken a nasty knock. Back in Overend Road, I silently held it in my mother's direction, valiantly attempting to mime pleasure and gratitude. It could not have been easy, but she said it. 'That thing,' she told her aunt, 'is quite unsuitable. How much did it cost?' I cannot remember the amount, but it was certainly sufficient to convince my mother of the gross immorality of wasting such a sum on something which would just be left to rot in the coalhouse, together with the junior-size cricket stumps, the fretsaw, the Indian clubs and numerous well-intentioned but wholly unwelcome 'Worksop' gifts. All of us – Aunts Annie and Lot, my mother and me – went back to the shop. After some haggling, we swapped the tennis-racket for an antique-type coal-scuttle. I had grown old enough to feign amusement at moments when I was near to tears of disappointment. 'What a present!' I said to my father as I put the bronze-painted-tin bucket in front of the fire. It was, he assured me, in the Great Tradition of 'Worksop' gifts. In the desperate days of the depression, they had given him a hobbin-iron, the more easily to sole and heel his own shoes.

The hobbin iron (cobblers' lasts, south of the Trent) took its place in family folk lore alongside all the other tokens of Christmas remembrance – each of them matching affection with economy. Between the wars, there were sixpenny pairs of Woolworth cuff-links for Syd and George, 3B pencils and lined paper for my grandmother and strange trinkets bought by my father and given by me as our joint gift to my mother. Just after the war, we chose a sugar-sifter from the window of a Hillsborough jewellery shop. The little card, to which it was attached by elastic, said 'genuine silver plate'. We paid our two and sixpence and asked the shopkeeper what it was used for. Syd was sometimes more imaginative and usually unreasonably generous. And not only at Christmas.

So it was natural for Syd to come to the rescue. With a brand-new racket, all that I needed to complete my impending tennis triumph was a pair of white shorts – for white shirt, socks and pullover I possessed; if not in abundance, at least in sufficient quantity to satisfy the Wadsley Cricket Club. Since I was still convinced as to which was the senior summer game, I took it for granted that what was good enough for wicket and outfield would more than suffice for baseline and net. The shorts I acquired in one of those complicated schoolboy multiple exchanges during which all sorts of goods change hands and everybody ends up bitterly dissatisfied. I think that today the shorts would be of a fashionable shape and size. In 1949, they were small and tight to the point of indecency. Thus armed, I began to play tennis regularly in the park. I did not join the club at once. But I made a point of playing on neighbouring courts while the Club was at practice.

At first my opponents were the same crew of cricketers and homework-borrowers with whom I spent the rest of my spare time – Alan Siddall, waiting to go to Oxford, Geoff Kirkby on summer holiday from Loughborough College, and whoever else would make up a doubles match and contribute to an hour's hiring of the dusty red court, with its lines marked out not with whitewash, but with strips of lead nailed into the ground. Gradually I developed a new coterie of tennis cronies; youths I vaguely knew from the City Grammar who had played tennis in the park for years and already possessed the essential white apparel that set them out as either 'professionals' or would-be 'professionals'. Principal amongst them were the brothers George and Michael Beeley. George was already in the sixth form and a languid member of the First XI. Mike – two years younger – batted with me in the second team. Both played tennis with a frenzied enthusiasm which bordered on sporting hysteria; long curly hair trailing behind them in their slip-streams, rackets waving in manic determination to return the ball. They brought with them to the park Keith 'Kedah' Redfern and Peter Middleton, who I believe now does some sort of job in the Treasury. We became a sort of tennis circus – meeting on most holiday mornings and playing throughout the day until our money or our stamina ran out.

We often arrived at the far side of Hillsborough Park before the gate in the tennis courts' wire fence was unlocked. And on our more affluent and energetic days we were still there when the park-keeper was sweeping out the pavilion, in anticipation of a quick getaway the moment the closing bell was tolled. In between our matches we sat on a grass bank that separated the tennis courts of my adolescence from the model-yacht pond of my childhood, and watched others playing on the scene of our recent glory. For we really were good tennis players – better than almost all of the riff-raff who played in braces, and better than most of the 'professionals' who played in the club. We were young, enthusiastic about all ball games, and played for hours on every summer day. Even before the holidays began, we squeezed in a couple of hours on several weekday nights, and rushed from our Saturday morning cricket matches to get in half-a-dozen sets before the light faded and the nets were allowed to hang slack for the night. The enthusiasm persisted for three summers.

With the years, I began gradually to acquire the trappings of the tennis fellowship. The classic bag – canvas and leather facings – came at Christmas. When Syd found the demands of teaching and tennis incompatible, I inherited the white all-weather racket and 'Worksop' made amends for the junk-shop fiasco by buying me a windcheater – one of the fashionable sporting garments of the moment. The windcheater proclaimed the sort of tennis which I played. It was made in American style from one of the new synthetic fibres that had come to Britain with the war, and it had a 'crew neck' – a feature which proclaimed its origin and the tennis temperament of its wearer. For while whoever designed it probably thought of 'crew' in some maritime or naval context, to me it was simply the adjective which qualified 'cut'. Crew-cuts belonged in my mind not to sailors but to the cannon-ball service and volley school of American tennis. Men who sustained long rallies from the baseline kept themselves warm between sets and after matches with V-necked sweaters knitted in a cable-stitch pattern and bordered with the colours of their Home Counties club. Men who rushed to the net and smashed every return which was more than shoulder-high wore windcheaters whilst they rested between victories. So I abandoned the giant sweater that my mother had knitted for me out of rug-making wool and let it emit its perpetual smell of wet sheep from the bottom of the wooden cupboard which I called a wardrobe.

It was onto my greying windcheater that I stitched the badge of the Hillsborough Park Lawn Tennis Club when, during my second summer of backhand drives and half-volleys, I formally joined the 'professionals'. I was never an enthusiastic member. One year I played in the Under-Eighteen team. And I always made some progress during the club's own knockout tournaments, before I was forced to scratch from the later rounds which were played on Saturday afternoons, and therefore came into head-on conflict with the cricket matches, which had the first and indisputable claim on my time and affection. But I never felt at home in the club. Its members did not make the same irreverent sort of jokes as the Beeleys made as we all took it in turns to use the pavilion's one bakelite beaker to pour pints of lukewarm water down our throats, and they did not take the interest in passing girls that we took. Above all, whether they played tennis badly or well, they played the game with a solemnity which I thought wholly inappropriate to what was, after all, essentially only an athletic diversion. Some of them seemed actually to prefer tennis to cricket, and the relationship between the two games was causing me mounting concern. I began to suspect that I was a better tennis player than a cricketer. The discovery caused me increasing anguish as I became gradually reconciled to the dream of centuries for Yorkshire and England fading forever. One of the many lessons that it taught me was that affection is not always reciprocated, and love does not always bring joy. I was no more ready to admit that I was better at tennis than at the game of my life-long infatuation than I was to concede that my football team, my school or my political party could be estranged from my affections. I went on playing tennis as if it were a passion rather than a pastime. But I told myself – and anyone else who would listen – that I only ran from baseline to net behind my service in order to keep fit for cricket. After our games we re-lived the volleys and drives in the way that we reincarnated the snicks through the slips and umpires' mistakes that resulted in our innings coming to an early and unjust end. We also went together to a herbalist drink-shop and had pints of sarsaparilla pulled from pumps that would have done credit to a Victorian public house. While other patrons ordered ounces of liquorice and mandrake root, we talked about cricket, school and politics. Occasionally we spoke of girls in the forced, artificial language of young men who thought they ought to be preoccupied by sex but could not quite simulate the obsession. Occasionally we were excited by the suspicion that a customer whose order we could not hear was buying contraceptives. But such diversions were the trivia of our drink-shop conversations. We chose to walk a mile to a shop in Malin Bridge because its Central-European proprietor – known to us as Karl the Capitalist – was prepared to argue politics. He spoke for individualism and free enterprise. We countered with bogus quotations from the works of Marx – which we had never read. For the Beeleys and I were socialists. More – we were members of the Labour Party. And I, at least, was playing an increasingly active part in its local organisation.

21

The People's Flag

—

Despite their apparent familiarity with Marx and the philosophers who followed him, the Beeley brothers, like me, made modest claims about their ideological commitment. In the Hillsborough constituency, nobody described themselves as 'socialists'. Members of the political family in which I was born and bred were 'Labour men' or 'Labour women', and the male of the species was far more visible than his mate. Labour women – my mother apart – met in the sexual seclusion of the 'women's section' or the Co-op Women's Guild. For Hillsborough was Co-op as well as Labour and its Member of Parliament, the Rt Hon A. V. Alexander, fought under the rainbow banner as well as the red flag. His agent, Councillor Albert Ballard, was paid by the Sheffield Co-operative Party. The 'dividend cheque' which we were given with every purchase at the Brightside and Carbrook Co-operative Society was a political symbol as well as an assurance that when Christmas or the summer holidays came there would be enough 'divi' in the little blue book to buy train tickets to Bridlington or pay for the chicken and the presents in the pillowcase.

My mother took 'divi' very seriously indeed. I was required to return from errands with the little slip of flimsy pink paper sufficiently uncrumpled to confirm that the proper amount had been credited to our share account. Each shareholder in the B and C was entitled to a bonus of one shilling in the pound on every purchase. And five per cent on a whole year of coal and groceries made summer holidays and mistletoe possible for families who, without the 'divi', would never have seen the sea or hung the holly. Of course, my mother never bought a whole year of anything at the Co-op. She 'shopped around' long before the expression was invented, walking long distances in pursuit of cut-price biscuits and making a second exploration later the same day to search for the Maypole Dairy with the 'specially reduced' butter. Each expedition ended in double triumph with the acquisition of groceries which were unrivalled in either price or quality. It was only when bargains were not available that my mother allowed ideology to interfere with home economy. And even in areas where private enterprise bargains were not available, the B and C was not our only provider. We had inherited from 'Worksop' strong views about 'new-laid eggs' and 'real' milk which was uncontaminated by either bottling machine or pasteurisation plant. My mother's theory of real milk concerned the time that passed and the distance that was travelled between teat and tea. So whilst other little boys lived in a lactic sub-culture of gold top, red top, silver top and TT-tested, I only knew about a man with a churn and a measuring-can from which he filled up our jug each morning. He was called Shepherd, and I remember with awful clarity the day on which he turned to bottles. Our only consolation was that the bottle-tops were cardboard rather than tinfoil which, according to 'Worksop', destroyed what purity was left in the pint which lay below.

After the milk and the eggs and the meat – which came from a man who was perversely praised for 'slaughtering his own animals' – had been extracted from our weekly budget, we spent very little at the Co-op. Yet the dividend which we earned obsessed my mother. Even at the age of sixteen, whenever I was sent for soap or sugar I was required to repeat our dividend number before I set off. If by mistake I allowed the shop assistant to write down something other than 25431, the wrong shareholder received our rightful recompense. I was also obliged to repeat instructions concerning 'own brands' – the jam and pickles, custard powder and salt produced by the Co-operative Wholesale Society and sold in competition with the more famous names of Chivers, Heinz, Birds and Saxa. My mother did not believe in 'own brands' and I was always told to resist the blandishments of the Wheatsheaf trademark. And I was also always required to hand over the dividend cheque with the change. In vain did I explain that the dividend was safe in the Co-op bank whether or not we kept the 'divi cheques' in the kitchen table drawer. They were all preserved, crumpled and undecipherable, but essential evidence in the prosecution which would certainly have followed any attempt to pay us less than our proper dues. And as we prepared to protect ourselves against the B and C's peculation, we preached the Co-operative gospel. Two donkeys tethered at opposite ends of a rope could reach neither the bale of hay nor the lush pasture if they pulled in opposing directions. But when they *co-operated* and marched side by side in the common cause, they could first share the fodder and then gorge themselves on the succulent grass. In the B and C's old cobbler's shop, we never considered a tug of war between donkeys of unequal strength, or the pair dying from overeating.

In the old cobbler's shop, I joined – and soon became Treasurer of – the Labour League of Youth. I had longed for the Chairmanship and aspired to be Secretary, but both offices were denied me. So I took officious control of the few shillings which we had in the bank. Rosemary Emans – a girl I had met at the Christmas conference of the Student Christian Movement – came to our branch when I spoke on the need to abolish the House of Lords. She was sufficiently impressed with my radical zeal to meet me on alternate Friday and Saturday nights at the Hallé concerts held in the City Hall. We each had concessionary tickets (provided virtually free by the Education Committee), which allowed us to sit on the platform behind the orchestra. For a whole winter of weekends, I looked down the back of a double-bass's neck. It was a strange introduction to serious music. But I saw John Barbirolli's every smile and frown, and after his last flamboyant bow I walked Rosemary to the Totley bus stop via the Pond Street bomb-site. I had never been so happy. For I was sixteen, with the hated fourth form behind me, I had something approximating to a girlfriend, and I had discovered the great excitement of my life. It was called the Labour Party.

The party had claimed and caught me long before that year. But until 1950 I was a member in the same way that I was a Hattersley – naturally, inevitably, and without a thought of why it should be so. It was in my sixteenth year that I began to understand the reason, and I also began to understand the excitement of commitment to a great cause. The excitement certainly outpaced the commitment. I had begun to read the simple texts – *The Makers of the Labour Movement* by Margaret Cole, and the Hammonds on the life and times of the industrial poor. And I learned more important lessons from the stories of pre-war poverty that were told after the meetings were over. But my real passion was for the practice – not the theory – of politics. From the moment I knocked on my first door and announced that I was 'calling on behalf of the Labour Candidate' I was infatuated by the business of politics. I enjoyed canvassing above all other political activity. But when there were no doors to knock, I gladly addressed envelopes or pushed leaflets through letter-boxes or under draught-excluders. I even started a collection of broadsheets and pamphlets, and stuck them in an old pattern-book which had once displayed samples of fashionable cloths and the up-to-the-minute styles into which Aunts Lot and Annie could make them. I had adapted 'Worksop' pattern-books for years – first as scribbling-pads and then as albums to immortalise the exploits of the British Army as initially recorded in newspapers. When the peace was won, the pattern-books became the chronicles of county cricket. Until 1950 my *magnum opus* was the epic of Ramadin and Valentine bowling out England and Worrell, Weekes and Walcott scoring the runs which made victory certain. I decorated the cover with poster-paint fantasies of palm trees, bananas and rum, and wittily printed 'West Indian Summer' across my Caribbean abstract. But even that masterpiece could not compare with the collection I called 'Election Material'. The case for food subsidies, the story of the Health Service told in pictures, the reason for rationing and a cartoon account of why the mines were nationalised were all included. The volume's prosaic title was in absolute contrast to the drama and romance which I stuck onto every page. I was in thrall to politics. I was election material myself.

We had begun to prepare for the 1950 General Election long before Parliament was dissolved. A. V. Alexander – anticipating a peerage and, according to his detractors, defeat at Hillsborough – announced that he would not contest the seat again. So a new Labour candidate had to be selected. George Buttery – B and C tailor turned Christmas Club collection agent – came to see us on behalf of George Darling, the Co-operative Party's contender, and told us we had a duty to support our fellow dividend recipient. Mr Buttery was in a strong position to argue on behalf of duty's irresistible call. He had briefly been councillor for our area – elected during a year of unusual Labour fortune. And when, three years later, he was engulfed in inevitable defeat, he remained for years the candidate in a ward he could not win. In the end virtue found its own safe seat, but in 1950 he was out of office and had plenty of time to urge loyalty in others. My mother and father agreed at once to support the Co-op line. Uncle Syd stubbornly insisted on judging the rival contenders on their merits as displayed during the selection conference. Despite their choice of different routes, they all arrived at the same destination on the appointed Sunday afternoon, and voted for George Darling MA, industrial correspondent of the BBC. I lay in bed for night after night pondering the competing merits of unthinking loyalty and high-minded independence. It was the first occasion that

I realised that politics posed such conundrums from time to time.

When the election came – two months after my sixteenth birthday – I began to canvass 'on behalf of George Darling, your Labour candidate' with a passion which was wholly inappropriate to so safe a seat. My command-post was established in Sid Osgothorpe's front room. Sid was the sort of stalwart on whom local Labour parties depend. He had neither wish for office nor hope of preferment, but simply devoted his time and energy to politics for no better reason than that he believed in the cause for which he campaigned. He was typical of his Sheffield class and generation – softly-spoken and gentle-mannered despite his employment in the city's hard and heavy industry. He was immensely proud of his daughter (a student at the Rachel MacMillan Teachers' Training College) and he urged everyone under eighteen to follow her into higher education. He wore a cap and scarf on days when the weather was far too warm to justify such self-protection – a foible I put down to a working life spent within sweating distance of steelworks furnaces. The romance of his connection with heavy industry heightened my affection. But even without the false glamour of the glow of white-hot metal I could have recognised him as an admirable man. I have only to remember Sid Osgothorpe to feel certain that the Labour Party is built on secure foundations.

Although we canvassed from Sid Osgothorpe's front room, tramped mud over his carpet and drank his tea, Sid himself was not in charge. The responsibility for the campaign in the Hillsborough Ward of the Hillsborough Constituency was shared between my Uncle Syd and Les Higgins, an ex-railway guard who had forsaken green flag and amber light to become a Co-op milkman – an occupation which left afternoons free for window-cleaning rounds, allotment cultivation or (in the case of Mr Higgins) politics. Sid Osgothorpe was merely the 'poll captain' for Wisewood. My mother accepted the same position in Wadsley. And in those highly organised days an activist with the same title was in charge of every locality. On the top of the vast administrative pyramid was perched Albert Ballard himself – bald, round-faced and a smooth, shiny, smiling pink. At the bottom was me, with dozens of other infantrymen in the Labour army. We saw Albert Ballard, Councillor and agent, only rarely. And when we did meet our commander-in-chief we treated him with a respect that was indistinguishable from awe. For he was one of those self-educated men who never let their education end, and as well as quoting from the Thomas Hardys and George Eliots of his WEA past he could produce long passages from the fashionable authors of the day – Hemingway, Waugh, Huxley, Orwell and, above all, Bernard Shaw – with a facility that the City Grammar's teachers could not match. But it was his rank rather than his erudition that impressed us most. He was in charge of the election. The law required that his name be printed on every pamphlet and poster. On him the campaign hung suspended. For he told us at the first workers' meeting – and George Darling unhesitatingly agreed – that elections were won on canvassing not candidates, poll cards not policies and, above all, the accurately-marked electoral register shrewdly used on Polling Day for the rallying of the faithful.

I was so convinced of the importance of organisation that, during that first election campaign, I denied myself the pointless pleasure of swelling the audiences at our own public meetings. Or, at least, I never wasted time listening to sermons when there was a chance to march towards the sound of gunfire and engage the enemy. On two evenings, when it had become too dark for successful canvassing and I had been assured that the day's ration of election addresses had been tied into bundles, I left the Committee Rooms before the lights were switched off for the night. And I hurried to witness the last moments of democracy's ritual being acted out in the dingy schoolrooms of the constituency. In Shalesmoor, the meeting was almost over when I arrived. I heard and saw no more than the Chairman's valedictory remarks, which urged the audience 'not to be put off because George has got letters after his name'. He spoke as if the MA was a mistake which the candidate would never have made if he had realised what risks were faced by working men who sampled education. In the school hall at Marcliffe Intermediate, there was so much *sotto voce* criticism from the back rows that the Master of Arts was totally inaudible. My comments to the mannerless Tories who surrounded me were somehow mistaken for an attempt to start a fight. I was still explaining that what I had said about cowardice was not a challenge but a rebuke, concerning the honourable obligation to heckle loudly enough to be identified or not at all, when Albert Ballard came in. He drew me aside, and in a voice that revealed the pain he felt at the discovery that I had learned so little, taught me another political lesson. 'Don't waste your breath on them,' he said; 'they've made up their minds already.' For all his enthusiasm for William Morris and his devotion to the works of the ethical socialists, Councillor Ballard took an essentially pragmatic view of the way in which his job should be done.

Only once did I allow myself to be diverted from my search for the marked register – a prize I pursued as if it were the Holy Grail. The causes of my sudden desertion I have blocked from my mind. But I still only recall with shame that on one Friday night, Syd and I (abetted and accompanied by Les Higgins) swelled the audience at a public meeting addressed by the Tory candidate – Sir Knowle Edge, Bart. Sir Knowle – it was generally agreed in the Labour Committee Rooms – was as much victim as villain. For the rumour was passed from canvasser to committee-room clerk and from poll captain to sub-agent that he had been deceived into believing that he would win the seat, and that he had offered to finance his own election as a down-payment on the fame that would shortly be his. He already possessed a fortune, for he was the owner of a company which manufactured and marketed 'Dolly Dyes'. In vain I tried to convince myself that there was nothing intrinsically ridiculous about 'Dolly Dyes'. I knew that we had used them at Airedale Road, mixing the contents of the little cloth bag of chemicals with the final rinse of the living-room curtains in order to turn them from faded blue into streaky brown. But in the heady atmosphere of the hustings, confronted by the Union Jack-covered table, the rosetted platform party and Sir Knowle Edge himself, I joyously joined in the weak-minded catcalls about true colours, and attempts to tart up the old and threadbare to look as if it were new. Sir Knowle faced all the barracking with a bemused stoicism, confirming my view that the Tories were the stupid party. He was marvellously archetypal in black jacket, double-breasted waistcoat, striped trousers and clipped toothbrush moustache. I felt like a hound who had scented and seen his quarry. The prospect of tasting blood was so exciting that I was home, in bed and half asleep before I remembered that I had been absent without leave from the real battle. I was unconscious before I had completed my calculation of how many houses I might have canvassed had I not chosen the romance rather than the reality of politics.

My sudden self-indulgence must have been forgiven. For I was included in the list of praetorian élite who were allowed to defend George Darling's interests at the counting of the votes. It was so rare an honour for one of my tenderish years that Margaret Hatch – a girl from Abbeydale Grammar School with whom I swapped ambiguously Freudian abuse on the way to school each morning – refused to believe that I was to be trusted with the huge responsibility of making sure that Labour ballots were not piled on Conservative heaps. But Miss Hatch's contention that it was 'just another one of your stories' was wrong – as I proved by confronting her mother in the street and requiring her to read my name on the letter of appointment. I took the letter with me when, on the Sunday before Polling Day, I attended the meeting of all Labour's scrutineers. One by one, we took the oath of secrecy. Collectively we rehearsed what Councillor Ballard assured us was a vital performance. The secret of success was, he emphasised, in taking up a position on the right of the counting clerk and concentrating on every ballot paper that moved from hand to table. I did not have the courage to ask if I should take up a different position in the event of my counting clerk being left-handed. Nor did I understand the stern injunction that we must not enjoy ourselves. I knew that a formal celebration was planned back at the Co-op when the votes were safely gathered in. And I meant to concentrate on the exact positions of the pencilled crosses harder than I had ever concentrated on anything before. But I intended to enjoy it.

On Polling Day, determined to justify the confidence which Mr Ballard had placed in me, I went straight to the Committee Room from school. I was joined there by Rosemary Emans, who had agreed to 'knock out' with me as the Labour Party capitalised on our thorough canvass and carefully-marked register to remind our 'promises' that the time had come to redeem their pledges. I suppose that Rosemary and I exchanged brief and furtive embraces in the 'ginnels' between the rows of Hillsborough's terraced houses. But she was there for reinforcement, not romance, and together we hammered away at the locked and bolted doors until the polling booths were closed. Because we worked longer than anyone else, I arrived back at the Committee Rooms after all the other scrutineers had left for the Town Hall and the count, taking with them the pass with which I was to gain admission. They had, I was told, been released from all comradely obligations by an angry Uncle Syd who had announced that I was 'hanging about somewhere with a girl'. I was too anxious to be angry myself and too determined to get in to the count to stay anxious for long. Abandoning Rosemary, I set off in hot pursuit of a city-bound tramcar, and the pass which would get me in to the count.

At the Town Hall's side door I was confronted by a friendly, gullible or perceptive inspector of police who readily agreed to accompany me to the Council Chamber where, I assured him (with an authority which was enhanced by the very sound of the name) Councillor Ballard expected me. Relieved rather than embarrassed, I took up my place on the right hand of a counting clerk and stared hard at the confusion of ballot papers which he was about to sort into neat piles. Of course, George Darling won. And because we had done our canvassing so well, marked our registers so clearly, and knocked out with such determination, Councillor Ballard was able to predict the size of the victory before the official result was declared. As we awaited the arrival of the Lord Mayor and the formal declaration, I humbly approached George Darling who sprawled on the steps of the Aldermanic Bench more like a conquering Roman general than a Labour and Co-operative Candidate. He signed my scrutineer's pass (which I had recovered from an unrepentant Uncle Syd) and added M.P. after his name for the first time. It had, he assured me, been another landslide victory for Labour. When Alderman Mrs Grace Tebbutt — Mrs Beadows of *South Riding* made flesh — read out '. . . and is therefore elected to serve in Parliament . . .' I felt the stirring of emotion that begins at the back of a bristling neck and ends at the tips of tingling fingers. I would like to pretend that the declaration of the Hillsborough result in the General Election of 1950 was the moment when I decided that one day those words would be used about me. But it would be no more than 'one of Roy Hattersley's stories'. I had made up my mind weeks before that dramatic moment. It had been love at first sight — not with Rosemary Emans, but with the irresistible canvass-cards and the marked-up registers that could not be denied.

22
Deed and Vow

—

The Labour Party shone through my fifth form year at the City Grammar like a vein of silver in a lump of grey Pennine stone. My interest in the theory of socialism was heightened by two masters who admitted their political enthusiasms in a way which was wholly exceptional in those reticent professional days. They did not wear badges on their coats or attempt indoctrination badly disguised as history and current affairs, but simply made no secret of their socialist allegiance and talked to younger members of the fraternal faith in a paternal, though rarely patronising, way. As I managed to insinuate socialism into every classroom discussion and casual conversation, both of them had innumerable opportunities to calm my ardour in a way which increased my enthusiasm. I suppose that to them I seemed to have been redeemed by politics. A year earlier I had been the truant who hid sets of homework essays in the pathetic hope that his indolence would not be discovered. By 1950, I had become the assiduous student of all subjects relevant to the past and prospects of the Labour Party – nineteenth-century history, economic geography, literature as represented by anyone who wrote about politics, Parliament and the working-class struggle which I had just discovered. All that connected last year's villain with this year's visionary was the abiding affection for cricket and football.

Derek Walker, games master and aspiring historian, bridged the gap between the two enthusiasms. During the winter of 1950, he spent whatever time he could spare from selecting me to keep goal for the second football team in reading for an external degree from the University of London. I suspect that it was our mutual interest in history that encouraged him to talk to me on the buses which carried us to away matches, and that our common attachment to games united us at the meetings of the History Society which we attended after school on Tuesday evenings. It was at one such meeting when I – to the distress of the insouciant members of the sixth form who were present – was denouncing 'the capitalist Press' that he gently reminded me that the *Manchester Guardian* was owned and controlled, not by an earl or baron, but by a trust. At the time he seemed to have proved conclusively that at least one paper could be trusted to report and comment with honest objectivity. When the meeting was over, we both agreed that Neville Cardus was the best cricket correspondent in the world, and that 'Old International' wrote about football in a way that the 'ball-flew-from-his-cultured-instep-with-the-speed-of-light' school could not match. Unlike Mrs Potter, he did not assume that the *Manchester Guardian* was as alien to my life and experience as rugby football, an activity which – as I knew nothing about it – I despised.

Rugby was being introduced into the school by Mr Turner, the temporary senior history master who presided over the study of the Great Reform Bill and the Dissolution of the Monasteries whilst the elegant A. W. Goodfellow was away lecturing at the Brincliffe Emergency Teachers' Training College. Mr Turner was more than a Labour supporter. He was a member of the party and an active worker for the cause. Indeed, when Mr Attlee had come to Sheffield to speak at the General Election rally in the City Hall we had smiled at each other across the gangway which separated the Hillsborough contingent from the supporters of Arnold Jennings in Heeley. At some time during my fifth form year, Mr Turner determined to make me into an historian. He told me what general texts to read, and suggested that I tried biographies – 'the most digestible form of history'. For the first time, my father and I were sharing the same book from Hillsborough's public library – *The Second Empire* by Philip Guedalla (for nineteenth-century France was part of our syllabus), Lytton Strachey on *Eminent Victorians*, and a strange, idolatrous life of Napoleon by Lord Rosebery. He also nudged me away from infantile leftism. Queen Mary received much publicity that year for a tapestry which she had woven with her own regal hand and sold on behalf of some military charity. For days the *Sheffield Telegraph* ran articles praising both her talent and her devotion. After the fourth or fifth encomium, I drafted a searing letter comparing the lot of the dowager of Windsor with the life of working wives in Shalesmoor. I proudly showed it to Mr Turner before I posted it to Kemsley House, expecting support – indeed admiration – for the polemic which I had lovingly constructed without having made acquaintance with the word that described my work. We sat down together at the back of the school hall amongst the desks which had been crowded into one of its corners to provide an occasional extra classroom for the overcrowded City Grammar. Safe from disturbance under the brass *Pro Patria Mori* plaques, we discussed the merits of putting my letter in the post. It was the first time that I had been accused of self-indulgence. The letter, he assured me, could serve no purpose other than the glory and gratification of its author. Better silently to improve the conditions in Shalesmoor than loudly to complain about them. I do not believe that I was wholly convinced by his argument. But I tore the letter up and symbolically flushed it down the 'Boys Only' lavatory.

Shalesmoor had become an important symbol of my nascent socialist philosophy. It was certainly one of Sheffield's more dilapidated areas, but it was not more spectacularly decrepit than the districts which surrounded it. But Shalesmoor, like its neighbouring slum of Philadelphia, lay below the Middlewood Road, nearer to the floor of the Don valley and nearer to the factories that huddled along the river's banks than the patches of terraced and back-to-back houses that hung on higher parts of the hillside in Walkley and Crookes. The view of Shalesmoor from the top of passing tramcars (with the water coolers of Neepsend power station in the background and the steelworks chimneys rising from amongst the little houses) made that particular crowded hill a dramatic example of the way in which the dark satanic mills had overrun the green and pleasant land. The power station's official address was Salmon Pastures, a name to which my father always drew my attention as we clanked above it on our way to the city centre. Shalesmoor came to represent all that Blake and Cobbett had written about the ravages of the Industrial Revolution, the Enclosures and the dispossessed who were driven from rural Yorkshire to cough themselves to death in the cutlers' shops of nineteenth-century Sheffield. When I first read Robert Blatchford's *Merrie England*, I thought of Shalesmoor when salmon still swam within walking distance of its then unspoilt hillside. And the *Ragged Trousered Philanthropists* seemed to paint their way to other men's fortunes from the slums that ran their zigzag course between the two arterial roads that joined Sheffield to the Woodhead pass and a different world called Manchester.

Perhaps its grim grey aspect would not, in itself, have been enough to make Shalesmoor the totem which it became. But in one of its shabby streets, I met a family that I imagined to be poor in a way which I had not previously experienced – the grinding, visible, unashamed industrial poverty of the Labour Party pamphlet and the history books of inter-war England. I was canvassing in one of the crowded yards amongst the shared lavatories and communal dustbins when the milkman arrived to exchange pint bottles for little bakelite tokens which working families bought from the Co-op on pay-day as an investment in the daily delivery throughout the coming week. One lady asked for 'tick' – the slate, credit, payment deferred. The milkman was sympathetic. But it was the third time in a week that she had asked for milk without providing the reciprocal token. And since the B and C sold milk only for cash, he could only respond to her request by either paying out of his own pocket or defrauding his employees. The milkman chose the second course, and poured the contents of a full red-top into the 'empty' which was standing on the step. He then smashed the milk-smeared bottle from which his charity had flowed and carefully collected the half-dozen pieces of broken glass. Neatly piled on the back of his electric float, they became evidence that one full bottle had been dropped and that its cost should be written off in his daily account. I was fascinated by the milkman's ingenuity. And I was outraged to observe the real iniquities of the capitalist system which – until that day – I had only hated from a distance. It impoverished working families and it drove honest milkmen to perform acts of complicated fraud. I never considered for a moment that the woman might have been feckless or dissolute, that the weekly wage had been squandered on Woodbines and ale, or that the housekeeping money had been gambled away at the Owleston greyhound track. And I never wondered in what circumstances the milkman had learned his benevolent trick. I had acquired the characteristic that critics of socialism call sentimentality, and which socialists themselves call charity in the best and most noble meaning of that word.

I carried my schoolboy socialism to ridiculous extremes. When Mrs Potter (preparing an inventory for some staff party) asked if any of the currently assembled class could recall the price of butter, I volunteered an estimate of the cost per pound without the subsidy which the caring Labour Government had provided. Mrs Potter smiled, confirming my hope that despite her bourgeois tendencies she was a Labour voter. I investigated, with the determination of an intelligence officer at the Russian Embassy, the political allegiances of the staff who taught me. Mr Turner actually gave me a list of labels – Miss Foster (religious instruction) 'honest reactionary'; 'Buzz'

Hum (senior science master) 'long-standing Fabian'; Mr Withington (junior history) 'really a communist' and Mr Parsons (classics) 'an idiot in the literal sense of the word: no interest in politics at all'. Two members of the staff spoke for themselves. Mr McIver (geography) accosted me in the corridor after an announcement had been pinned to the Debating Society notice-board advertising that I was to propose the motion that 'Property is Theft'. He told me that as Proudhon's proposition was self-evidently ridiculous. No self-respecting person would spend an hour after school considering such a notion. Mr Etchells, on the other hand, revealed quite the opposite philosophical sympathies in the most attractive of circumstances. He had travelled with the second football team to Nether Edge Grammar (where I had saved a penalty), and to my surprise stayed on my homeward-bound tramcar after it had passed through the city centre. Indeed, he found me in the front bay when the other survivors of our massacres had, in the best traditions of second football teams, leapt from the platform. In those days, grammar school football teams played their matches on Saturday mornings, and it was clear that, like me, Mr Etchells was on his way to Hillsborough and Sheffield Wednesday.

We began with some desultory conversation loosely related to the proposition that I might (indeed, should) have saved five of the seven goals which had been scored against us. Mr Etchells, it seemed, had not realised that I had been un-sighted for the first, that the second had been deflected and that the scorer of both the third and the fourth had been offside. I was just about to describe how the sixth and seventh had been the direct responsibility of the incompetent centre-half, when a familiar head appeared at the top of the iron staircase which joined platform to top deck. The head, which slowly turned into a whole person, belonged to Paul Beard, sometime head boy of the City Grammar and, more recently, undergraduate in the University of London and pillar of the Conservative student organisation. I heartily disliked Beard, for he patronised me unmercifully, and possessed expensive clothes, a posh voice and a smooth face which always looked as though it had been bathed during the past hour. I took it for granted that Beard would join us in the front bay. So did Mr Etchells. To my astonishment and delight, he reacted to that prospect with a word which I had never before heard outside church. 'Christ!' he said, 'Beard.' His opinion of the ex-head boy was, he later assured me, based on previous incidents in their brief acquaintance.

During his first year at the school, they had both boarded a tram going in the same direction as the route which we travelled that day. Mr Etchells had foolishly enquired if the football match was their mutual destination, and had been rewarded by a look of outraged disbelief. Beard was incapable of participating in such a mindlessly proletarian pastime. Beard had then expanded views on working-class fecklessness, with special reference to the miners. The County Durham accent suddenly reappearing as if in tribute to his collier forebears, Mr Etchells uttered the astonished condemnation, 'I think he's a Tory.' The emotion which he engendered within me by the surprise discovery of our common passion was so strong that I almost admitted responsibility for the fourth goal. Unfortunately, class solidarity did not prevent my new-found comrade from telling Mr Walker that the blame for the second team's annihilation must be placed on me. The following Saturday, a little boy called Carter (a competent footballer with no political opinions) kept goal.

In the week that I was dropped from the second football team, I dropped French from my curriculum. At the time, the first of the two rejections appeared an intolerable humiliation, whilst the second seemed a merciful relief. In fact, it was absurd to deny me even the chance of obtaining the package of School Certificate passes which were necessary for matriculation and entrance into university. But when I discovered that the potentially damning decision had been taken I rejoiced, regardless of my doom. All I could think of was escape from the constant indignity of Mr Thompson's genial abuse. In the French class we sat in order of linguistic merit – the most fluent boy in the back right-hand corner, and me on the extreme left of the front row. Our lessons took the form of a catechism and the interrogation seemed always to begin with me. I could never respond to the sudden invitation to translate, conjugate or spell, and after a moment's flushed silence some more talented pupil would be invited to lighten my darkness – 'tell him, Newman.' (Or Wilson, Nicholson or Oxley, Stacey or Almond.) And tell me they always did, right up to the moment when I 'dropped' French and began to waste the daily forty minutes that pupils with the gift of tongues spent on the sex of nouns and the irregular behaviour of verbs. I pride myself still that I wasted my time constructively. The rule said that 'private study' periods could be occupied with any 'serious' book. I chose volumes that were serious to the point of absurdity, the by-product of whatever crazy political and philosophical notion I was dabbling in that week. I recall Mr Curtis – a handsome, middle-aged mathematics teacher and tennis-player of the 'professional' variety – doing a sudden check of all the books which lay under his supervisory eye in front of the 'private study' participants. Mine – bought from the Market Hall second-hand bookstall the previous week – was Hilaire Belloc's *Answer to Mr H. G. Wells' History of the World*. I suppose that I had bought it on the strength of the author's reputation as the essayist of fourth-form joys. But I became fascinated by his refutation of natural selection and read on even when, instead of fifteen hundred words on 'Winding Streets' or three pages concerning 'Crossing the Channel', it turned out to be full of rhetorical questions concerning the inability of sea-lions nimbly to climb onto ice-floes, despite ten thousand years in which only the fittest survived. 'Are you really reading this?' Mr Curtis asked. I gave him the sealions right between the eyes and he passed on before I could explain that it was not the survival of the fittest but the survival of the fittest to survive – a very different thing.

Of course, I should have been spending my time on unseens and dictation. For without a modern language or Latin at School Certificate level most universities would have been closed to me. By the spring of 1950, a degree was at least an aspiration which we openly discussed. And the minimum entrance requirements were common knowledge to both my parents and to me. Yet for a combination of reasons, which ranged from awe of authority to fear of failure, we allowed ourselves to be talked into accepting a potentially lethal academic handicap. Mr Northeast assured my mother that I would fail in French. But he did not add that it was the habit in grammar schools of the period to withdraw all examination candidates who were not certain of success in order to keep the ratio of 'candidates entered' to 'candidates passed' admirably high when the results were published in the local papers. He did however talk airily about 'pumping a bit of Latin' into me when School Certificate was over. My mother accepted his judgement because she knew no better. I welcomed it because part of me was still a feckless fool who fantasised about a life in Labour politics rather than worked towards its achievement. We were all dreaming the most destructive dream of all – the one in which, somehow, everything always turned out right in the end.

And there were plenty of pleasant distractions behind which I could hide myself when reality – as represented by School Certificate

– became particularly unpleasant. One was the selection for the First XI. I did not open the batting or field at first slip as were my proper deserts. But going in at number six and patrolling the third-man boundary provided pleasures which were wonderful to experience and better still to contemplate. I also acquired a dog from our butcher, whose pedigree Labrador had provided an unwelcome litter of mongrel pups. My mother and I visited his farm to make our choice and were shown the unwanted whelps sound asleep on old sacks in front of a coke fire. Their owner bent down and gently (at least for a farming butcher) shook them awake to display their lovable, puppyish characteristics. Three of them slowly tottered – legs bowed and eyes still half closed – across the stone floor. The fourth bit his hand. Of course, she was the one we chose.

I doubt if Dinah (as we chose to call her) ever bit a human being again. She did, however, cause her owners every problem that a dog is capable of inflicting on its best friends. Her affection for men, women and children was not matched by regard for other living creatures. She fought dogs of every size and chased cats of any colour. She caught bees and butterflies in her mouth, and once (having demonstrated the speed of her reflexes on a wasp) was so badly stung on the roof of her mouth that she ran screaming through the churchyard and was only found after two days of assiduous searching, and three expensive advertisements in the *Star*. As we were opposed to 'unnatural operations', we spent weeks of each year protecting her from male assault. And since she had no concern either for honour or chastity, she broke through or burrowed under every fence and barricade which we built around the garden. So we pursued her through street and churchyard, determined to save her virginity. She contracted every ailment known to dog. The hair on her shoulders fell out, leaving patches of black, scaly skin exposed like leather epaulettes. The pads of her feet split unless she had constant paw-baths. Her ears were infected, and she had an extraordinary talent for getting corn-stalks stuck up her nostrils. She was run over by an Austin Seven whilst overcome by an uncontrollable fit of pre-walk hysteria, and I had to hold her down on the veterinary surgeon's bench as he sewed her leg together. Bandaged from dew-claw to haunch, she turned her one great virtue into a vice. My mother had trained her never to defecate in the garden. Too old a dog to learn new tricks, she sat on the grass which we had begun to call a lawn and waited to feel nature call her to Wadsley Common. The only way that we could be certain that she would not burst like a baked apple was to carry her – overweight to the point of Labradorian obesity – each day over the mile of road that separated 101 Airedale Road from open ground.

And saving her life was very important to me. For she represented the quality in life which I admired the most. She was incurably hopeful. On holiday in the corrugated-iron bungalows which we rented for a week each summer, I would watch her chase seagulls along the littered beach. She was fat and she was unhealthy and when on form she could jump eighteen inches into the air. But until the end of her life she believed that one day she would catch a bird in mid-flight just below the clouds.

23

High Summer

—

I never looked forward with any pleasure to our summer week by the sea. Indeed I regarded the whole business, from the evening when I had to pack the old cardboard suitcase to the afternoon when it was empty and back on top of the wardrobe, as a profound nuisance. My aversion to holidays was the result of being easily satisfied rather than hard to please. Despite the regular disasters which overtook me, I immensely enjoyed the routine by which I lived for fifty-one weeks of the year, and I was deeply reluctant to abandon it for the fifty-second. Indeed, all that I was prepared to do during our annual trip to the sea was to transport the portable parts of Airedale Road to Humanby Gap, Theddlethorpe St Helen or wherever my mother had chosen. The Labour Party had to be temporarily left behind. But books – more than I could possibly open between Saturday and Saturday – weighed down my suitcase. And the tennis rackets were packed in the certainty that Uncle Syd (who came with us in the early Fifties, when he had lost contact with his training college cronies) could be persuaded out of retirement and onto the nearest public court. Whatever event or outing was prepared, I had to be back at our asbestos-and-corrugated-iron bungalow at ten minutes to two when the BBC broadcast the 'lunchtime scoreboard'. But even when I had re-created some of the pleasures and pastimes of home, holidays still involved an almost literally intolerable inconvenience. I could never reconcile myself to the Elsan. It was not the hygiene of the chemical closet which concerned me, but its comfort. I had become an inveterate lavatory reader – having made acquaintance with many of the world's greatest poets in circumstances which I found ideally suited to a quick excursion through a couple of sonnets or a lyric of modest length. In a dark, draughty tin hut literary defecation was impossible. Robbed of one of life's great pleasures, I would morosely button my braces and watch Dinah kick sand and seaweed high into the air with her back legs as a symbol that she had completed a more satisfactory experience. My envy sometimes bordered on hatred.

In the summer of School Certificate, we went east for our usual week. Then I actually pestered for permission to go on a second holiday of my own. Geoffrey Kirkby (by then a games master, magnificent in a Loughborough blazer with a Greek discus thrower on the pocket) and Harold Woolhouse (about to work for a year in a market-garden for a year as preparation for his botany course at Reading University) invited me to join them at a farm camp – an institution invented by the Ministry of Agriculture to enable students and the indigent poor to earn a few pounds by helping to bring the harvest home. My parents were against it from the start. But after a campaign of persuasion which really amounted to unremitting persecution, I was given a couple of pounds and allowed to pack the fast-disintegrating cardboard suitcase in preparation for my journey to Cannock Chase.

It rained all week. For the first two days the downpour was so heavy that apart from a quick and damp journey to the mess hall in the decaying mansion from which the camp was run, we just sat on our beds in the old Nissen hut and listened to the storm beating on the roof. On Monday the pattern of the deluge changed. Each morning the crops were given enough drenching to ensure that they could not be picked, cut or lifted during the rest of the day. Then, our prospects of employment having been extinguished, the sun came out and after a few hours of misty uncertainty we were surrounded by a fair imitation of a pleasant early autumn afternoon. We played scratch games of cricket, for I had providently brought the older of my two bats. We improvised a sort of rugby against a party of French students, one of whom intentionally kicked me on the head. And we deeply resented the presence and behaviour of a group of Egyptians who were clearly too rich to need the £5 a week maximum wage, and were only posing as prospective peasant labour in order to meet the girls who inhabited another group of Nissen huts on the other side of the compound. Despite their money and their Levantine good looks, we possessed an asset which they could not match. It was Geoff Kirkby's blazer. Among the hopeful female farmers were four hockey and lacrosse enthusiasts who were whiling away the weeks before they became students at a ladies' college of physical education. They found the discus thrower irresistible. His glory was reflected on Harold Woolhouse and me.

Mine (though the possessive pronoun was never really accepted by her) was called Olga George and came from Wimslow. We ate together each day in the dining hall, played desultory games in the damp afternoons, and went together to the local public house during the balmy September evenings. I did not feel at all comfortable in the pub for – unlike the others – I was wholly innocent of alcohol. Whenever it was mentioned in our living-room my father was vaguely disapproving and my mother was violently opposed to anything other than total abstinence. The difference in their attitudes sprang from a difference in their childhood experiences. My paternal grandfather drank heavily, sang in public houses, and wasted money which he could not afford; but drunkenness made him sentimental, not violent. My mother's father drank as a by-product of his major vice, but the penniless Brackenburys drew no moral distinction between the gambling away of his wages and the stealing of the grocery money to buy drinks in the places where the card-schools were arranged. In almost seventeen years I had come into direct family contact with drink only once. Sometime in the early Forties, Uncle George, on leave from the Government Audit office in Watford or St Albans, had visited his old friends at the Sheffield Assistance Board. Instead of getting home for lunch as promised he had not returned by mid-afternoon. The family's natural assumption was that he had been run over by a bus or knocked down by a tramcar. Our equally inevitable response to the tragedy was to stand in the front window anxiously awaiting the arrival of policeman, ambulance or bloodstained uncle. At about seven o'clock, George appeared at the end of the road. For a few seconds we noticed nothing unusual about his appearance or his gait. Then we realised that as well as looking dishevelled he was making slow and unsteady progress in our direction. Indeed, he only remained upright with the assistance of walls, fences and railings. When he actually tottered in through the back door, he had the sense at once to make his silent way to bed. We all behaved typically. I giggled nervously. My mother was both disgusted and outraged. My father explained that, 'not being used to it', George had, no doubt, succumbed to a relatively small quantity of alcohol.

Ten years later as Olga and I trod the path which led to the farm camp's local pub, the spirit of George walked by our side. My most vivid memory of him remained the last sad parting – the saying of things which should never be said, and my mother's error in believing that my uncle (rather than his new wife) had fastened the crooked sergeant's stripes to his sleeve. Her innocent explanation that she had 'never for a moment thought that they had been sewn on by a woman' provoked George into the ultimate retaliation – the removal of his old dressing-gown from behind the bathroom door, despite the implicit understanding that it had been hung there when he left Sheffield in 1938 for my father's exclusive use. And together George, Vera and the dressing-gown abandoned us for ever. As I crossed the tap-room threshold I feared that, like George, my degradation would begin with drink and end with a permanent parting from Airedale Road.

I took the fateful step and stood before the bar, uncertain and embarrassed. Fortunately our athletic young ladies seemed accustomed to the proceedings and procedures, and the only question left for me to answer was whether my 'half' should be mild or bitter. I chose mild because I assumed from its name that it contained a less lethal dose of alcohol. Our companions – unusual for those unemancipated days – insisted upon buying their rounds. Indeed when, on the Tuesday, Olga and I hitch-hiked in search of Lichfield Cathedral and only got as far as the outskirts of Walsall and a matinée performance of James Mason and Margaret Lockwood in *The Wicked Lady*, she insisted on paying half the cost of both the tickets and the fish and chips which sustained us during the journey home. By Wednesday, we had run out of money. I agreed to be the one who wrote home and asked for emergency funds, which the others would help to repay on our return to Sheffield. And on Friday morning – the day before our departure – I received the £5 note which I knew my mother would register to us by the first available post. It was pinned to a message which I also anticipated with dread certainty. 'Surely,' the reproachful letter concluded, 'with so little time left before you are *supposed* to return home, five pounds will be enough *for you all*.' My friends all agreed that I was lucky to have parents who responded so quickly and generously to my appeal. Having kept the letter to myself, I knew (though I did not say) that they were almost right.

Despite my mother's forebodings (for the letter, though it was in my father's hand, expressed her sentiments) we arrived home in time and I began to prepare for the City Grammar sixth form. I had done adequately – though not spectacularly well – in my School Certificate. With two distinctions and six credits it was foolishly assumed that despite the absence of the necessary modern language qualification I was bound inevitably for university. Indeed the school's irrational faith in my future was underwritten by a decision that I should take the S-level history paper after two years in the sixth. I was part of the bridging passage between the old School Certificate and the new General Certificate of Education, and I suppose that the decision to cram three years' history into six terms was, in part, an experiment with the new regulations. I felt an undeniable pleasure in the thought that after losing a year of my life in the fourth form, I was about to save half a year in the upper sixth. But in reality, half a year was no better than none. For State Scholarships were only awarded to candidates with high marks in two S-level papers. And, in any event, the State Scholarship for which I could not qualify had little other than kudos to offer the pupils in Sheffield schools. University admissions were decided before the third year results were known. And thanks to almost thirty years of Labour rule, every one of the city's university students received a grant of State Scholarship value. So for all practical purposes my 'scholarship paper' was a waste of time. I would have been far better employed working on the Latin which was essential to my matriculation and university entrance. But nobody — teachers, parents or pupils — chose to take that practical course. The nearer I got to the higher education which my parents determined should be mine, the more difficulty we all found in overcoming our ignorance of the brave new academic world for which I was destined.

I was coached for pointless success in my Scholarship Level paper by A. W. Goodfellow MA, who had returned from the Brincliffe Emergency Teachers' Training College to reclaim his City Grammar kingdom. It was an inheritance about which he felt ambivalent emotions. For it was his clear and open conviction that he should have become the school's headmaster when Mr Northeast retired and was succeeded by Mr Davies. On the basis of the inadequate evidence available to a sixth form boy, he was right, for he combined an interest in education in general with a real affection for the City Grammar in particular. And even the insensitive teenagers of the sixth form recognised his genuine concern for the welfare and reputation of the school at which he had learned as a boy and taught when a man. But to us his tribal loyalty was nothing like so impressive as his appearance and demeanour. He was the most elegant man that we had ever seen. Whilst other masters came to school in Harris tweed jackets and check shirts, A. W. Goodfellow wore a pinstripe double-breasted suit and a starched white collar. When he used the word 'parliament' he pronounced every syllable. And he complimented the style of his dress and his language with an intellectual elegance which we were, even then, able to recognise – although it was beyond our powers to describe. He taught proper reverence for the improving passion of Victorian England and for the radicals who wanted to build social reform into the industrial revolution. I learned from him that William Ewart Gladstone was the greatest of all Prime Ministers and that piety is acceptable in politics if it is genuine. He introduced me to John Bright and Samuel Smiles and he persuaded me to read Kitto's *The Greeks* and Eileen Power's *Medieval People*. And it was from A. W. Goodfellow that I discovered the Great Exhibition, the civic arboreta with their labelled trees, the botanical gardens with the learned notices hung on the plants and the Mechanics' Institutes – all seeking to teach working men about the wonders of the world.

He was the first man I ever met who ruthlessly exploited the power of the self-deprecatory joke and the attraction of the carefully calculated indiscretion. He always apologised for invented inadequacies in a way which made it absolutely clear that no apology was either necessary or really offered, and he talked about his own imagined deficiencies in a way which clearly demonstrated his confidence that no such deficiencies existed. When he illustrated a point about the Enclosures with an aside about a loutish agricultural labourer called Hodge, he affected embarrassment that he had inadvertently chosen to illustrate bucolic barbarism with the name of the senior geography master, and insisted that any name was preferable to that of a 'silly Shakespearean fairy'. He allowed his four male scholarship candidates to overhear an aside about the sixth form lacking a single bedworthy girl, and raised his hand to his face in counterfeit consternation that we had been subjected to his unthinking indecency. Hand to face was his characteristic pose, and he spent much time and muscular effort smoothing down with crooked little finger his already smooth hair. His left elbow seemed always to be in the air. We thought that we had come face to face with sophistication. Perhaps we had. At least we had learned that the word did not have to mean Noêl Coward and long silver cigarette-holders.

Mr Goodfellow became my form-master when I entered the lower sixth (boys), and when I moved on to the upper sixth for my final year he moved up with me. So our little community – pastoral and academic – was preserved for six terms. Within it I had two particular friends, neither of whom could abide each other. Michael Beeley of the Hillsborough Park Tennis Club and the youngest of the cricketing Beeley brothers was, like me, a Labour supporter who concentrated his scholastic enthusiasm on history and English. Malcolm Tyson, an orphan of uncertain age with whom I had struck up an acquaintance in the lower forms, could play no games, supported Sheffield United instead of Wednesday and was, we suspected, a secret Conservative. But the ties that bound Tyson and me in the fourth and fifth forms still held us close in the sixth. And because both Beeley and Tyson were friends of mine they at least behaved as if they were friends of each other.

Together we faced Mrs Potter for at least one lesson every day. Beeley insisted that he and the myopic English mistress had always worked together in complete harmony. Tyson found her irredeemably intolerant and intolerable. I warmed to her as my two years in the sixth form progressed. For she, like Mr Goodfellow, was privileged to introduce me to previously unknown delights. With Mrs Potter I worked my way through the glossary of the Warwick *Hamlet*, and weighed the evidence for the Prince of Denmark's flesh being 'sullied' rather than the more commonly accepted 'solid'. I discovered that Satan could become a hero when John Milton wrote about him, that T. S. Eliot had some interesting things to say about difficult poetry and that Robert Browning had written verse of a complication that readers of *The Golden Treasury* would never have expected. When we argued about *Saint Joan*, Mrs Potter's views about nationalism confirmed that, despite her élite habits, she was a socialist at heart. She also talked to me about writing itself; about clarity being the essential ingredient of any acceptable style, and clarity being the product of conscientious concentration as much as natural talent. 'There are no synonyms in the English language,' Mrs Potter used to insist. Selecting the precisely correct adjective and noun was, she made me believe, a great and noble enterprise.

I actively looked forward to the time I spent each day on history and English, and I even enjoyed my daily lesson in geography – the third subject in my A-level syllabus. There was never the joy and glory in tracing maps and learning how the glaciers changed the face of England that I found in Shakespeare, or G. M. Trevelyan on the

Italian Risorgimento. But I convinced myself that a passing acquaintance with the principal exports of the South American states and a working knowledge of the European railway system would be invaluable preparation for the life of politics which lay ahead. In fact, the only objectionable part of my work was Latin which, since I was learning by rote like a child, I treated with the silly irresponsibility of a child five years my junior. Homework was once more cribbed and copied. The consequences of failing the all-important O-level examination were thrust out of my mind. Edgar Parsons, the genial eccentric who struggled to teach me, became an ogre whose absence through sickness was a cause for rejoicing and whose physical presence made me shudder with aversion and antagonism. But not even the horrors of *North and Hilliard* could significantly diminish the peculiar sensation of being happy at school. I set off unnecessarily early each morning after impatiently consuming the cooked (but by some strange alchemy usually cold) breakfast that my mother insisted upon frying as the proper preparation for the day. I looked forward to seven out of the day's eight lesson periods. And I thought of the staff — Etchells and Walker as well as Goodfellow, Potter and Hodge — as my senior friends to be treated with a fraternal respect. If one cloud darkened my horizon it was not the prospect of the impending examinations nor the scramble to find a place in a university. It was the realisation that, as I was growing up, reality must now take the place of fantasy. I had become a far greater success in lessons than I had ever been on the playing field, and I had to adjust my life accordingly.

24
In that Dawn

—

For the academic survivors who had cleared the eleven-plus hurdle
and completed the five-year steeplechase to School Certificate, the
old grammar school sixth forms provided a life which was entire in
itself. The City Grammar was certainly my place of work. And I
worked in it and for it harder than I had ever worked before. But it
was also the scene of my pleasure and the site of my entertainment. I
still went occasionally to the pictures with my parents, and remained
a rigidly regular attender at Ward Labour Party meetings. My father,
Syd and I continued our traditional winter excursions to see Sheffield
Wednesday play. Indeed, our football horizons widened. For one
Saturday, as we made our way to the ground, Uncle George appeared
around the corner of Marcliffe Road. He was searching for his
long-lost brothers and had anticipated the route which they would
follow at half-past two when Wednesday were at home. My father
openly wept. Syd behaved as if it was not the first time they had met
during the years of official estrangement, and George expressed
astonishment to find 'little Roy' six feet tall and wearing a trilby hat.
And during the slow weeks of reconciliation which followed, we
joined him on Sheffield United's Spion Kop as often as he travelled
across the city to Hillsborough. But despite these extended delights,
the centre of my existence was the City Grammar. I practised football
and played club cricket after representing the school in the morning,
listened to *Take it from Here* only when my homework essay was
written, and generally saw the rest of my life as an adjunct of and
extension to the delights and diversions which were offered me in
Orchard Lane.

There was only one need that the City Grammar could not meet –
girls. There were, of course, a lot of them about. Indeed, more than
half of the school's population was female; for as well as containing
girls of conspicuous talent the sixth form included others with
inadequate School Certificates and little hope of success at A-Level,
who simply hung around waiting for places in teachers' training

colleges. But none of my peers ever attracted me. In the fifth form I had worshipped from afar the head prefect, whose name I now forget. And in my final term I felt a brief (and unreciprocated) infatuation for a sixteen-year-old replica of Anne Baxter. But neither the older woman to whom I never spoke nor the child who rebuffed my every advance sat with me in class between nine and four. It was, I have no doubt, a weakness in my character. But I could never feel any attraction for a girl who confused the two Home Rule Bills, or could not understand why Andrea del Sarto was not satisfied with being called 'the perfect painter'. The girls I met outside the school did not face the constant humiliation of returned essays with 'C' on the bottom. Nor were they obliged to run about in navy blue knickers holding hockey sticks in their hands as if they were as adept at women's sports as I was at men's games. No doubt the girls I saw outside school were less scholarly than my colleagues and contemporaries in the sixth form. And, Olga George apart, they were certainly less athletic. But their deficiencies were not as cruelly exposed as the shortcomings of Pat Taylor, Pat Coulson, Olga Bennett and Shirley Jago. Towards the very end of what our school magazine would have called my 'school career', I did make an unsuccessful foray in Miss Jago's direction. But when she contemptuously ignored me I felt neither pain nor embarrassment. I simply assumed that she was experiencing the aversion that I felt when I listened to her friends attempting to read Shelley or Keats aloud. Romance was struck dead by one touch of cold philosophy – or (to be more precise) history, English, geography and Latin.

For the first few sixth form months I preserved my friendship with Olga George. Indeed, the whole farm camp menage re-assembled in Manchester for a sort of reunion. I visited the George family in suburban Cheshire, and Olga came to Sheffield for a day and was given tea at Airedale Road. We wrote to each other twice each week and, after one of the visits, her next letter to me contained an implication of mild carnality. My mother decided that my father must express the disgust she knew that he felt – and so reveal that she had been regularly intercepting and reading my mail. It was not the sort of task at which he excelled. So instead of feeling embarrassed by the revelation that I had dallied in shop doorways, or angry at the discovery that my privacy had been so grossly infringed, I simply felt sorry for my father as he struggled to do my mother's bidding. In any event, I knew that Olga was a passing pleasure, which would not survive our months of separation. She was, no doubt, caught up in the delights of her training college, and I was enmeshed in the joys of the City Grammar sixth form. For a child first fed on Greyfriars and Billy Bunter, and then weaned on *Tom Brown's Schooldays*, the mere fact of being in the 'sixth' was a cause for rejoicing. So assuming all the offices and honours that the municipal grammar schools had copied from the ancient foundations on which they were so assiduously modelled made certain that all the little stars in my life revolved round the single sun of the City Grammar School. Anything outside its orbit was not in my universe.

In the lower sixth, I first became captain of Zulu House and then, in the summer, captain of cricket. City Grammar preferment was decided by a form of guided democracy. Candidates were first judged by their peers – the whole house assembled for Tuesday morning prayers, or the two cricket teams which had been selected for the first fixtures of the season. But the victor's election was only confirmed after it had been endorsed by a designated member of staff. In 1951 not even Miss Foster (still teaching religious knowledge, and the school's oldest inhabitant) could remember an occasion when the popular will had been denied. The secret of the double decision's invariable success lay in the sophistication (and sycophancy) of the pupils, who never made a choice of which their elders and betters disapproved. And after the Zulu House and the cricket teams had been polled Mrs Potter and Mr Walker duly announced that they had no objection to the choices that had been made. My second year in the sixth form began with two simultaneous elections. In my final year I was qualified to become a prefect. The day after I had been confirmed as house captain, Mr Goodfellow read out the list which was to be submitted for the headmaster's approval. He clearly believed that Mr Davies's endorsement was a formality. Mike Beeley and I congratulated each other, and prepared for a year of glorious authority; patrolling the corridors at lunchtime, keeping little boys in after school and tyrannising teenage girls as a substitute for more intimate relationships. We would have to submit to the rule which required prefects to wear a City Grammar tie on all occasions. But that was a small price to pay for the inestimable advantage of being able to announce the recognition of our leadership-potential on our university application forms.

When, the following day, the new prefects were summoned to the headmaster for the laying-on of hands and the lecture about keeping the crates of milk-bottles tidy, two of the names on the list did not receive an invitation. One of them was a girl whose exclusion was not unexpected. She had transferred from another school a year before and always wore the navy-blue uniform of her previous Alma Mater, rather than the bottle-green of the City Grammar. Despite warnings that Mr Davies was a stickler for proper dress, she had made it plain that she was not prepared to throw away a perfectly good gym-slip and blazer just for the dubious privilege of pinning a fancy badge on the new livery which she would be forced to buy. Even then, in the heyday of selective education and the symbols of superiority with which the grammar schools surrounded themselves, we were all appalled by the irrationality of Mr Davies's insistence that the colour of clothes should be a crucial factor in the decisions on how to distribute the City Grammar's greatest honour. I was even more outraged by the Headmaster's refusal to accept another of the names submitted to him. For it was mine.

Mr Davies, being that sort of man, had made sure that the putative prefects were called to their initiation ceremony just as afternoon school was ending. When the four o'clock bell rang I left for home, passing on my way Mr Alan Goodfellow, little finger on head, MA gown flapping in the draught which blew along our corridors, and enthusiasm all aroused for the task of congratulating the recently-anointed. He enquired where on earth I was going. 'Home,' I answered in a way which made clear that much was amiss, but did not acknowledge that he was in no way responsible for my misfortune. There was no attempt to detain me; only a scrupulously polite – but entirely irresistible – suggestion that I should see him in the sixth form room at half-past eight next morning. Despite a sleepless night, I turned up on time. It was, Mr Goodfellow announced before I could open my mouth, essential that I did not keep the headmaster waiting. There followed some convoluted courtesies concerning the respect properly due to so august and distinguished a figure, and I hurried off trying to look as serious as the portentous occasion demanded.

I was invited to become a prefect in a conversation which seemed wholly relaxed and natural, even though it made no mention of my absence from the previous night's more general soirée. I was reminded of my obligation to eschew all neckwear except the school tie, and warned that in a week or two I would be asked to nominate a passage from the Bible to read at morning assembly, and to choose a hymn to follow my reading. I told Mr Davies – perhaps a little too quickly – that I could offer him my selection at once. It was Chapter 21 of the Revelation of St John the Divine, verses 1–8, and William Blake's *Jerusalem* set to music by Hubert Parry. There was a pause – caused, I now suspect, by the headmaster's surprise at my swift response. I filled the silence with an explanation that the extract from the scriptures and the sacred song were both concerned with the same theme – redemption. For a moment Mr Davies looked both startled and impressed. Was I, he enquired, religious? Before the cock crowed thrice, I had decided not to explain that I had learned both the words and music in the Labour Party.

Mr Goodfellow seemed to enjoy my account of the interview, and assured me that I had been right to avoid all reference to socialism. I expected him to go on with a detailed account of how, the previous evening, he had confronted Mr Davies in the headmaster's study and insisted upon my elevation. He did no such thing. 'Look here, old man,' he said; 'I had a frightful job last night. I had to plead and I had to make promises. He had looked up your record. Something about stealing books and pretending to look for them. Something else about truancy to watch a cricket match.' Mr Goodfellow had not enjoyed the conversation. But he had insisted that new leaves had been turned and old habits abandoned. He had also 'given his word' that I would be an exemplary prefect, and he was beginning to wonder how he could fulfil his pledge. He need not have worried, for I had abandoned my life of crime. But for the rest of the year he took no chances. Even after two terms of meritorious conduct he was still cautious. When Auntie Annie died, my parents irresponsibly arranged the funeral on a Thursday when Yorkshire were playing at Bramall Lane. I made my advance apologies without a thought. But on the evening before our solemn journey to Worksop, Alan Goodfellow 'phoned me at home and led me through a highly artificial conversation during which I was manoeuvred into repeating over and over again that on the following day I would be in Steetley Churchyard when Uncle Ern once more performed his duties as Chief Mourner, Principal Mute and Undertaking Consultant. After Mr Goodfellow and I had been through every detail of the burial service, I suddenly realised the object of the bizarre duologue. Affront and impatience combined. Impertinently I asked if he would like to speak to my father and confirm that I was not lying. He sounded genuinely hurt. 'Of course not, old chap. Never for a moment thought you were.'

By then, it was too late to alienate me from life in the City Grammar sixth form. For it had provided delights which, without its improving influence, I would never have realised existed. Now, all the joy seems to have been based on a single sentence from one of Bernard Shaw's prefaces about which Mrs Potter and I argued. It concerned the necessity of confusing pleasure with work. During my last two years at school, I found it more and more difficult to distinguish between the emotion and the activity. When I wrote a poem for *The Holly Leaf*, the City Grammar's magazine, I loved every agonising minute of the hours it took to beat it into publishable form. Yet when I handed it over, I was treated as if I had just written an 'A+' essay. It was, of course, concerned with politics, and was dedicated to the Labour Government that lost office as I was taking my Advanced Level trial examinations. All that I now remember is the puerile opening couplet:

They might have done much better, but they could have done much
  worse;
What has left the rich man's pocket is now in the poor man's
  purse . . .

— and the anonymous peon of poetic praise for Lord Woolton that some member of staff was persuaded to write to maintain proper political balance. In the same edition of *The Holly Leaf* I published my account of a 'geography expedition' to Ingleton. It proved my first lesson in the dangers of irony.

Ingleton is an area and Ingleborough is, perversely, not a town but one of the three peaks which stand in triangular guard over the area. Together with Mr Hodge and five fellow candidates for A-level geography, I climbed the 2,600 feet and placed a stone on the cairn which marked the summit. We also climbed Whernside and Pen-y-Ghent, and in three days we learned more about limestone country than books could have taught us in a year. We saw Malham Cove and Gordale Scar — great white cliffs cut into the land like a Yorkshire version of King Solomon's Mines. And I stood breathless at the sight of Malham Tarn, a glacial lake of such agoraphobic beauty that I expected a hand holding a sword suddenly to break the silver surface of the water. I wrote about it all when we returned to Sheffield, not in an attempt to put on paper the lyricism that the scenery made me feel but in the brittle language of a seventeen-year-old embarrassed by an unaccustomed aesthetic experience. One of our little party – I think it was a girl – had developed a stomach complaint on the second day. And I described her misfortune (and our decision to press on despite the absence of one of the team) in the vocabulary of Scott's last expedition. Such pretensions were, I was assured by the junior English staff who edited the magazine, wholly inappropriate to three days in the North Riding. When I explained that the language was intentionally unsuitable, they threatened to withdraw the article from *The Holly Leaf*. Fortunately, a last-minute excision proved impossible. So the piece appeared, and I began to experience a frustration that has persisted for over thirty years. The irony was taken literally and I was abused for overstating the drama of the occasion.

I did not mind. I knew what I intended to write and I judged my account a great success. In those two happy years, I could not recognise failure when I saw it. I was the one house captain who could neither run nor jump. But I entered my name in the athletic heats, was cheerfully knocked out in the early rounds and turned up, smiling, on Sports Day to watch more fleet and agile boys breast the tapes and win the cups. When I was asked to play one of the eponymous heroes in *Androcles and the Lion*, I gladly accepted the feline part. And when, because of my inability to walk downstairs on all fours whilst wearing a lion-suit, I was asked to resign from the cast, I gladly stood down and turned up to every public performance in the genuine hope that I might be able to help with behind-stage chores. The sixth form engulfed me in euphoria and I was unable to understand how anyone connected with it could find it in any way unrewarding or unattractive. When I was discarded from the first football team, I rejoiced that I had once played in the first football team. When I scored a duck for the first cricket team I marvelled that I was captain of the first cricket team. Pollyanna had come to male life in the Sheffield of the 1950s. The contentment that turns into complacency was most dramatically demonstrated during the winter of 1951. Aping the Festival of Britain, the school had decided to have a celebration of drama and music of its own. My only role was aesthete and critic. Together with other intellectually-inclined members of the sixth form, I sat in the front row of the school hall as assorted junior pupils played Chopin nocturnes on the old piano, recited poems learned from the elocution classes which they attended or acted out little playlets chosen and rehearsed in their classes. Then in the Music (Individual Performance) Class, a nubile girl from the fifth form shuffled barefoot onto the stage and began to sing, with excruciating incompetence, a popular song of the time called 'Keep Your Shoes on, Lucy'. There was suppressed commotion amongst the panel of judges. Mrs Potter was visibly close to collapse. Neither Mr Walker nor Mr Goodfellow (usually, in their different ways, the most self-protective of men) attempted to disguise their embarrassment. Mr Etchells seemed to be enjoying the performance hugely. Miss Foster appeared to be making a formal complaint to the headmaster. I just sat back and enjoyed it. It was all part of the brave new grammar-school world.

25
Through the Hoop
—

Much as I enjoyed those last two years at school, I never forgot that the City Grammar had a serious purpose. Even before the successful sixth form days I realised – with varying degrees of confidence and understanding – that there was a specific goal at which it was my duty to aim. On the afternoon which followed the second half of the eleven-plus examination my father had suggested that I spent my unexpected free time in an exciting visit to the Weston Park Museum. As the three surviving members of our close-knit family had made our way to the cases of stuffed birds and cabinets of stainless steel cutlery, my mother had waved her hand in the direction of Sheffield University's administration building. 'Today,' she said, 'you have taken your first step towards there.' And she pointed dramatically towards the red brick. I had no clear perception of what she meant. But I realised that the concept of her message was as portentous as the manner of its delivery was dramatic.

The message was constantly repeated. At the end of the City Grammar's first summer term, the headmaster invited morning assembly to applaud a parade of sixth-formers who had been offered university places; I realised that it was my duty to receive an equivalent ovation in six or seven years' time. Sometimes the dream faded. But it was always the prospect of gaining admission to a university against which my performance was measured. My first form result almost extinguished my mother's atavistic dream. But in the second year the flame spluttered again. In the third it always burned fitfully and sometimes it did not burn at all. Yet by the time that I had taken the School Certificate Examination it had become an unquenchable obsession as well as an unavoidable obligation. Hope was partly sustained by the City Grammar School itself. For the annual parade of next year's undergraduates did its intended work as both encouragement and encomium. I can still remember the names – Oliver, Hobson, Jacqueline Betts; Bullivant, Beard, Bennet and Oliver again, two years after his elder brother. But the whole school knew – as we stood to pay tribute to the chosen few – that the glittering prizes were not available to all the anxious new pupils who, each September, crowded into the Chemistry Lecture Theatre for enrolment. Of the hundred and thirty little boys and girls who entered the school during their eleventh and twelfth years, less than twenty left for university or training-college places. Theoretically we were the intellectual cream of our generation, the tested and proved top ten per cent of our age group. So every child with a bottle-green blazer was a potential candidate for a long striped scarf. Yet eight times out of ten the metamorphosis never took place. Sometimes, economic necessity took promising students early out of school. More often, the City Grammar's determination to distinguish sheep from goats (when in reality the whole flock were lambs) convinced children of real ability that higher education was beyond their talents. That disincentive was only overcome by pupils with character of unusual strength or parents of remarkable confidence and determination. In the Forties and Fifties, the Yorkshire working classes were doggedly determined for their children's success. But the world of minimum entrance requirements and Joint Matriculation Boards was wholly foreign to them. It was my good fortune to be born into a family which – not least because of its extraordinary origins – was passionately committed to my success. Yet neither my mother nor father – nor even Uncle Syd – attempted the difficult task of doing business with Assistant Registrars (Academic) and Deputy Directors of Education (Student Grants).

My mother was anxious for me to 'do well' in every way. Sometimes her enthusiasm for my success was simply an embarrassment. On the one occasion when I played at Bramall Lane, I walked out to bat in the shaming knowledge that the only spectators on the acres of otherwise empty terraces were my parents. Sometimes her eagerness for me to succeed was acutely painful to us both. In the second big match of the Bramall Lane season when I was out for a duck, she demanded to know why I was not still at the wicket scoring runs like the other opening batsman. There was never any question of her disappointment becoming public. But when I failed – failed myself and therefore failed her – the extent of my error was never hidden from me. Yet even the reproaches were in themselves a sort of encouragement. I cannot pretend that my mother treated triumph and disaster just the same. But she took a detailed interest in the visits of both impostors. My father wanted my success, but always accepted – indeed, almost expected – failure. Between them they sustained in me the most important confidence of all – the certainty that they were always interested. The rule applied to examination results as much as to cricket scores.

The second rule, applied by my mother with equal ruthlessness, concerned the importance of never giving up. The cardinal importance of carrying on was one of the principles by which she lived and by which she expected those around her to survive. That spirit got me through the school examinations and into university. But the unremitting drive forward was sometimes more characterised by its fervour than by the careful zeal with which the target was selected. Indeed, the desire for me to enter a university was so strong that it now seems ridiculous that the pursuit of a place was carried on so incompetently.

In those distant days, applicants wrote to individual universities. None of us had a very clear view about the rival merits of alternative courses – the advantages of subsidiary archaeology as compared with supplementary theology. We just filled in batches of apparently identical forms, distributed literally identical passport photographs and held ourselves available for all the interviews to which we were invited. I offered myself to the history departments of all save one of the universities which were members of the Northern Joint Matriculation Board. The exception was Sheffield. For I had decided that the last summer at school should be the turning-point of my life, the historic moment when I left home and lived alone and independent. Nottingham and Liverpool turned me down almost by return of post. Manchester, however, immediately offered me a provisional place which would be turned into a certainty as soon as I confirmed that I had passed all three A-level examinations and also obtained the O-level pass in Latin for which I struggled with so little satisfaction. Birmingham and Leeds summoned me for interviews, and I set off for those great provincial cities, nervous, alone and without the slightest idea what lay ahead. Indeed, I never realised that I ought to have a view about the nature of the ordeal which I faced, and made no attempt to prepare myself for the half hour of close scrutiny which awaited me. I just turned up at the stipulated time.

I remember nothing about the interview in Birmingham except that I arrived at New Street Station over an hour before it was due to begin. I spent the spare time in the great Municipal Art Gallery, missing the Pre-Raphaelites but standing in the shadow of Epstein's

'Lucifer'. Birmingham, like Manchester a week before, offered me a provisional place. The Leeds experience I remember more clearly, for it took place on the same day as the football match between representative sides from Leeds and Sheffield grammar schools was played on the old Elland Road ground. Mr Walker (in charge of the South Yorkshire side) put me into the squad as reserve goalkeeper, although we both knew that I was nothing like good enough to justify my inclusion. Although I was delighted by my selection I was terrified that the real goalkeeper would not turn up on time, and that I would make an idiot of myself on the Leeds United ground. Fears about the football weighed much more heavily upon me than concern about the day's earlier engagement. I therefore faced the seven assembled academics with something approaching equanimity.

Amongst them was Bonamy Dobrée, professor of English, expert on literary style and (as far as I was concerned) wholly unrecognised. Like every other applicant, I had listed reading amongst my hobbies and Professor Dobrée – taking my entry at its face value – cross-examined me about the modern novel. Fortunately he mentioned Jean-Paul Sartre, and I was able to tell him that during the previous week I had seen *Crime Passionel* at the Sheffield Playhouse. I mumbled an approximation of the Patent Potter Child's Guide to Existentialism, and had the wit to pick up his point about enjoying the play being more important than the hunt for hidden meanings. We both then moved backwards, without any noticeable crashing of gears, to Charles Dickens – an author regarded by me as something approaching private property. I gave a quick résumé of my Dickensian scholarship, and sat back waiting to be asked when I had first read *Nicholas Nickleby*, when a young man on Professor Dobrée's right asked me what I thought of *Pickwick Papers*. Rashly I told him that I had 'never been able to get into it.' The youth looked shocked. 'Surely, after Falstaff, Mr Pickwick is the great comic figure in English Literature?' It was, I decided, too late to turn back. So I took refuge in the truth. I had never found either of them funny. The pale young man turned paler still, and I made a diversionary comment about the amusing qualities of Herbert Pocket in *Great Expectations*.

Professor Dobrée offered me a provisional place in his English Department if I 'cared to give up History', and I left for the second interview of the day at a hall of residence which I hoped to inhabit.

The Warden, a retired naval officer, gave me tea – pushing the bread-board towards me and inviting me to cut my own bread from his Hovis loaf. He accepted me into his 'band of brothers' and promised that I would 'not be asked to share a room with a black man'. In the evening, Sheffield Grammar Schools' first choice of goalkeeper turned up on time. So I sat in the stand next to Mr Walker, relieved of almost every anxiety and elated by the discovery of what can be achieved by honest effrontery.

The one anxiety which remained was the Advanced Level examinations. For all my offers were provisional. It never struck me that I would do anything except exceedingly well in my main subjects. But without Latin, there would be no place in a university for me. And the alternative to three years of study was two years of National Service as a conscript of the Queen. On the day that I 'registered' at the Labour Exchange, the papers were full of fierce fighting on the thirty-ninth parallel between the two Koreas. 'Just in time,' said Mr Walker with a cynicism which masked his sympathy.

I decided to prepare for the worst by planning a temporary military career. My first instinct was to become a soldier, for the lead infantrymen who had marched out of my Christmas stocking in 1940 had done their romantic work. Indeed, thanks to them and the spirit of northern patriotism in which I grew up, I knew the exact line regiment in which I wanted to serve – the York and Lancasters. But then Harold Woolhouse came home one weekend from his market garden, and together we went to Worrall for a forbidden drink in the company of another Old Boy of High Storrs School. He was called Mike Smith, and he possessed an MG sports car with wire wheels – the reward of his remunerative employment in the RAF. For Smith had signed on for a couple of extra years in addition to his National Service and become a fighter pilot. I never had any doubts that I preferred to read rather than to fly. The runway would be my reserve path to the stars. For some reason I believed that the best escape route would be the Fleet Air Arm, and in pursuit of my contingency plan I visited the Royal Navy's recruiting office. I decided not to tell the gnarled Sergeant of Marines that a life on the ocean wave was my fallback position. I simply told him that I expected three A-level passes and would like to fly Skuas and Fairey Swordfish. He looked at me as if I was mad. Did I know, he demanded, what happened in the Fleet Air Arm? Planes were catapulted into the air from the swaying decks of ships at sea and then landed on aircraft carriers – if their headlong progress towards destruction was halted by a rubber band stretched tight from port to starboard. As he described the lunacy which I contemplated, he waved his hand in a way which suggested a force ten gale. His advice was specific. I should put all notions of glory out of my head and apply for university instead. If I contrived to stay a student for ten years I would miss National Service altogether. I did not confess that my problem was less concerned with staying on then with getting in. I just thanked him for his interest and returned to the view that if I could not be a student I would become a soldier. I spent the weekend on Gladstone's Second Administration, *L'Allegro* and the Great Lakes of North America. *North and Hilliard* remained unopened.

Back at school, downstairs in the basement geography room, Mr Hodge continued to urge us to consider the merits of the university colleges – the institutions which entered their students for London external degrees. He was himself the graduate of such a college and could not understand why so many of his colleagues were prejudiced against them. Although I had no enthusiasm for Stoke, Exeter, Leicester or Hull I filled in four more sets of application forms. The University College of Hull replied by return of post, inviting me to sit their scholarship examination. In the dusty equipment room behind the chemistry laboratory Mr Goodfellow supervised my work on the written papers, and a week later I was invited to meet Professor Dickens. He asked me for an example of defence policy influencing economic prospects, and I answered NATO and Marshal Aid. I now think that he expected railways in Bismarck's Germany.

Michael Beeley – not a student of geography and not, therefore, subject to Mr Hodge's blandishments – was extremely offensive about Hull. And whispered mysteriously that he had a better idea that he would share with me. In the sixth form cloakroom, between the blue gabardines and the wet swimming trunks, he showed me a cutting from the previous Saturday's *Times*. Yorkshire boys were invited to apply for the William Ackroyd Scholarship 'tenable at the University of Oxford'. Beeley demanded an oath of secrecy, which I gladly gave. He was anxious to avoid competition from aspiring Oxonians who did not read *The Times*. I was afraid of appearing ridiculous when it all ended in tears.

We both wrote to the William Ackroyd Trust and confirmed that – to the best of our knowledge – we were not 'founder's kin'. I was preparing myself for the journey to Leeds and the written examination when – like Mike Beeley – I received an extraordinary letter. Two scholarships were available every year, and that year there had only been two applications. Michael Beeley and Roy Hattersley were, therefore, William Ackroyd scholars. The bursary itself was worth only £50. But the trustees anticipated that the local authority would make up the difference between their munificence and the normal maintenance grant. We could barely believe our good fortune. Virtue and initiative had been rewarded. We both wrote to 'The Secretary, Oxford University', explaining that we would be reading English and History respectively, and asking when term started. The reply which we received by return of post was couched in language as kind as it was crushing. 'There are many such awards . . . none of them provides admission rights . . . admission is determined by individual colleges . . . list of bursars and tutors attached . . . too late to apply for the forthcoming year.' I gave thanks to whichever saint looks after the naive that we had kept our academic success a secret.

I was still recovering from my disappointment when Hull held out its hand. The letter came at the beginning of a busy day. For Syd was to be married that morning, and Sheffield United were at home to Barnsley that afternoon. The wedding of my bachelor uncle came at the end of a brief (though I suspect not tempestuous) courtship of a widowed fellow teacher. They had decided – despite my father's badly concealed bewilderment and my mother's open antagonism – to live in her bungalow in one of Sheffield's Derbyshire suburbs and take up employment at the village school. When the Hull letter arrived we were about to leave for the Register Office – my father worried that Syd had made the wrong decision, my mother more offended than astonished by his desertion, and me worried about missing the kick-off of the local derby. Syd was almost forty, had served three years with the Eighth Army and had survived most sorts of personal and vocational upheaval. But my mother really believed that he was incapable of looking after himself, that no one would care for him as she did and that the new Margery Hattersley would prove a particularly unsuitable partner.

The letter which the postman pushed through the door, when my father and I were already in our best suits, was written in tantalisingly ambiguous language. The University of Hull had not awarded me a scholarship. That at least was plain. It was equally plain that I was wanted by its history department. But the extent of the enthusiasm was not clear. Other universities had made the crucial distinction between 'firm' and 'provisional' offers. Hull seemed to be firm, but did not say so in plain language. Syd, looking anxiously at the living-room clock, suggested that when I got home from wedding and football match I should write with a formal request for clarification. It was, no doubt, a well-intentioned proposal, combining common sense and self-interest. But my mother detected in the suggestion a lack of interest in my academic welfare, an absence of family feeling and an insensitivity to the needs of others which she thought it necessary to redress. I must, she said, draft a letter at once. Syd wondered if time that day really did permit. My mother was categoric. My academic prospects were a great deal more important to her than prompt arrival at the ill-fated marriage ceremony. The bridegroom sat in one of the living-room armchairs curled up in anguish. What might have been a ghastly confrontation between my mother's last assertion of authority and my uncle's natural desire to attend his own wedding was averted by my impatience. The letter — signed 'C. R. Meggitt, Registrar' — carried the telephone number of the university college and, for once, my mother allowed me to make a trunk call. She was, I suppose, part nervous about my prospects and part anxious to end with honour the crisis she had created for Syd and his bride. Ignorance of the Registrar's status made me ask for C. R. Meggitt himself and assume that he had both heard of me and was familiar with my application. I demanded to know, at once, if I had been made an unconditional offer, and what were the minimum requirements for admission to the history department. Mr Meggitt gave the answer Syd feared — 'Put it in writing'. But by the time the telephone call was over, my mother's ire had passed. At last we climbed into the waiting hire-car. There was a difficult moment during the ceremony when its secular nature caused my father to say (in a loud voice) that it hardly seemed like a wedding at all. But apart from that, the day passed well. George, my father and I arrived at Bramall Lane well in time for the kick-off and the results board on the pavilion registered an away victory for Sheffield Wednesday.

But a new element was still to be added to the anguish. George Darling — like the good Member of Parliament that he was — called round to see us with a belated wedding gift for Syd. As my mother led him through a résumé of recent family fortunes, he expressed his horror that I was contemplating the irrelevant study of history. He had assumed that it was my intention to read economics. For no other discipline served the Parliamentary apprentice so well. Was it too late to change? My reaction revealed both the depth of my political naïvety and the strength of my political commitment. I was utterly convinced that I must put history aside and that Bonamy Dobrée's suggestion that I might spend three years studying English literature was an impertinence. I wrote to all of the universities to which I had originally applied asking if I could be considered for entrance to their economics departments. And to the universities and colleges on which I had not previously smiled I wrote cringing letters asking if it was too late to be considered for their economics or commerce courses.

In the weeks that followed, I worked harder than I have ever worked in my life. I read and revised each night from the minute when I got home from school until the moment that I was incapable of assimilating another fact or theory. I then took Dinah for a brief walk on Wadsley Common and repeated to her the acronyms I had constructed to help me recall details of the War of the Spanish Succession and the *Nun's Priest's Tale*. When the examinations were over, life was half apprehension and half anticlimax. I hung in limbo, able to enjoy nothing. I captained the school in the last cricket match of the season and for once pupils beat staff. But all I could think of on my way home was the crossroad which I was so quickly approaching. The path I had followed for eighteen years was almost at an end. Yet I was still not sure in which direction my new route would go. Providently, we prepared for me to be either a scholar or a soldier.

Appointments were booked at the dentist into whose surgery I had leered from the top deck of my school-bound tramcar, and the neglect of a decade was remedied by four extractions and eight fillings. Having forestalled the brutality of military dentistry, I then began to accumulate an undergraduate's wardrobe – a plaid woollen dressing-gown to replace the one which my mother had made from an old army blanket, and a double-breasted suit from Burton's. The corduroy trousers which I had worn at school were judged to be still fit for everyday wear. So was a Harris tweed jacket that I had persuaded my father to give me, even though his need was greater than mine. Most of my shirts had been re-collared with cloth cut from the tails. My mother had knitted me a bottle-green cardigan with a zip fastener up the front. It seemed just the thing to wear on the journey that lay ahead. But my mother judged it unsuitable for the solemnity of the day on which I left home so it was packed in the wooden trunk which I had bought to safeguard possessions that were worth far less than the cost of their portable protection. When the day to leave eventually came, my father left for work as usual. But before he went, he shook hands with me for the first time in my life. My mother took me to the station, and on our way we waited outside Wadsley Church for the number eighteen bus that used to run from Worrall to what we still called Town. The cemetery and the school yard lay behind us and up the hill, beyond Well Lane and Rydlehurst Avenue (where Miss Rhodes had once attempted to teach me French) was Wadsley Common. Walter Colley – the last remnant of old Yorkshire – joined us at the bus stop, his clean sweat-rag proclaiming that he was on his way to work. 'Are you off then?' he asked. 'Aye,' I answered. 'You should say "Yes",' said my mother. 'Yes, Mr Colley.' There seemed no point in arguing.

Ralph Glasser
Growing up in the Gorbals £4.99

'A remarkable piece of work . . . vividly written, with a rare blend of sympathy and intelligence' THE TIMES

'. . . a classic . . . he has caught both the people and the place . . . and there are passages which stand comparison with Zola and Gorky' OBSERVER

'At least three stories are mated in this fine and sombre memoir. First there's the Jewish story . . . The second story is of the naturally brilliant boy making his way towards a life of scholarship . . . Thirdly, there's the story of the Gorbals itself . . . It is a pleasure to know that there is to be a sequel' NEW SOCIETY

'. . . a classic . . . He reveals a hidden face of Glasgow and gives a unique and fascinating insight into his early life . . . All the "No Mean City" ingredients – the filth and the squalor, the gang fights, the religious bigotry, the violence of the "tallymen", the mating rites of the midden, the pleasure of the "steamie" – are present' GLASGOW EVENING TIMES

'*Growing up in the Gorbals*, and its promised sequel, may well take their place beside the *Wesker Trilogy* as prime evidence of what culture has been for the most conscious working people in these last two generations' LISTENER

'Glasser has performed a service in recreating that ambivalent world of iciness and warmth, material poverty and spiritual richness, the hopes of dreamers and the dour resignation of "Expect nothing and you will never be disappointed"' JEWISH CHRONICLE

Leslie Thomas
This Time Next Week £3.99

The autobiography of a happy orphan

'A work of rare beauty and skill' SUNDAY EXPRESS

'It's a school. Down in Devon. The masters play soldiers in the woods and the fields with the boys. I've heard they have a very good time. But you will write, won't you?'

One minute twelve-year-old Leslie Thomas and his brother Roy were ordinary kids at home – and then they were packed and leaving, having kissed and wept with their dying mother by her bed.
It was the last they ever saw of her. By Christmas 1943 the cancer had taken its toll. Their father had been killed the previous year, trapped in the engine room of a torpedoed merchantman in the South Atlantic.

Leslie's vivid reminiscences of life in Dr Barnardo's homes in Kingsbridge in Devon and later in the house at the corner of Galsworthy Road and Kingston Hill in London are often hilarious and sometimes unbearably touching. It was all a strange and wonderful misadventure which also provided the seed-bed for the talent that was later to flower so spectacularly.

'Every childhood is a meadow. Ours was stubbly and had weeds and stony places. But there was sweet grass too in patches, and days of sun and freedom and happiness. And at its end, there was the gate to the Outside . . .'

'Mr Thomas's book is all humanity, to which is added a Welshman's mastery of words' OBSERVER

'One of the funniest and also one of the most moving accounts of childhood that I have ever read' DAILY EXPRESS

Vera Gissing
Pearls of Childhood £3.99

The poignant true wartime story of a young girl growing up in an adopted land

In 1939, shortly before her eleventh birthday, Vera Gissing escaped from Nazi-occupied Czechoslovakia, leaving behind her parents, family and friends. Vera survived the years of war in Britain. But when she returned to Prague in 1945, her loved ones had perished in the Holocaust.

It was not until nearly forty years later that Vera Gissing found the strength to return to the diary she kept during her wartime childhood.

Here she faithfully recorded her private thoughts – the pain of her separation from her mother and father, her hopes for the freedom of her native country, but also the happiness she found, first with the Rainfords, the family who adopted her, and later at the Czech school for refugees in Wales.

Now, drawing on her diary and the letters she received from her parents, Vera Gissing describes her wartime exile in *Pearls of Childhood* – a record of courage as powerful and moving as *The Diary of Anne Frank*.

Glyn Hughes
Millstone Grit £3.95

A Pennine Journey

Photographs by Peter Hollings

*'I am writing about, I am living in, that block of the Pennine hills
made of millstone grit and ringed by textile towns: Yorkshire wool to
the east and Lancashire cotton to the west. Majestic places, they
once were . . .'*

Written as an account of a journey on foot, *Millstone Grit* is a
captivating and impassioned evocation of the Pennine landscape, its
towns, villages and wild places.

Combining the poetic and the humorous, Glyn Hughes threads
together personal experience, local lore, history, myth, and legendary
names from a byegone age, to bring vividly to life the beauty of this
remarkable region and the unique qualities of its people, past and
present.

'The work of a subtle poet with the ear of a stand-up comic and the
eye of the most delicate of watercolourists. It is a work of sadness
and savagery . . . of gentle compassion . . . a grand book. Grand'
THE TIMES

'It is not a guide, but captures the essence of the place so well that
many readers are sure to want to travel that way themselves'
YORKSHIRE POST

'Enjoyable both verbally and visually . . . You can hear the brass
bands, you can smell the gas and coke and you can hear the winds
moaning over the moors by just looking at the magnificently gloomy
and absolutely appropriate photographs'
DERBYSHIRE LIFE AND COUNTRYSIDE

'The best book I have read on the North of England for a long time'
ALAN SILLITOE

George Clare
Last Waltz in Vienna £4.99

Winner of the W. H. Smith Literary Award 1982

On Saturday, 26 February 1938, seventeen-year-old Georg Klaar took his girl Lisl to his first ball at the Konzerthaus.

His family were proudly Austrian. They also happened to be Jewish.

Just two weeks later came the Anschluss. A family had been condemned to death by genocide . . .

'So many names on the family tree have death dates of 1942, the year in which Baldur von Shirach sent the wire: My Führer, I joyously report that Vienna has been cleansed of all Jews. Mr Clare's beautiful, eye-pricking book makes us understand what that meant'
DAILY TELEGRAPH

'Mr Clare leads us gently, but inexorably, to the edge of the pit and then leaves us to look down into it'
EDWARD CRANKSHAW in THE OBSERVER

'They are like actors in a Lehar operetta suddenly cast in the roles of a Greek tragedy' ARTHUR KOESTLER in THE SUNDAY TIMES

'A deeply moving book. I felt enriched and grateful after reading it'
JOHN LE CARRÉ

'An admirable book, combining very cleverly the historical and the personal' GRAHAM GREENE

'A beautiful book: a fascinating piece of history . . . a work of art'
BERYL BAINBRIDGE

All Pan books are available at your local bookshop or newsagent, or can be ordered direct from the publisher. Indicate the number of copies required and fill in the form below.

Send to: Pan C. S. Dept
              Macmillan Distribution Ltd
              Houndmills Basingstoke RG21 2XS
or phone: 0256 29242, quoting title, author and Credit Card number.

Please enclose a remittance* to the value of the cover price plus: £1.00 for the first book plus 50p per copy for each additional book ordered.

*Payment may be made in sterling by UK personal cheque, postal order, sterling draft or international money order, made payable to Pan Books Ltd.

Alternatively by Barclaycard/Access/Amex/Diners

Card No. | | | | | | | | | | | | | | | | |

Expiry Date | | | | | |

_____

                         Signature:

Applicable only in the UK and BFPO addresses

While every effort is made to keep prices low, it is sometimes necessary to increase prices at short notice. Pan Books reserve the right to show on covers and charge new retail prices which may differ from those advertised in the text or elsewhere.

NAME AND ADDRESS IN BLOCK LETTERS PLEASE:

....

Name _____

Address _____

_____

_____

_____

                                                          6/92

No of copies   Books by Roy Hattersley

[ ]   The Maker's Mark   £4.99

[ ]   In That Quiet Earth   £14.99
           (*Hardback*)

[ ]   A Yorkshire Boyhood   £3.99

[ ]   Goodbye to Yorkshire   £3.99